The Illustrated History of Humankind

TRADITIONAL PEOPLES TODAY

Continuity and Change in the Modern World

AMERICAN MUSEUM OF NATURAL HISTORY

The Illustrated History of Humankind

TRADITIONAL PEOPLES TODAY

Continuity and Change in the Modern World

General Editor
GÖRAN BURENHULT

Foreword by MARVIN HARRIS

HarperSanFrancisco
A Division of HarperCollinsPublishers

TRADITIONAL PEOPLES TODAY: *The Illustrated History of Humankind.*
Copyright © 1994 by Weldon Owen Pty Limited/Bra Böcker AB.
All rights reserved. No part of this book may be used or reproduced in any manner
whatsoever without written permission except in the case of brief quotations
embodied in critical articles and reviews. For information address HarperCollins
Publishers, 10 East 53rd Street, New York, NY 10022.

FIRST EDITION

Conceived and produced by
Weldon Owen Pty Limited
43 Victoria Street, McMahons Point NSW 2060, Australia
Fax 61 2 929 8352

and

Bra Böcker AB
S–263 80 Höganäs
Sweden
Fax 46 42 330504

The Illustrated History of Humankind
Publisher: Sheena Coupe
Series Coordinator: Annette Carter
Copy Editors: Jacquelin Hochmuth, Margaret McPhee, Bruce Semler
Editorial Assistant: Vesna Radojcic
Picture Research Coordinator: Jenny Mills
Picture Editors: Karen Burgess, Annette Crueger, Jenny Mills
Index: Garry Cousins
Art Director: Sue Burk
Design: Denny Allnutt, David Roffey
Airbrushed shadows: David Wood
Design Assistant: Andrée Dysart
Cartographic Assistants: Peter Barker and Dianne Regtop
Production Director: Mick Bagnato
Production Coordinator: Simone Perryman

Weldon Owen Pty Limited
Chairman: Kevin Weldon
President: John Owen
Vice-President, International Sales: Stuart Laurence
Coeditions Director: Derek Barton

Bra Böcker AB
Publisher: Anders Janson
Editorial Director: Claes Göran Green
Editor: Christina Christoffersson

Library of Congress Cataloging-in-Publication Data

Traditional peoples today / Göran Burenhult, general editor. — 1st ed.
    p. cm. -- (The Illustrated history of humankind : v. 5)
  Includes index.
  ISBN 0-06-250268-9
  1. Ethnology. I. Burenhult, Göran. II. Series.
GN303. I4 1994 vol. 5
[GN316]
909 .04 -- dc20

          94-6217
          CIP

94 95 96 97 98 WOHK 10 9 8 7 6 5 4 3 2 1

Manufactured by Mandarin Offset
Printed in China

A WELDON OWEN PRODUCTION

Endpapers
Feather fans are traditionally used in
many Native American ceremonies.
This fan, of macaw feathers, was made
by a Navajo artist.
LOIS ELLEN FRANK/AUSTRALIAN PICTURE LIBRARY

Page 1
A transformation mask representing the
hero Born-to-be-Head-of-the-World, used
in the potlatch ceremony by the Kwakiutl
people of the Northwest Coast of the
United States.
LYNTON GARDINER/AMERICAN MUSEUM
OF NATURAL HISTORY, NO. 4578/4

Pages 2–3
A cattle camp belonging to the Dinka
people, near Bor, in southern Sudan.
ROBERT CAPUTO/AURORA

Pages 14–15
A group of Nenets women and children
from Yamal, in Siberia, attend a spring
festival held out on the tundra.
BRYAN AND CHERRY ALEXANDER

C O N T E N T S

8

THE FIRST STATE SOCIETIES arose in Africa and Eurasia about 5,000 years ago, and somewhat later in the Americas. Wherever they formed, states embarked on expansionist careers that profoundly influenced their stateless neighbors. Some neighboring groups became fully integrated members of the state system, eventually merging physically and culturally with the rest of the population. Others endured as ethnic enclaves within the state, paying taxes and obeying common laws but preserving their own language, economic specialties, religions, and philosophies. Still others, reacting to the threat of being conquered, formed political and military alliances that led to the development of new state systems, which, in turn, embarked upon their own expansionary careers.

But the pre-industrial state was not universally triumphant. On every continent, many different modes of human social life persisted. Among these were hierarchically complex, multivillage chiefdoms, some with hereditary rulers but with no regular forms of taxation. The majority of these chiefdoms, such as flourished on the islands of Polynesia, were based on intensive agriculture, but where habitats were especially bountiful, as along the Northwest Coast of North America, chiefdoms based on hunting and gathering modes of production prevailed. Small, more or less permanent villages that were essentially independent political entities also flourished, especially in Melanesia, in the mountains of New Guinea, and in the interfluvial portions of the Amazonian rainforest. Led by headmen and, more rarely, head-women, these village societies relied for their subsistence primarily on a mix of gardening and the hunting and collecting of wild animals and plants. Pastoral peoples have also long resisted the encroachment of the state. The great centers of pastoralism developed in Asia's vast expanses of dry lands, and in North and East Africa. In the Americas, the absence of domesticated herd animals in the pre-Columbian period (except for the Andean llama), precluded the development of pastoral societies. Pastoralism was also rare or nonexistent in Southeast Asia and Oceania. Finally, on every continent except Antarctica, there endured bands of other more or less mobile peoples who hunted and collected for a living. These band societies, whose populations ranged from 25 to 150, were especially common in the more remote and adverse habitats, such as the Arctic, the southern tip of South America, and the perimeters of North America's Great Plains (before the Spanish introduced the horse). In Australia, however, band communities flourished over the entire continent in a great variety of habitats.

As this volume so vividly demonstrates, the Earth still teems with a staggering assortment of chiefdom, band, and village societies. But ever since the onset of the Industrial Revolution, these traditional societies have been subject to exponentially quickening pressures for incorporation into state systems, and for drastic cultural change, primarily in the form of wage labor, taxation, the disintegration of kinship ties, loss of lands, and despoliation of the habitat. The world will be a much less interesting place if it comes to contain nothing but industrial states. There are signs, however, that this need not come to pass, if both governments and traditional peoples themselves recognize the value of preserving the old, along with the necessity of adapting to the new.

Marvin Harris
Graduate Research Professor
Department of Anthropology
University of Florida

◄● An Australian Aboriginal dancer from
Arnhem Land, in the Northern Territory.

THIS IS THE FINAL VOLUME of *The Illustrated History of Humankind*. The historical roots of our human family tree run deep; and as the millennia passed, our species branched out to embrace an entire planet. It is a tale of colossal dimensions, and appropriately enough, the first four volumes of *The Illustrated History of Humankind* were phrased largely in the past tense—befitting our millions of years of human history and prehistory. But as we celebrate our global pedigree, it is important that we move from past to present tense. A century ago, it was generally assumed that the world's indigenous peoples would simply disappear, literally or culturally, along with the wilderness they inhabited. And many did. It is a shocking, ghastly story. Yet despite the biological and cultural disruptions, the remarkable fact is that many indigenous populations survived.

W. Richard West, Jr, founding director of the Smithsonian Institution's new National Museum of the American Indian—and himself a Cheyenne-Arapaho Indian—is often asked what it's like to be an American Indian living in twentieth-century America. He tells a story from his own childhood, when his father took him to visit one of the world's great natural history museums: *"The museum had an excellent Indian collection and it had an equally excellent natural-history collection. After spending several hours viewing each, I posed a question to my father that had been on my mind for much of the visit: 'Why do they show Indians with all the mammoths and dinosaurs?' My father replied, in a comment that came as close to sardonicism as his usually gentle nature permitted, 'I believe they must think we, too, are dead.'"*

Native Americans, of course, did not become extinct. Today, more than two million American Indians, from hundreds of tribes, live in the United States and Canada alone. Modern census data even suggest that more Indian people may live in America today than when Columbus arrived more than five centuries ago. The story of contemporary Native America is told, in part, by George Horse Capture, a member of the Gros Ventre tribe and an internationally recognized scholar on Plains Indians.

So it's easy to dispel the myth of the "vanishing savage". In these pages, we also disprove the oft-repeated suggestion that the Tasmanian Aborigines were wiped out by white contact. They were not. And who better to tell the tale than Greg Lehman, himself a Tasmanian Aborigine? These remarkable stories not only underscore the tenacity of such peoples, but also provide a surprisingly upbeat postscript to the often disastrous story of European contact.

But in celebrating the indigenous presence in the modern world, we must be wary of a second fallacy: the antiquated image of the noble savage. We feel it necessary, for instance, to dispel the false notion that modern Australian Aborigines still roam the outback as "pure" or "traditional" hunter-gatherers. They do not. Nevertheless, like so many indigenous populations throughout the world, Aboriginal people have maintained substantial parts of their own culture as they adapted to "progress" in modern towns and cities.

So, on the one hand, we shall chronicle and appreciate our uniquely human past, paying especial attention to those traditions, languages, belief systems, and values that have become extinct. But we are also mindful that many such traditions still survive. Native people fit "traditional" and "modern" together in their own unique cultural mix—not as living fossils, but as living links to our long-term human past and active participants in today's global village.

◄● In the Amazonian rainforest of Brazil, Yanomami
Indians work over a hollowed-out tree trunk, grating
manioc to make soup for a feast.

David Hurst Thomas

DEFINING WHO is "traditional", and who is not, is not an easy task. In a sense, we are all more or less traditional, each society having its own history and its own set of beliefs, customs, and values, its own forms of behavior and bodies of knowledge. Most of us, however, would consider Alaskan Inuit at the turn of the twentieth century or the Papuans of the New Guinea highlands in the early 1930s, for instance, to be more traditional than industrialized Americans or Europeans in those same periods. But it is difficult to draw a sharp line. For example, where do we place the Japanese culture, which, in spite of an unparalleled process of industrialization, has retained its ancient beliefs and customs to a quite remarkable extent?

We must also remember that no society is static. The historical processes of social, economic, political, and religious change, so clearly illustrated in the previous volumes of *The Illustrated History of Humankind*, can be difficult to link to the concept of "the traditional", which is generally associated with cultural persistence and continuity.

Yet, we are brave enough to name the fifth and last volume of the series *Traditional Peoples Today*—a title that refers to the rich, but steadily diminishing, variety of nonindustrialized cultural forms all over the world, in most cases maintained by indigenous minorities. All of these cultures, however, have to varying extents been incorporated into, and have adapted to, the modern industrialized world.

For a long time, the European colonizers' view of non-Westerners was marked by the firm conviction that Western civilization formed the spearhead and the peak of human development. The "natives" were in every way regarded as inferior, a conception that paved the way for the racist elements so common in Western societies, which have become such a major problem in our time. The Western industrialization process strengthened these cultural differences even further. But it would be fundamentally wrong to look at world history only as a story of Western expansion. Rather, it is the result of thousands of cultural forms coming into contact with, and influencing, each other.

The first chapter, "The Evolution of Races, Populations, and Cultures", examines the enormous global variety —physical, cultural, and linguistic— displayed by our species, *Homo sapiens*. The following eight chapters provide detailed accounts of indigenous societies in Asia, Southeast Asia, Australia, the Pacific, Africa, the Arctic, and North and South America: their customs and beliefs, their economies and social life. Finally, "The Future of Humankind" ponders the challenges that lie ahead. Will our species be able to keep up the evolutionary pace, and will the great variety of human existence continue?

Göran Burenhult

◀ A man from Papua New Guinea's Trobriand Islands decorates his face in preparation for the yam festival.

14

16

THE EVOLUTION OF RACES, POPULATIONS, AND CULTURES

180,000 YEARS AGO – THE PRESENT

The Global Animal

WULF SCHIEFENHÖVEL AND FRANK KEMP SALTER

WHEN WE WALK the streets of São Paulo, New York, New Delhi, or any large city in the world, chances are that we will see and interact with people of strikingly different physiques, colors, faces, customs, and values. Since the development of seagoing ships and the rise of empires from the middle of the second millennium BC, peoples from widely separated geographic regions have been mixing to a much greater extent than they did in prehistoric times. It is only within the last few hundred years, however, that the technology has existed to allow millions of people to be transported between continents within a short space of time. Because of this, the physical characteristics of different populations have, in general, remained sufficiently distinct for them to be traced back through a family tree to a specific place of origin, where a particular hair form or skin color or facial structure evolved. Thus, an ancient evolutionary process is still the ultimate source of biological differences as well as similarities between groups.

◄● People in different cultures all over the world use a rich variety of techniques to produce tools and other goods. These women skillfully weaving baskets belong to an ethnolinguistic group found in southern Burkina Faso and northern Ghana, in Africa, known as the Gurunsi, which includes such peoples as the Lyela, Kasena, Nankana, and Nuna.

◐ A Makonde helmet mask. The Makonde, a Bantu-speaking people of northeastern Mozambique and southeastern Tanzania, are renowned for their elaborate woodcarving.
BONHAMS, LONDON/THE BRIDGEMAN ART LIBRARY

♂ A young Akha woman from the hill districts of northernmost Thailand. An agricultural people, the Akha are famous for their headdresses, elaborately decorated with such objects as silver coins, beads, buttons, fur, and feathers. While smiling is a universal feature of human behavior, basically conveying friendliness, the situations in which it is used vary among different cultures.

♀ A richly decorated villager of Mumeri, in the Eastern Sepik Province of Papua New Guinea. In traditional societies, both men and women adorn themselves with colorful and often spectacular forms of decoration. In the Sepik River region, many traditions are still alive today, while others, such as initiation ceremonies for adult men, have been reintroduced in some places.

Why are there so many different types of peoples and cultures on this planet? When we think about differences between groups, we tend to confound biological and cultural features. This can confuse the issue of racial variation, because culture varies much more, and also more obviously, than does biology.

Some cultural differences are known to have a genetic origin, one example being alcohol intolerance (which will be discussed later). Certainly, more differences of this kind are likely to emerge in the future. But such exceptions only go to prove the rule that, at least in principle, most aspects of culture can be transferred from one group of humans to another. This is because culture is acquired in the form of ideas, habits, and utensils, while biological traits, including the universals of behavior and psychology, are transmitted genetically. For instance, while there are many ways of describing emotions such as anger, fear, happiness, sadness, surprise, and disgust in different languages, these emotions are universally communicated by the same facial expressions. Culture is thus an "extrasomatic", or nonbiological, cause (and form) of behavior.

Human groups have the capacity to learn new ways of performing practical tasks, such as hunting or making clothes, to learn new words, to adopt different belief systems. These capacities are only dimly visible in other primates. Members of all traditional cultures (which generally means people who do not live in cities and do not manufacture goods by industrial methods) have built up a rich repertoire of techniques to meet the universal challenges of existence: finding food and shelter, bearing and rearing children, trading with neighbors, managing intragroup and intergroup conflict, and so on. Although many of these motivations and goals are biologically determined,

they are largely expressed and achieved culturally. Ideas and techniques are invented, improved, kept, or changed by individuals or groups of individuals over the course of time.

In principle, most or all of a group's language and customs can be transferred to a different population. But why does this not happen much more often? Why do we still find the colorful mosaic of cultures around the globe? At the biological level, why have our ancestors not mated outside their local populations sufficiently to create one cosmopolitan physique, color, and physiognomy? We shall be much closer to answering these questions when we know more about the origins of modern humans, *Homo sapiens*, because we would then know how far back in time these group differences began to evolve.

The Question of Origins

The origin of racial differences remains controversial. Debate has tended to polarize into two camps, one relying mainly on DNA analysis, the other largely on fossil evidence. The most extreme version of the idea that races or distinct populations are a relatively recent phenomenon and reflect only minor genetic differences is the so-called "Garden of Eden", or "Eve", hypothesis, which postulates that modern humans originated in one gene pool in Africa between 90,000 and 180,000 years ago. This time range was estimated by measuring the differences in DNA found in the mitochondria, a part of the cell outside the nucleus that is passed on only by the mother. (See the feature *DNA: The Code of Life*.)

According to this hypothesis, pre-existing hominid populations in various parts of the world were completely replaced by groups coming out of Africa. In particular, these African groups are thought to have replaced groups of *Homo erectus*, a species of hominid known from fossil evidence to have reached Asia long before *Homo sapiens* appeared on the scene. The proponents of this view acknowledge that it does not explain the failure of modern humans to interbreed with archaic native hominids. Perhaps this was due to profound differences between the two groups in the capacity for speech, or to different degrees of resistance to infectious diseases.

Other scientists take the view that scattered populations of prehuman hominids in different parts of the world evolved into humans independently of each other. Known as the "candelabra", or multiregional, model of evolution, this hypothesis is supported by fossil evidence. For instance, there is a high frequency of "shovel-shaped" incisor teeth among *Homo erectus* fossils, currently estimated to be two million years old, found in East Asian sites, and such teeth are still typical of the people of modern Asian countries. On this view, modern Chinese, Japanese, and other Asian peoples are not children of "Eve" but descendants of early humans who evolved in parallel with other human populations, all of which exchanged genes sufficiently to retain the

JENNY MILLS

JEAN-PAUL FERRERO/AUSCAPE

unity of the species. Proponents of this multiregional model dispute some of the DNA methodology that underlies the Eve hypothesis, pointing to the many assumptions involved—in particular, that the "mutation clock" in the mitochondria runs at a steady rate. The question of whether the major geographic races —negrid, mongolid, and caucasid—predate the evolution of modern humans is the subject of much heated debate among scientists at the present time.

The world's population was small, perhaps between 1 and 10 million, before the so-called Neolithic transition, when peoples in certain parts of the world began independently to domesticate animals and cereal plants. Genetic differences within isolated small populations could translate into major genetic distance between groups in different regions once members of those populations spread to distant parts of the globe. In an ambitious project carried out at Stanford University, in California, a team of researchers led by L.L. Cavalli-Sforza has analyzed and mapped the genetic variation found among the populations of the world on the basis of data relating to 120 genes. From the picture that has emerged, they postulate that there were at least 10 major expansions. The greatest genetic variation was found along the east–west axis, indicating that this was the predominant direction of these population expansions.

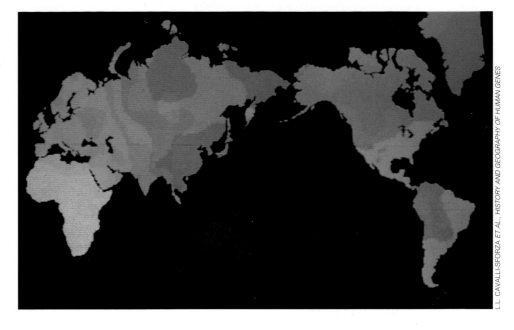

Races and Populations

The terms population and race need to be clearly distinguished. Groups large and small have been called races, and systems of racial classification range from a broad grouping into three major geographic races (negrid, mongolid, and caucasid) to more detailed groupings distinguishing between many smaller populations. Race has often been confused with cultural features, such as bodily adornment, habits, attitudes, and gestures. The concept has also been subject to political abuse, the most notorious case being the Nazi policy of repression and genocide towards Jews and Gypsies in the 1930s and 1940s. Some scholars argue that the concept of

race serves no scientific purpose and that the term should be dropped altogether from the scientific lexicon. This view has received some support from modern DNA analysis, which goes beyond visible differences to trace the ancient family connections of diverse groups. It is argued that, viewed against the background of the great genetic similarity of populations, the genes coding for visible differences are not significant. But such arguments do not alter the fact that there are striking visible differences in physiognomy, hair form, and other physical characteristics associated with different climates.

Races are the result, not the cause, of evolution. They are the outcome of biological processes operating on individuals and populations: natural selection, genetic drift, and the so-called founder effect. The process of natural selection operates on differences between individuals. Sexual reproduction and mutations provide an endless source of variation, expressed in slight differences in appearance or behavior. When a new trait leads to more healthy or better-adapted descendants than are produced by other individuals, it becomes more widespread in the population—as individuals with the new trait produce more children, grandchildren, and so on.

Genetic drift, on the other hand, is a wholly random process. It is also called "genetic sampling error", indicating that genes can be lost by accident, as it were, from a small group. Genetic drift can be accelerated if a group splits or is reduced in size—as a consequence of tension within the group or natural disaster, for example—which results in a fraction of its members founding a new, usually geographically separated, population. This is also called the "founder effect". There is some evidence that the anatomical differences evident between different populations have resulted from cycles of near-extinction and regrowth during the Pleistocene glaciations, which provided repeated opportunities for genetic drift to occur in small, isolated populations. These changes

☙ A genetic map of the world, synthesized by correlating the occurrences of 120 genes. These data represent about two-thirds of the entire range of human genetic variation. The areas shown in green account for half of this variation, and being centered in Africa, support the hypothesis that modern humans evolved on this continent. The greatest contrast can be seen between these areas and the regions of Australia and New Guinea, showing that the latter have been genetically isolated for the longest time.

◄❸ Selling flowers at a street stall in Bangalore, the capital of the southwestern Indian state of Karnataka.

❸ Selling food in a Beijing street. Such small-scale, urban economic enterprises tend to flourish in places where there is a busy, passing trade of office workers.

⚱ Body painting and scarring and the wearing of ornaments have important religious meaning in Australian Aboriginal societies. Among the Tiwi, of Bathurst and Melville islands, off the northwestern coast of Australia, men use earth-based pigments to decorate their faces and bodies for funeral and yam ceremonies: the different designs mark an individual's relation to ancestors, totemic animals, and tracts of land. In other parts of the world, the meaning of body art varies from deeply religious to secular and sexual.

⚱ A Kayapó child from the Xingú River basin, in Brazil, decorated with body paint and a feathered headdress. In spite of the hot and humid climate, Amazon Indians have not developed the frizzy hair and dark pigmentation typical of peoples in other tropical regions.

then became fixed as populations expanded in more favorable periods, since drift occurs mainly in small populations.

As a method of classification, the concept of geographic race is limited in its ability to draw fine distinctions. Since the concept is based on different frequencies of phenotypic (or visible) traits, and since most groups possess at least some of the characteristics included in the clusters of traits that distinguish other groups, definitions can easily be too narrow or too broad. The finer-grained concept of population avoids most of this problem of definition, and is compatible with the concept of race. A population is (or was in the past) an inbreeding group: in general, sexual partners come from the same "gene pool", and members only rarely mate out of the home group. This pattern is clearly changing rapidly in some parts of the world, under the impact of modern means of travel.

How does the concept of race stand up to DNA analysis? The Cavalli-Sforza team classifies peoples in terms of the major geographic races, negrid, mongolid, and caucasid, but argues that racial characteristics—such visible, measurable traits as skin color, hair form, and skull shape— are heavily influenced by "climatic selection". This means that peoples living in similar climates over a relatively short period of time should be expected to develop similar racial characteristics. (For evidence to the contrary, see the discussion of skin color, below.) This theory of climatic selection envisages change occurring over thousands of years, in contrast to the multiregional model of evolution, which has a time frame of hundreds of thousands of years. If this is so, then these kinds of racial markers and the genes coding for them are poor indicators of genetic history. One problem for this

view is the apparent resistance of racial markers to change. If a hot, humid climate "selects" for frizzy hair, why do the Yanomami Indians and other aboriginals of the Amazonian basin have straight hair? In all likelihood, this is the form they inherited from their ancestors, who migrated from northern Asia some tens of thousands of years ago.

Skin Color

A heavily pigmented skin is very useful under conditions of intensive sunlight, because it shields the tissues beneath the skin from the ultraviolet (UV) frequencies that form part of solar radiation. This is why populations in some regions close to the equator, where the radiation from the sun is particularly intense, are heavily pigmented. In areas of less sunlight, such as northern Europe and northern Asia, this impenetrable shield of pigment is a distinct disadvantage. Our bodies need a certain amount of UV light to penetrate the skin in order to turn the provitamin D present in the subcutaneous tissue into its bioactive form, vitamin D3. This latter is an important protective element, which is necessary to form straight bones. Without vitamin D, bones grow crooked—a condition called rickets. The pelvis is often affected, and in women, this deformation can cause severe problems in childbirth.

It is more than likely that our early ancestors in Africa had heavily pigmented skin. Once the descendants of these first modern humans started to move into areas with much less sunlight, individuals who had dark skin were less likely to survive and have offspring than those who had a lighter skin. Through this selective process, populations that settled in regions of low-intensity sunlight became white.

One hypothesis put forward to explain the dark pigmentation of aboriginal people in parts of southern India, Malaysia, Australia, and Melanesia is that this feature was introduced to these areas by populations migrating from Africa. The descendants of our African ancestors would have carried with them the dark-brown to black-brown skin color. They stayed pigmented, because their new homes were also situated in latitudes with intensive sunlight.

An alternative hypothesis is that, by a process of natural selection, populations in these geographical zones evolved independently with much more heavily pigmented skin than populations in regions further north or south. On this view, dark skin evolved many times in different regions—not just once, as proposed by the first hypothesis. The populations of southern India, Sri Lanka, Malaysia, and Indonesia present a mosaic of lighter to darker skin colors and therefore cannot easily serve as evidence for either hypothesis. But the second hypothesis cannot account for the fact that the original Indian population of the Americas, who migrated from Asia via the Bering Strait, is not heavily pigmented—whereas the period of at least 15,000 years that has passed since the immigration of these Indian people should have been long enough to produce the selective advantage of heavily pigmented skin for those living in equatorial latitudes.

This delay in adaptation sits well with the first hypothesis of slow change, as does the fact that the inhabitants of Melanesia and parts of Australia are as deeply pigmented as equatorial Africans and also have a similar hair form. The slow evolution of climate-adapted characteristics is also supported by examples of dark-skinned peoples who have lived in low-UV conditions for tens of millennia, such as Pygmies living under the canopy of the rainforest, or southern Australian Aborigines. These examples remain a puzzle: why did these peoples not suffer from rickets as a consequence of vitamin D deficiency? In the case of the Pygmies and other rainforest inhabitants, one suggestion is that they have adapted by becoming shorter in stature, thereby increasing the proportion of skin relative to bone mass and reducing their need for vitamin D.

Blood Characteristics

Some of the invisible bodily characteristics typical of certain populations are also products of natural selection. For a long time, it was thought that the distribution of the major blood groups (A, B, AB, O) among populations represented a chance effect, possibly an outcome of genetic drift. But when German geneticist Friedrich Vogel compared the distribution of people with B-type blood with the occurrence in former times of smallpox—a disease that until recently was often lethal—he discovered a significant degree of correlation between the two. For a still unknown physiological reason, individuals with B-type blood are better protected against smallpox than those belonging to other blood groups. They have, therefore, increased in numbers, relative to other population groups, in regions once stricken with the disease, such as the southern half of the Indian subcontinent.

Biological Determinants of Culture

At first sight, biology and culture seem to be very different entities. Research in recent years, however, has shown that these two elements of human existence have more in common than was formerly thought. First of all, humans are cultural beings by nature. That is to say, our biology forces us to acquire culture—language, beliefs, habits—by virtue of the intricate processes taking place in our central nervous system, where emotions, thoughts, words, concepts, and philosophies are generated. Culture, or at least its precursors, also comes naturally to our closest relatives, the primates. Chimpanzees, for example, have developed techniques for fishing termites from their nests with twigs and for cracking nuts with stone tools. As with humans, these particular forms of behavior are not biologically determined, but the capacity and curiosity to learn are. There are, therefore, positive links between biology and culture. There are also negative links,

where biology constrains or limits the type of culture a population can adopt.

Modern genetics have given us important insights into the ways in which culture is developed and diffused, as have the findings of anthropology, linguistics, and archaeology. Sometimes, differences in single genes or a small set of genes have been found to cause localized, clearly defined changes in the biology of a particular population. In such cases, researchers have had the opportunity to examine the very complicated interplay that takes place between the genome (the assemblage of all our genes), the phenotype (the appearance and functioning of our bodies), and the environment. One clear genetic difference relates to the capacity to digest alcohol.

Through one of these genetic mutations, roughly half of the mongolid population (Japanese, Chinese, Korean, and Amerindians) lack a specific enzyme, called aldehyde-dehydrogenase, that is necessary to break alcohol down into less toxic components. Individuals without this enzyme experience a flush after ingesting even small amounts of alcohol: a reddening, or blushing, of the skin, accompanied by dizziness, nausea, and loss of motor control. The fact that a high proportion of the population lacks this minute element of physiological machinery means that Japan, for instance, has proportionately far fewer alcoholics than, say, the United States. But it has also had a much wider and more important historical impact. The Japanese and other Asian cultures are nonalcohol cultures. Although they know how to make alcohol from various sources, alcoholic products, such as rice wine or rice liqueur, are used mainly in rituals, not for everyday consumption. One small and seemingly insignificant difference in the genome of Asian people has caused their culture to take a different course from that found in many other regions of the world. This example helps us to understand how important our biological outfit can be for the formation of specific cultural traits.

D. AND J. HEATON/AUSTRALIAN PICTURE LIBRARY

♨ Some mongolid populations, such as the Japanese, have low frequencies of an enzyme, called aldehyde-dehydrogenase, that is necessary to break down alcohol. Alcohol was, therefore, not part of traditional, everyday Japanese culture, although rice wine was sometimes used in ritual contexts. This is one example of how biology can influence cultural traits. Ritual tea drinking originated in China and was introduced to Japan about the thirteenth century by Zen monks, who drank tea to stay awake during long sessions of meditation. Later, it became more widespread as an expression of hospitality.

♀ People's environment largely determines their eating habits. Here, a Nenets boy eats raw reindeer meat. The Nenets are a reindeer-herding mongolid people who inhabit the northeasternmost parts of Europe, on the edge of the Arctic Ocean, between the White Sea and the Taymyr Peninsula.

BRYAN AND CHERRY ALEXANDER

DNA: THE CODE OF LIFE

Lutz Roewer

SKELETAL REMAINS of five people who had been shot that were found in a burial pit near Yekaterinburg, in the Urals, in 1991, were alleged to be those of the last Russian Tsar, Nicholas II Romanov, his wife, and three of their daughters, all of whom were executed by the Bolsheviks in 1918. Where once such a find would have remained a matter for speculation, thanks to the modern science of genetics, Russian and British scientists were able to provide us with an unequivocal answer. By comparing DNA extracted from the cells of the 73-year-old skeletons with that from blood cells obtained from direct relatives of the royal family, they were left in little doubt as to the skeletons' royal identity. What is DNA, and how does it allow us to link individuals so precisely through the generations?

DNA stands for desoxyribonucleic acid, a complex molecule found in the nuclei of the cells of all living organisms that contains, in chemically coded form, the genetic information necessary to build, control, and maintain life. The characteristic form of the DNA molecule is a double helix, formed of two intertwined chains of subunits called nucleotides.

All species, including humans, have the vast majority of their DNA in common. In fact, only one-thousandth of human DNA differs significantly from one

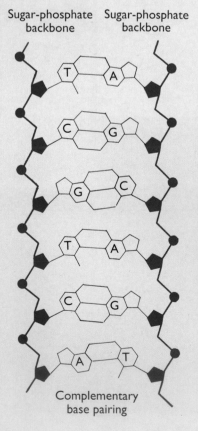

Sugar-phosphate backbone **Sugar-phosphate backbone**

Complementary base pairing

❂ DNA consists of a polymer formed of four repeating subunits, called nucleotides, which are composed of three entities: a sugar (desoxyribose), a phosphate group, and a base. There are four bases commonly found in DNA nucleotides: adenine (A), guanine (G), thymine (T), and cystosin (C). Nucleotides, when linked together, form a polymer composed of a sugar–phosphate backbone, which is always the same, and the attached bases, which vary. These bases bind not only to the sugar, but specifically to each other: adenine always pairs with thymine, and guanine with cytosin. This binding occurs across separate strands of the sugar–phosphate backbone, with the result that DNA is generally in a double-stranded state, with one strand wrapped around the other, forming a double helix. The marvelous regularity expressed in the double helical form is what qualifies the DNA molecule as a carrier of information.

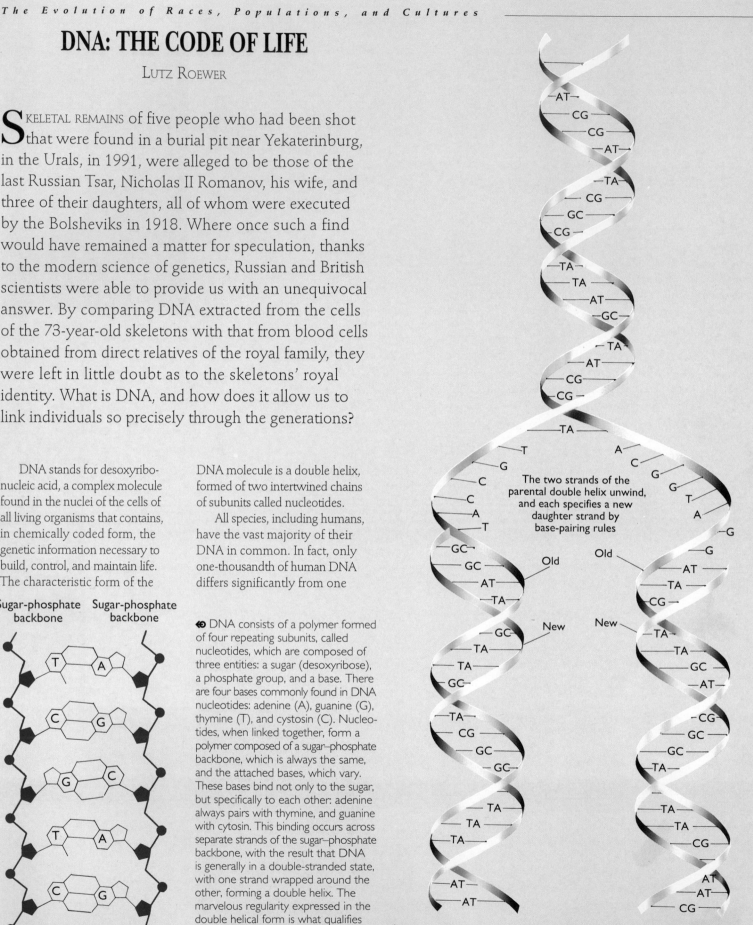

The two strands of the parental double helix unwind, and each specifies a new daughter strand by base-pairing rules

Old   Old

New   New

❂ During cell division, identical daughter double helices are generated through the replication of DNA. After the initial separation of the double-stranded DNA molecule, each single strand serves as a matrix for the synthesis of an identical duplicate. DNA polymerases catalyze the process of identical DNA replication.

person to another, but this is enough to make us all genetically unique, with the exception of monozygotic (identical) twins, who each inherit an identical set of genetic material, or genome, from their parents. Defined more precisely, a genome is the complete genetic material for any cell carried by a single set of chromosomes—the chromosomes being the structures in the cell nucleus, each consisting of a long, coiled and folded strand of DNA, that carry the genes.

One of DNA's major functions is that it codes for (or specifies) the structure of protein molecules, which, in their various forms, are fundamental to life. In cells, proteins serve either as structural elements (such as keratin and collagen), forming the substance of skin, bones, ligaments, and so on, or as enzymes, which function as catalysts, regulating all aspects of metabolism. This includes controlling and, when necessary, repairing the identical, newly synthesized DNA strands formed during the process of replication leading up to cell division.

DNA Fingerprints

But only 5 percent of an individual's genome codes for proteins. The remaining 95 percent of DNA does not contribute to an organism's visible characteristics (or phenotype), and minor changes (mutations) in this component do not, therefore, lead to hereditary diseases or lethal defects. Such variants, or polymorphisms, can remain undetected by the enzymatic repair system, and are thus able to accumulate, passing from parents to offspring and forming a pattern of DNA variants specific to groups of closely related individuals.

Surprisingly, dried DNA is usually so stable that it can resist decomposition for millions of years. Old DNA molecules get more and more fragmented over time (becoming rather like a pile of rubble), but segments up to 5,000 base pairs long have been identified in ancient Egyptian mummies, and one section 790 base pairs long was isolated from a 16 million-year-old magnolia tree. Such fragments are sufficiently long to allow meaningful comparison with the DNA of more recent species.

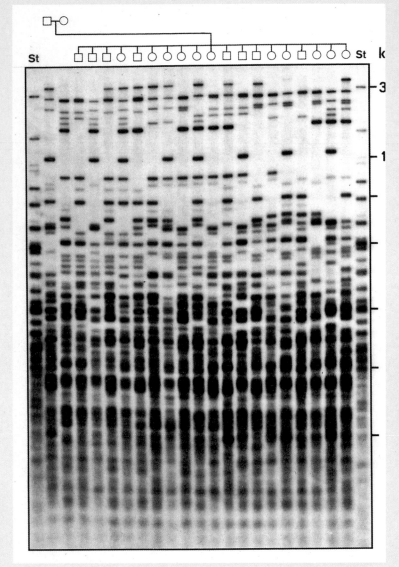

How do we find such an informative needle in a haystack of genetic material? A technique called polymerase chain reaction (PCR) has made it possible to pinpoint and copy selected DNA fragments to build a whole stack of such needles for analysis. PCR-derived DNA "fingerprints" have proved to be sufficiently discriminating to provide a statistically reliable method of establishing relatedness between individuals.

An Evolutionary Clock?

Relationships over two or more generations can be traced by analyzing DNA located in the mitochondria, the "powerhouses" of the cell responsible for respiration and energy production. These intracellular organelles have an independent genetic program controlling their functions. They contain DNA that codes for organelle-specific proteins, and rep-

licate themselves independently of the nuclear DNA. The control and repair mechanisms in mitochondrial (mt) DNA, which is inherited exclusively maternally, are not as accurate as those in the nuclear DNA, and mutations occur 10 times more frequently there than in cell nuclei. Mt DNA thus accumulates a number of sequence variants over time. By counting the number of observed point mutations—changes in the position of base pairs—family relationships can be established over shorter (historical) and longer (evolutionary) time spans, provided that the maternal line has not been broken.

All related individuals within a couple of generations (maternally related, in the case of mt DNA) have the same number and/or pattern of point mutations. This is how the skeletons of the Russian royal family were identified (with a probability of

Variable DNA patterns ("DNA fingerprints") recorded in a large human family. The "fingerprint" of an unrelated individual is shown at either side for comparison.

○ = Women   □ = Men

In humans, as well as in other species, "DNA fingerprinting" visually identifies DNA polymorphisms (variants). For particular sequences in the overwhelming abundance of genetic material to be differentiated, the polymorphic DNA fragments have to be arranged according to length by separation in an electric field. The resulting genetic bar codes can be used to determine individual identity and parentage and to estimate relatedness. All the bands in an individual's DNA fingerprint should also be identifiable in the fingerprints of his or her father or mother.
COURTESY OF P. NÜRNBERG, BERLIN

A light micrograph of human DNA.
PHILIPPE PLAILLY/SCIENCE PHOTO LIBRARY/ THE PHOTO LIBRARY, SYDNEY

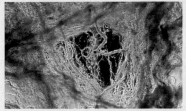

98.5 percent). In longer, evolutionary time spans, point mutations theoretically accumulate at a constant rate—giving rise to the notion of mt DNA as an "evolutionary clock". If such a clock can be calibrated (in terms of *n* mutations per *n* years), it is possible to construct evolutionary trees that link recent and extinct species.

Extensive analyses carried out over the last 20 years show that different populations differ significantly in their level of mt DNA variation. For example, the mt DNA lineages of coastal Papua New Guinea populations have been traced back to Southeast Asia. These Austronesian-speaking people show significant genetic distance from the older Highland populations, who speak Papuan languages. It is the aim of the ambitious Human Genome Diversity Project at Stanford University, in California, to analyze about 400 human population groups. This may help us to understand where and when the human gene pool started, and how it diversified and produced the many physically and culturally distinct peoples on Earth.

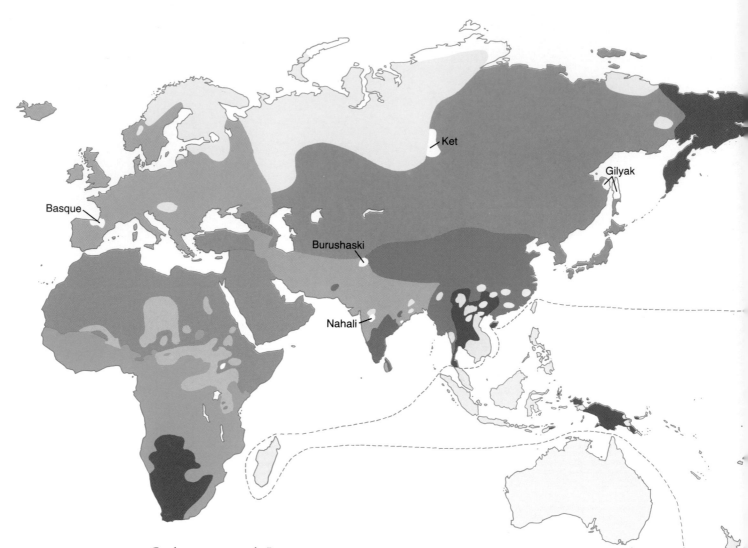

Ket

Gilyak

Basque

Burushaski

Nahali

PETER SANDERS

⚹ One of the most influential inventions in the history of humankind, writing developed only within the last 5,000 years or so. In many cultures, it is connected to religious activities. Here, a student in a school in Khartoum, in Sudan, is writing in the Arabic script.

Cultures and Languages

Most cultural differences are, of course, unrelated to genetics. Culture is developed, changed, abandoned, and replaced for a multitude of social, economic, and historical reasons. Because of this, it is often portrayed as a domain completely separate from biology, almost as if our brains are like computers into which any piece of software can be installed. To a certain extent, this is a useful analogy. A child from any part of the planet adopted soon after birth learns the language of the adoptive parents, along with their manners and habits—whether this be how to build a shelter or to drive the family car.

The computer analogy is important, because it stresses the relative autonomy of human culture compared to the cultures of other species. In many species of birds and mammals, behavior has been found to be based on learned information rather than being coded in the genes. Chimpanzee mothers, for example, have to learn how to care for their young, and many bird species will learn any song presented to them at the critical stage of their development. Individuals of these species are genetically primed to learn particular lessons, just as human children are primed to learn speech. But humans have taken the learning process much further by developing a generalized ability to acquire knowledge and base decisions on it. Language is a crucial facilitator of this ability, and one possessed by no other species. The computer analogy cannot be taken very far, however. True, like computer programs, cultures change over time as ideas and inventions are developed, borrowed, and abandoned. But they do this under their own steam, without the intervention of a master programmer.

While a culture cannot be identified with any single element of appearance or behavior, there are features and combinations of features so distinctive that they allow us to place most individuals in their home group with a high degree of accuracy. Language is one central marker, and as more features are taken into account, such as clothing, diet, and manners, our predictions are likely to be even more accurate.

Although largely free from direct biological control, culture itself appears to develop according to evolutionary laws. In recent years, anthropologists have started to make use of models derived from evolutionary biology to explain the processes of culture formation. W.H. Durham, for instance, argues that the Darwinian principles of descent

LANGUAGE FAMILIES OF THE WORLD

A language family can be defined as a group of genetically related languages—that is, languages that share a common ancestor. Language families are divided into different subgroups, which, in turn, are divided into specific languages and dialects. Recent theories suggest that all language families have their roots in a so-called "protoworld" language, which is thought to have been spoken by early *Homo sapiens*. Shown here is the distribution of the world's language families before European colonization. Language isolates—languages without known relatives, such as Basque—are also included.

CARTOGRAPHY: RAY SIM, ADAPTED FROM M. RUHLEN, *A GUIDE TO THE WORLD'S LANGUAGES* (1987), VOL. 1, STANFORD UNIVERSITY PRESS, CALIFORNIA

- Indo-European
- Uralic-Yukaghir
- Altaic
- Chukchi-Kamchatkan
- Afro-Asiatic
- Nilo-Saharan
- Niger-Kordofanian
- Khoisan
- Dravidian
- Austro-Asiatic
- Hmong-Mien
- Papuan
- Australian
- Tai
- Caucasian
- Eskimo(Inuit)-Aleut
- Na-Dene
- Amerind
- Sino-Tibetan
- Austronesian

and modification are also useful to describe cultural evolution. Descent means a process of splitting or branching off, in which a parental culture gives birth to new cultures. Durham accepts the possibility of culture formation through fusion—that is, a merging of different parental cultures leading to a thoroughly "hybrid" culture. But this process does not seem to be very common in fact. Of the many thousands of languages spoken on Earth, one global inventory lists only 37 mixed languages (usually called Pidgin or Creole languages). Recent European history also demonstrates that the fusion of various cultures to form a synthetic national culture has not been as easy and successful as theoreticians and politicians have sometimes thought. Durham argues that there "exist a number of effective barriers to hybridization—ecological, psychological, linguistic and cultural". Other mechanisms lead to the creation of new entities, including subcultures and in-groups. This process has been termed "pseudo-speciation", indicating that the separation of human cultures is, in some respects, similar to the formation of different species in the rest of the animal kingdom.

Linguistics have proved to be one of the most productive areas of study for researchers investigating the process of culture formation. Because peoples tend to retain their language over long periods of time, languages are almost as resistant to change as are our genes. The Basques of southwestern France and northeastern Spain provide a good example, being genetically very distinct from the peoples around them (and possibly representing the descendants of an early European population) and also speaking a language completely unrelated to the languages of their neighbors. The opposite can also happen, however, as is shown by the Hungarians. Genetically, Hungarians are a Slavic people, but many centuries ago, they took over a Uralic language spoken by a Siberian population that at that time occupied, or at least influenced, much of the land to the west, including present-day Hungary and Finland.

❂ A Basque farmer in Lapurdi, southwestern France, sews a wreath of red peppers. The Basques are a distinctive European population that has retained its ancient genetic and linguistic heritage.

Ethnicity: A Powerful Motor in the Formation of Cultures

Ethnicity is the outcome of the coevolution of biology and culture within particular populations, and continues to have a profound impact on the contemporary world. Groups of humans have a notable tendency to develop identity markers that distinguish them from other groups. This tendency is expressed in the variety of dress, bodily adornments, hairstyles, architecture, gestures, rituals, and the like that are identified with particular groups, from subcultures to entire societies. It is clear that the inclination of humans to form defined units is one of the most powerful mechanisms generating culture, and it seems reasonable to assume that it is based, at least partly, on our psychobiological make-up.

We can only speculate about the reasons for this. It was most likely an advantage for our early ancestors to limit their cooperation and gift-giving to people whom they knew well and trusted, and to whom they felt emotionally attached—their relatives and friends. In our species' evolutionary past, it was advantageous to be a member of a defined group, because it provided protection in case of attack. As Richard Alexander of Michigan University has argued, modern nationalism, with its intense loyalties and destructive wars, may be the result of once-adaptive propensities being enacted out of context. In the band societies of our evolutionary past, the advantages of showing loyalty to one's extended family might have selected for predispositions that, in mass society, lead to nationalism and racism.

The intertwining of biology and culture can also be detected at other levels of behavior, particularly when one looks at the way in which children adapt to social speech patterns. Children invariably adopt the dialect, the speech melody, and the specific way of pronouncing phonemes that are characteristic of their community. It is very difficult—in fact impos-

🔔 Prayer wheel in hand, a Drukpa elder and his grandchildren, in Bhutan, watch the Buddhist Tsechu, a dance portraying in mime the nine different aspects of Buddha's second incarnation, Guru Padmasambhaba. Older generations have a very important role to play in transmitting culture and a sense of ethnic identity to the young.

↪ Religious events typically serve to bind communities together. At the annual Sani festival in northern India, Buddhist rituals are performed over two or three days. The festival is also a marriage market, since local unmarried girls come here in the hope of finding suitable husbands.

☞ His digital watch held high, a heavily adorned young Masai man, from East Africa, awaits the start of a dance performance. The wonders of technology are universally attractive.

♀ Powwows, featuring traditional dances, are one of the means by which Native North Americans have reclaimed the heritage that defines their identity in a modern society.

JIM BRANDENBURG/MINDEN PICTURES

sible, in most cases—to shed this specific tinge to one's language when one moves to a different speech community after about the time of puberty. From this, we know that this kind of linguistic imprinting can, as a rule, happen only once, when we are children.

What is the function of this language imprinting? It seems most likely that we have a particular neurological program in our brain that leads us to absorb the language of the community in which we spend our early childhood and adolescence. There seems to be a reward mechanism built into our psychobiological machinery that makes us feel good when we are in our own culture, hearing familiar sounds and seeing familiar sights.

The intricate processes involved in the coevolution of biology and culture have generated the astounding variety of human societies we find around us. The many different ethnic identities represent the outcomes of successful coevolution, and are thus a valuable biological and cultural resource. The societies of the industrialized world, in contrast, can be likened to the vast monocultures of the modern farm, with kilometer after kilometer of a single crop—highly efficient enterprises, yet inimical to diversity and vulnerable to disease. The continued coexistence of many cultures provides working alternatives to failed social experiments. Ethnic diversity is a living reminder of the possibilities for change, demonstrating that there are multiple paths to the good life. A cultural détente will require us to place intelligent limits on the relentless drive towards economic efficiency. Material goods are important, but cultural identity constitutes a large part of our quality of life. Culture is as much a part of our environment as air and water, trees and wildlife. While change is inevitable, self-determination by members of the world's many peoples will allow them to retain the essence of their ethnic identity—and thus afford future generations, too, the opportunity to experience the manifold and magnificent forms of human existence and identity.

FRANS LANTING/MINDEN PICTURES

WHO OWNS THE PAST?

J. Peter White and David Hurst Thomas

IT WAS IN THE MUSEUMS of natural history and ethnology that many of us bumped first-hand into different worlds. Through the high-security glass, we peered at our first Egyptian mummy, at Mayan stone carvings, and at stone axes from all over the world. From the recent past, too, were paraded seemingly endless rows of originals: enigmatic Chinese jades, deadly Amazonian blowguns, ingenious Inuit (Eskimo) harpoons, and strange African and Oceanic carvings.

For many decades, museums have displayed the vast, complex nature of the human experience, showing how different countries and cultures are, and that even our own past is often a foreign country. While today's television may give better images, only museums can flaunt the real thing.

Many countries and communities now want the real things back. How do we determine who "really" owns them? And to how much of the past does such ownership apply?

Descendants as Owners?

The answer to this question may seem obvious: to the people whose ancestors created the object in question. But a little thought will reveal that it is not so simple.

For instance, if the world's population is actually all descended from an African "Eve", do humans collectively "own" any knowledge of the human past that is more than 200,000 years old? What would such ownership mean? Certainly, not the right to go to Africa and dig up million-year-old skulls—the African countries where such remains are found are too conscious of their importance to the history of humanity to allow most of us anywhere near them. But perhaps we all have the right to attempt to interpret their meaning?

Take another example. There is an archaeological site at L'Anse au Meadows, an undisputed Viking settlement in Newfoundland, which has been radiocarbon-dated to about AD 1000. Does this site "belong" to the Canadians because it stands on

Canadian soil? Most of us would consider that it did, in the sense that we would not dispute their control over access to it. But some modern Scandinavians might argue that it belonged to them, because their ancestors lived there.

Then there is the bitter dispute surrounding the ownership of the famous Elgin Marbles, a carved marble frieze removed from the Parthenon in Athens nearly two centuries ago and taken to the British Museum. The former Greek Minister of Culture (and actress) Melina Mercouri argued that these sculptures symbolize Greece itself and were stolen from a Turkish-controlled Greece, an act that desecrated a major monument. She demanded their return. David Wilson, Director of the British Museum, pointed out that their removal was lawful at the time and that they are better protected in the museum than they would be in the acidic air of Athens.

The issue spans the globe. Iroquois people demand the return of "their" face masks, Australian Aborigines the return of "their" prehistoric skeletons, while New Zealand Maori insist that mummified "trophy heads" be removed from museum displays everywhere.

Many concerned scholars agree with at least some of these claims and urge that some objects, particularly those with personal associations or special cultural status, should be returned immediately to their countries of origin. On logical and legal grounds, they argue for the return of human skeletal material clearly ancestral to current groups, along with some of

This ancient bronze equestrian figure was manufactured in the kingdom of Benin, located in the tropical rainforest region of what is now Nigeria. Although the kingdom no longer exists, the culture of Benin survives among the Edo people of Nigeria's Bendel State. Some people argue that these bronzes, many of which belong to the world's major museums, are national treasures that should be returned to the modern descendants of ancient Benin craftspeople.

BRITISH MUSEUM/ THE BRIDGEMAN ART LIBRARY

the Benin bronzes to Africa, some Sepik River carvings to New Guinea, and the Rosetta Stone—a spoil of war—to Cairo. Some museums and universities have already begun returning such objects.

Different Frames of Reference?

The right to excavate or own materials from the past is one aspect: the right to describe them and tell their story is another. Problems with the

latter often arise in colonial situations such as Australia, New Zealand, the United States, Canada, and many South American countries, where minority groups (Aborigines, Maori, Inuit, and others) see the right to control accounts of the past as a way of regaining power over one aspect of their lives.

Australian Aboriginal activist Ros Langford summed up the conflict as "our heritage, your playground", implying that white Australians' interest in Aboriginal remains was merely playing around. Not being Aborigines, they could not properly understand or have any empathy with the period of Australian history before the arrival of Europeans. Similar statements are made in other countries, but few archaeologists or anthropologists would accept this view.

Questions about ownership have more recently been raised in noncolonial contexts, as radical archaeologists question whether the accepted framework (such as the one underlying this series) is not an imposition on nonscientists. If we accept American Indian, Black African, or Maori views of the past as legitimate, how can we deny legitimacy to Americans and Europeans who believe in Atlantis or the role of astronauts in creating great monuments in the past?

We accept that the answers to such questions are fundamentally political. Western science is the method of understanding the world that will be accepted by most readers of these volumes. This is because we have been educated within a scientific framework, and scientific techniques and explanations are in everyday use in the world we live in. "Science" underpins what most governments, and most people, are prepared to accept as the only reasonable way to explain how the world works. Scientific methods, that is, are politically dominant in the modern world.

But if we do not accept the basic premises of scientific reasoning, then none of the scientific account is acceptable. This is the position of some Christians, for whom the Bible is literally true: they know the world was created about 6,000 years ago, not millions of years ago, so a long period of human evolution is unacceptable. Aboriginal people, whose fundamental belief, the Dreaming, documents their eternal presence

in their own country, similarly reject scientific claims about their original status as migrants.

Ownership of the past is thus impossible to divorce from our beliefs about the past and who should write about it. But while there can therefore be no single answer to the question of ownership, this does not mean there must be constant conflict over it. Recognition that there can be honestly different views of what happened in the past is the first step. The next is to try to reach agreement on appropriate methods by which the past can be studied, so that it is accessible to the many people who are interested in it. "Who owns the past?", with its implied note of confrontation, may well turn out to be an unnecessary question.

☜ False Face masks, or "vision faces", are still worn by Iroquois members of the False Face Society, and are a powerful element in rituals in which participants seek understanding through dreams and visions. Many Iroquois people actively seek the return of these masks from museums.

PRIVATE COLLECTION/WERNER FORMAN ARCHIVE

☝ The Rosetta Stone was taken from Egypt in 1799 and is now in the British Museum. It is inscribed with parallel texts in Greek and in Egyptian demotic and hieroglyphic characters, and thus provided the key to deciphering ancient Egyptian hieroglyphics.
BRITISH MUSEUM/THE BRIDGEMAN ART LIBRARY

☝ A detail of a wooden statue from the Sepik River area of Papua New Guinea. Many such carvings have been made for ceremonial use and for sale to tourists; a few are of immense historical significance in their local region.

ENTWISTLE GALLERY, LONDON/WERNER FORMAN ARCHIVE

TRADITIONAL PEOPLES OF THE ASIAN CONTINENT

A D   1 2 0 0   –   T H E   P R E S E N T

Survivors from a Half-forgotten Past

E. PENDLETON BANKS

ASIA IS HOME to a bewildering variety of peoples, who speak many different languages and follow almost every known kind of religion. Together, they represent more than half the world's population. Even in highly industrialized countries, such as Japan, Asian cultures have retained a markedly traditional flavor, making them a source of great fascination to outsiders.

Ethnic groupings in Asia fall into two broad categories: those occupying a dominant position in large, powerful societies, such as the Han Chinese in China and the Hindus in India, and the smaller, less technologically developed societies. Often, the small societies occupy niches within the borders of the large societies, forming minority groups that differ from, and sometimes conflict with, the dominant ethnic groups. This is the fate of the Kurds in Western Asia and of such peoples as the Kazakhs and Uygurs in China. Even if one of the smaller, more traditional societies happens to find itself the dominant group in an independent nation-state, it is likely to come under the cultural or political influence of its more powerful neighbors. The Mongolian Republic, sandwiched between Russia and China, is a good example of this.

This chapter is concerned with the smaller societies, and draws upon a range of studies by archaeologists, historians, geographers, and ethnologists.

◆◎ Yaks crossing a snowbound pass in Nepal at 5,600 meters (18,500 feet) above sea level. These sturdy animals can find food under the snow, and enable the Bhotia people to live and travel at extremely high altitudes.

◐ Even nomads with meager possessions find ways of expressing themselves artistically in colorful designs. This painted design is from a Mongolian tent door.
NIK WHEELER

TRADITIONAL SOCIETIES IN ASIA

Traditional peoples are found in each of the major regions of Asia. The locations of some of the more significant groups are shown here. Mountains, deserts, and islands are the typical settings in which small societies are able to maintain their distinctive ways of life.

CARTOGRAPHY: RAY SIM

Minority societies sometimes represent the remnants of peoples who were more numerous or more powerful in earlier times. The Mongols, for example, were among the most powerful peoples in the world in the thirteenth century AD, under Genghis Khan and Kublai Khan. Invariably, they have adapted their way of life to extreme environments: deserts, steppes, cold mountain plateaus, tropical rainforests. The modern world has come to appreciate these adaptive strategies—sometimes too late to save the people concerned, but, it must be hoped, not too late to learn from them. Often, it is precisely because they have succeeded in adapting to an unusual situation that these societies have been able to survive and to maintain their cultural distinctiveness. But in the end, it is their wonderful human creativity that makes these peoples so appealing. They may be isolated and are often poor in material goods, but their lives are

rich with myths, songs, dances, rituals, and various forms of the visual arts. We should not think of them as "primitive", even while recognizing that, economically, their situation is marginal.

Ecologically, Asia consists of a series of latitudinal zones stretching more or less unbroken from west to east. The tundra extends across the Arctic from the northern Ural Mountains to the Bering Strait; the taiga, the northern forest, extends from the Urals to the Pacific coast; there

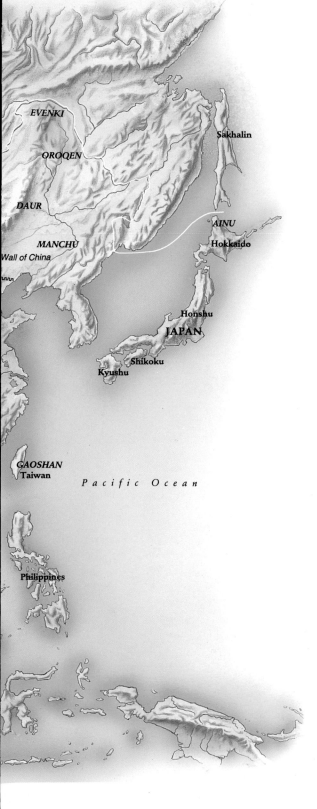

are the grass and steppe lands; and a belt of deserts reaches from the Arabian peninsula, through Iran and across central Asia, to the Gobi Desert of northern China and Mongolia, with a branch extending across southern Iran to Pakistan and India. The highland areas, between the northern and southern deserts, take in the Zagros and Elburz mountains of Iran, the Himalayas, and the ranges that separate Southwest China from its neighbors to the west and south. A discontinuous belt of forest runs across Sri Lanka, India, Bangladesh, Myanmar (formerly Burma), and Southeast Asia. (The peoples of the tundra and taiga, and of Southeast Asia, are discussed elsewhere in this series.)

It would be possible to group the peoples of Asia in terms of their habitat, but since political divisions do not conform to ecological zones, it is perhaps more useful to distinguish four major regions: western Asia, central Asia, East Asia, and South Asia. Nevertheless, the divisions become arbitrary at certain points: the boundary between central Asia and South Asia could run either north or south of Afghanistan; and China, clearly an East Asian nation, encompasses some peoples whose cultures are central Asian.

🔥 A flourishing field of grain awaits harvest in the Hunza Valley, under a towering peak of the Karakoram Range. Plentiful sunshine and glacial meltwater support farming here, in this otherwise bleak environment.

🔥 The Kazakhs spend much of their lives on horseback. Horses give them the mobility they need to tend their flocks and herds in the mountains of Xinjiang Uygur Autonomous Region, in western China.

33

NIK WHEELER

NIK WHEELER

☗ Unlike most Kurds, who are Muslims, this Kurdish woman is a Christian.

WESTERN ASIA

Western Asia includes Turkey, Syria, Lebanon, Israel, Jordan, Iraq, Kuwait, Saudi Arabia, Qatar, the United Arab Emirates, Oman, Yemen, Iran, Georgia, Armenia, and Azerbaijan. The region has been the home of some of the oldest civilizations on Earth. The Sumerians, Akkadians, Babylonians, and Hittites built their cities here long ago, and later, more powerful empires were based here. The Persians held sway over much of the area until the Macedonian king Alexander the Great swept through in the fourth century BC. Rome and its successor in the east, Byzantium, ruled over large parts of western Asia until the expansion of Islam, beginning in the seventh century AD, culminated in the powerful Ottoman empire in the fifteenth century.

Yet, western Asia has always accommodated smaller societies, with strong traditional cultures, that have resisted assimilation by the great empires. The Jews clung to a local religious culture between the Mediterranean coast and the valley of the Jordan River until the Romans scattered them during the first century AD, and Jewish and Christian colonies persisted long after the region was swept by Islam during the seventh century. Most of the Arabian peninsula was inhabited by Arab Bedawi (Bedouins), tending their herds and flocks and living in their traditional way, until the 1930s, when the exploitation of desert oil revolutionized their way of life.

Geography has often favored the persistence of traditional cultures. The Zagros Mountains of Iran have long sheltered groups of nomads, such as the Bakhtiyari and Qashqa'i, allowing them to live independently by herding livestock without

been a series of tragic conflicts between the Kurds and the majority peoples of each country, in which the Kurds have usually suffered the most.

Events outside the region have sometimes been influential in maintaining ethnic distinctions. Armenia and Azerbaijan, once incorporated into the Russian empire and later into the Soviet Union, found themselves independent nations once again after the collapse of the Soviet Union in 1990, and old animosities immediately fueled a war.

The spread of Islam over western Asia from the seventh century AD did much to break down cultural barriers. One can travel long distances in this region, crossing a number of national borders, and find in each town similar places of worship, with people praying in the same manner and reading the Koran in the same language. Moral codes, diet, and clothing also tend to be similar throughout Islamic regions. But religion can also create barriers, as in the doctrinal differences between the Shia and Sunni sects of Islam. Often, the emphasis on traditional culture seems to be a reactionary retreat from the modern world, arousing Western fears of a fundamentalist religio-political movement. Dealing with ethnic conflict in western Asia and elsewhere may well be the major problem for governments of the twenty-first century.

The Kurds live in a region divided among Turkey, Syria, Iraq, and Iran. Their towns and villages are often built in mountainous terrain, like this settlement at Ali Qosh.

The Arabic-speaking Bedouins of the Arabian peninsula lead a nomadic life, living in large tents of woven wool as they follow their herds of sheep, goats, and other livestock to the areas where grazing is to be found.

clashing with the settled farmers of the plains, who resent the damage caused by migrating herds and have no sympathy with the nomadic way of life. (See the feature *The Wakhi: Living on the Roof of the World*.) Sometimes, of course, these smaller ethnic groups are themselves the remnants of intrusive populations. The Qashqa'i, for example, stem from a Turkic-speaking people who invaded the territory of the Indo-European Iranians.

Mountains have also been significant to the Kurds, a people of Indo-European language who inhabit the highland area where Turkey, Syria, Iraq, and Iran adjoin. Each of these host countries has tried to assimilate the Kurds, offering them citizenship in return for their abandoning their ethnic distinction, but the refuge from the central governments offered by the sheltering mountains has encouraged the Kurds to keep alive their dream of Kurdistan, a nation of their own. The result has

35

THE WAKHI: LIVING ON THE ROOF OF THE WORLD

HERMANN KREUTZMANN

☉ Well adapted to rugged Pamirian conditions, yaks are used by the Wakhi for many purposes.

CHINESE PILGRIMS TRAVELING to the learned centers of Buddhism on the Indian subcontinent as early as the fourth century AD brought back reports of "the roof of the world"—the culmination point of the ancient silk routes in the Pamirian mountains. In the thirteenth century, Marco Polo admired the Pamirs' fertile meadows and abundant wildlife, which included the spectacularly horned wild mountain sheep (*Ovis poli*). He described the inhabitants of the little district of Wakhan as a Muslim people who had preserved their own language. The Wakhi have survived to this day, even though events over the past 200 years have scattered them across several borders.

The Wakhi habitat was fragmented when colonial borders were drawn by Tsarist Russia and British India in 1895. Separate groups of Wakhi now live in four different countries: Afghanistan, China, Pakistan, and Tajikistan. Their adherence to the Ismaili sect of Islam enhances their minority status, such groups being typical of high, remote mountain regions.

The Wakhi ethnolinguistic group belongs to the Indo-Iranian branch of the Indo-European language family, and currently comprises 30,000 people. The Wakhi's oral tradition suggests that it has long been their custom for several families to live in one-room mud houses within a compound, each household consisting of an extended family of three generations, including brothers and their families. Nowadays, however, brothers usually form their own households, and instead of up to 50 members, households comprise between 6 and 30 members.

A Harsh Environment

Survival in the harsh environment of the so-called Pamirian knot—the interface between the Pamirs, Hindu Kush, and Karakoram—requires a highly sophisticated approach to the use of natural resources. The Wakhi make use of all ecological zones, moving seasonally between them as they tend their crops and

♀ Wakhi houses are the center of family life, several generations living under one roof.

raise yaks, sheep, and goats. They build their permanent homes at the lowest point of their seasonal movements, at altitudes of between 2,500 and 3,500 meters (8,200 and 11,500 feet).

Single crops of barley, wheat, beans, and peas are cultivated on river terraces or alluvial fans in irrigated valley oases. These foods form the Wakhi's staple diet, and are supplemented by milk products, including butter, yogurt, and *qurut* (dehydrated whey). Meat is eaten only in the long, harsh winter months, when fattened animals are slaughtered and the meat is freeze-dried for storage. Traditionally, an economy of this kind assured the Wakhi a meager subsistence. Over the past 200 years, Kirghiz nomads have challenged their predominance over the Pamirian pastures, but most Kirghiz have now resettled in Turkey.

Changing Borders

During the "Great Game" played out between Russia and British India in the course of the nineteenth century, the Pamirian knot became the focus of international diplomacy. The end result was the creation of a buffer zone between these two powers in the form of the Wakhan corridor, a narrow strip of land controlled by Afghanistan. The northern part of Wakhan was taken over by Russia.

By this time, the Wakhi had lost their status as an independent

⚉ The collection of firewood often involves a long trek through mountainous terrain, across rivers spanned by crude suspension bridges.

⚘ Living at high altitudes, the Wakhi are close to their summer pastures, but must pay the price of long, cold winters.

principality. One group, which included the hereditary ruler, sought refuge in the neighboring Chitral Valley. Other groups moved to virgin lands in China's Taghdumbash Pamir. The Wakhi managed to turn their loss of sovereignty and the fragmentation of their society within a homogeneous ecological zone to advantage by developing a high degree of mobility. This was accentuated when the alien Afghan administration established in Wakhan increased taxes and imposed forced labor and military conscription. To avoid interference in their way of life, groups of Wakhi migrated to other areas in the mountainous regions of central Asia. During the end of the nineteenth century and the first half of the twentieth, their way of life thus came to resemble that of true nomads, until border control was enforced and international relations cooled off.

A Marginal Life

The Wakhi's situation changed as the "roof of the world" became marginalized. Although the core of their material culture has survived, the Wakhi have had to adapt to situations ranging from isolation to assimilation. Wherever they live, they are renowned for using marginal lands, but their circumstances often differ. In Tajikistan and China, farms have been collectivized in an attempt at modernization, while in parts of Pakistan and Afghanistan, the remoteness of Wakhi settlements has excluded them from such development programs.

All Wakhi are Ismailis, but the sect's spiritual leader, the Aga Khan, has focused most of his efforts on Ismaili peoples in northern Pakistan. This has brought about an educational revolution in the Hunza Valley, which now has the highest degree of literacy in Pakistan, while the Wakhi of Chitral are still living at subsistence level. No longer wholly dependent on agriculture, many Wakhi now earn extra income from trade and other activities outside their own settlement regions.

Recent changes in international relations have enabled Wakhi groups in different countries to communicate with each other once again, and to focus on their common heritage. As one very important step towards preserving their culture and identity, Russian linguists are developing a written version of the Wakhi language.

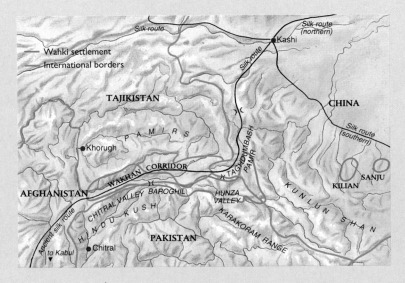

THE ROOF OF THE WORLD
Where once the remote settlements of the Wakhi were traversed by the ancient caravan routes of the Silk Road, today they are intersected by the borders of four countries.

CARTOGRAPHY: RAY SIM
(AFTER HERMANN KREUTZMANN)

⚉ Uygur men of western China, in costumes typical of an earlier time, pose with dignity for an unknown photographer.

TETTONI, CASSIO & ASSOCIATES/PHOTOBANK

☛ Samarkand, a central Asian city famed for its prosperity as a trading center, has often been threatened by fierce nomadic invaders over the course of its history.

⚲ A Kazakh man and his son tend their horses beside the aptly named Heavenly Lake in the Tian Shan (Heavenly Mountains) of the Xinjiang Uygur Autonomous Region, in western China.

CENTRAL ASIA

Central Asia may be seen as a pattern of deserts and steppe lands across which peoples moved as nomads or in trading caravans—a kind of "land–sea", which both separated and connected the societies that had formed around its shores. Traders carried silk from China to the West; pilgrims found their way to India to study Buddhist scriptures; styles of art and architecture spread from western and South Asia as far as China. Yet in the midst of central Asia, there were always islands of civilization: fabled cities such as Merv, Samarkand, and Bukhara, where the local rulers often lived in extravagant style. The Turkic peoples, who have lived in central Asia for at least 2,000 years, have also asserted themselves from time to time, and in the process played a significant part in world history.

The following five nations are usually included in the region of central Asia: Kazakhstan, Uzbekistan, Turkmenistan, Tajikistan, and Kyrgyzstan. Part of western China must also be included: the Xinjiang Uygur Autonomous Region is clearly central Asian, and both the Xizang Autonomous Region and Qinghai are areas that are culturally and ecologically distinct from eastern China.

The dominant physical feature of central Asia is a series of forbidding deserts and rugged mountain ranges. The Kizil Kum and Kara Kum (Red Desert and Black Desert), the vast Taklimakan Desert, the Tian Shan (Heavenly Mountains), and the Pamir, Hindu Kush, and Kunlun ranges make up an inhospitable landscape. Yet people have found ways of surviving in many parts of the region. Nomadic tribes of Mongols, Kazakhs, Kirghiz, Uzbeks, and Turkmen have been able to find grazing for their livestock in rich valleys such as the Fergana Valley—which produced the finest horses in the ancient world—or on the slopes of the high mountains, where winter snows bring forth summer grass. At the same time, although only a few rivers are to be found here, they have supplied water for irrigated agriculture. The resulting internal drainage, which

P. ROY/EXPLORER/AUSCAPE

MIKE LANGFORD/AUSCAPE

NIK WHEELER

MIKE LANGFORD/AUSCAPE

Kazakh yurts are usually erected in level, grassy areas, where livestock can graze and where household tasks can be performed in the open when the weather permits.

Kazakh women inside a lavishly furnished yurt. Yurts are circular felt tents of very practical design, which can be taken down and put up again in just a few hours.

is a feature of most of the river basins, has created large lakes with resources of fish. Sometimes, people have had a detrimental effect on the environment: the recent drying up of one of the largest of these lakes, the Aral Sea, was caused by the excessive use of water to irrigate cotton fields.

In some ways, this part of the world has been in decline for centuries. When the famous Venetian traveler Marco Polo crossed central Asia in the thirteenth century, the overland route was just beginning to lose its importance in East–West trade to the sea routes. By the time European travelers began to explore the region in the nineteenth century, it was a land of ruined cities, abandoned irrigation systems, and isolated peoples. These conditions were favorable to the preservation of small, traditional societies, many of which were described by these explorers as they made their way into central Asia. At the same time, much of the area was being incorporated into the Russian empire (later becoming part of the Soviet Union). The eastern part, which had intermittently been under Chinese rule for 2,000 years, was brought firmly under Chinese control after the Communist Party seized government in China in 1949. The traditional peoples, having lost their political independence, have thus been exposed to modern technology as well as to new political ideologies.

Not surprisingly, then, most of the remaining traditional societies are to be found among the nomadic pastoralists, including the Kazakhs, the Kirghiz, and the Mongols. Thanks to their mobility and isolation, they have been able to escape some of the pressures of modernization. In addition, some of the oasis farmers of central Asia—the Tajiks and Uygurs, especially—have been able to carry on their traditional way of life.

The Mongols: Riders of the Northern Steppes

The Mongol people occupy a vast area in East and central Asia, including the Republic of Mongolia, which is three times as big as France; the Inner Mongolian Autonomous Region of China, which is also larger than France; and portions of the Xinjiang Uygur Autonomous Region of western China. In cities such as Ulaanbaatar, the capital of the Republic of Mongolia (which has a population of 400,000), the people have learned to participate in modern industrial technology, but many Mongols still live as nomadic pastoralists, following their traditional way of life.

Living in a circular felt tent known as a *ger*, a nomadic Mongol family spends its days herding horses, cattle, camels, sheep, and goats—they themselves always list the animals in that order, indicating their relative importance. Much time is spent milking all of these animals and making yogurt, cheese, and an alcoholic beverage known as *airag*. Men, women, and children all ride with great skill.

The Mongols endure incredible hardship in the winter, when temperatures can drop to minus 40 degrees Celsius (minus 40 degrees Fahrenheit) and blizzards howl across the steppes. Wherever possible, they spend the winter in a relatively sheltered location on the south side of a mountain range. In the summer, they move their livestock to higher elevations on the north side, rarely traveling more than a few kilometers in the course of a year.

◄ Mongol herdsmen rounding up their horses with *urgas*, loops of rope attached to the ends of long sticks. The horse is central to the Mongol way of life: beautiful songs are composed in honor of favorite steeds.

NIK WHEELER

⚲ The Mongol felt tent, known as a *ger*, provides a snug environment in cold weather for tasks such as cheese-making.

⚲ The weatherbeaten faces of these Mongol riders express the pride of a people who must overcome the hazards of bitter storms and a rugged landscape to feed their families.

NIK WHEELER

⚘ This Persian miniature shows the mighty Genghis Khan seated on a throne, with two of his sons. The deferential figures surrounding them are, perhaps, kings the Mongols defeated as they swept across Asia in the thirteenth century.

⚲ The Mongols use carts drawn by yaks or oxen to transport their *gers* and other cargo.

In the time of Genghis Khan (who lived from about AD 1160 to AD 1227), Mongol society was based on clans, formed of groups of people descended from a common male ancestor. Clan leaders were loyal to a *khan*, who might lead the men of his subject clans to war. This clan system broke down in modern times for various reasons. The Qing dynasty of China replaced it with the "banner" system in the eighteenth century, under which people in different districts were governed by local leaders, while the communist rulers of China and Mongolia both tried to replace clan and family loyalties and rivalries with a system of communes. When the communist government of Mongolia collapsed in 1990, the nomads readily resumed family ownership of livestock, but there is no sign that the clan system will be revived.

Despite their historic reputation as ruthless conquerors, the Mongol people today impress the visitor as gentle and soft-spoken. Children are treated with great kindness, and everyone's favorite ritual is the celebration of New Year's Day, when family members embrace each other and feast together. Visitors, even total strangers, are always welcomed to the *ger* with formal hospitality, including the offer of refreshments, and if they stay overnight, a sheep will be slaughtered for dinner.

In the past, the Mongols worshiped Tenggeri, the god of the sky, and believed that their shamans could communicate with spirits. They exposed the bodies of their dead to vultures and scavengers, and built shrines, called *oboo*, to local spirits. An *oboo* consists of one or more piles of stones, and everyone who visits one is still expected to walk around it three times, adding a few stones to the cairn. In the sixteenth century, after contact with the Tibetans, the Mongols adopted Lamaistic Buddhism. This religion was suppressed by the communist governments in both Mongolia and China, but it is now being revived in many places, and old monasteries and temples are being rebuilt.

☝ Mongol men and women make felt from sheep's wool. A layer of wool is spread on an old piece of felt, and then rolled up in a leather cover and dragged across the plain to compact the fibers.

↩ Usually, *gers* are found in groups of only two or three, but some Mongolian cities have large concentrations of them. This *ger* settlement near Hovd, in western Mongolia, is unusually large.

↪ Lamas read Buddhist *sutras*, or scriptures, in unison in the Erdene Zuu temple at Karakoram, the ancient capital of the Mongol empire. Buddhism was outlawed by Mongolia's communist government, but since 1989, many temples and monasteries have reopened.

The Bhotia: Yak Herders of the Changtang Plateau

Tibet usually calls to mind the sacred city of Lhasa, with its temples and monasteries dedicated to Lamaistic Buddhism and supported by peasants laboring in fields of barley. Under the Chinese domination of recent decades, the traditional culture of Lhasa and the other Tibetan cities has changed beyond recognition. The Dalai Lama, the pre-eminent religious leader, went into exile in 1959, and the Panchen Lama, the second most powerful leader, who collaborated with the Chinese, died in 1989. Many monasteries have been destroyed, and there has been an influx of Han Chinese people. Armed police keep watch over the lamas, alert for signs of political activity.

In western Tibet, the Bhotia (as Tibetans call themselves) still lead the independent life of nomadic pastoralists, with little outside inter-ference. Living at an altitude above 4,800 meters (15,700 feet) in the vast Changtang Plateau, these people live by herding yaks, sheep, goats, and horses. Animals supply nearly all of their food, with the exception of wheat, barley, and tea, which they buy from other communities, and salt, which they collect from salt lakes. The barley is toasted to make their favorite dish, *tsamba*, and the salt is used to flavor their famous yak-butter tea.

The nomads live in rectangular woolen tents. In the winter, which is very severe at such altitudes, they pitch their tents inside depressions, surround-ing them with stone walls. Fires of dried animal dung keep the interior warm, but someone must still watch over the animals, despite blizzards and temperatures as low as minus 40 degrees Celsius. Yaks (the Bhotia call them *nor*) make this way of life possible, since they can find grazing even at high altitudes, can endure the coldest winter weather, and can carry heavy loads.

Each extended family, consisting of husband, wife, children, and one or both of the husband's parents, takes care of its own herds and lives in its own tent. Few occasions bring larger communities together, but marriage serves to link otherwise isolated groups, since husbands and wives obviously come from different families. The constant movement to fresh pastures—often in the same area used in previous years—dominates everyone's life. The only respite from the daily routine of moving, watching, and milking the herds is provided by occasional trading journeys or visits to Buddhist temples. Milk is used to make yogurt, butter, cheese, and a cosmetic known as *döja*, which women apply to their face.

Before the Great Proletarian Cultural Revolution in China in 1966, the nomads belonged to a class system. Some were rich and some were poor, and most were vassals of Tibet's ruling class. Vassalage and the private ownership of livestock were abolished by the Chinese authorities in favor of a commune system of collective ownership, but in the 1980s, communes were disbanded and livestock was returned to individual families. While it is unlikely that the old system of vassalage will return, there are signs that class is being re-established as some families prosper more than others.

With the relaxation of Communist control since 1980, there has been a revival of Buddhism in Tibet, and the nomads once again invite lamas to be present at funerals and other times of crisis. Some pre-Buddhist shamanistic practices have also been renewed, such as the use of mediums to communicate with the supernatural.

The Tibetan nomads are a proud people, and they look down on those of their neighbors who cultivate the land. To them, farmers are slaves to the endless toil of agriculture, while nomads live off the bounty of nature.

Bhotia men enjoy tea, seated within a stone-walled enclosure. In winter, the Bhotia erect their tents in enclosures like this to provide protection against storms.

A goat is milked into a container made of horn. Milking goats and other livestock is a task that occupies much of Bhotia women's time. The milk is then made into such products as butter or cheese.

Opposite page: In her spacious woolen tent, a Bhotia woman cooks over a fire of dried animal dung. Curiously, the Bhotia have not adopted the efficient round felt tents of their neighbors. A large slit in the roof lets the smoke out.

Goats are released from one of the stone pens the Bhotia use for milking and shearing animals, as well as to protect them from wolves and harsh weather conditions.

WORSHIPERS OF THE SACRED BEAR

E. PENDLETON BANKS

THE AINU HAVE long fascinated ethnologists. Although they live in the northern Japanese islands of Hokkaido and Sakhalin and the Kurile Islands, both racially and culturally they have more in common with Caucasoids than with the Mongoloid Japanese. The men wear full beards, and the women tattoo their lips. Were they the original people of Japan, driven by population pressure to seek refuge in the north? Are they, perhaps, the descendants of the Jomon of the Neolithic age? Despite centuries of acculturation, the Ainu still sing ancient songs and dance traditional dances. They keep alive the memory of the old days by reciting an epic known as the *Yukar*.

Heavily armed Ainu hunters of bygone days, in their traditional dress. The aboriginal religion of the Ainu centered on the ritual sacrifice of a bear cub, which was captured and carefully tended for two years before the ceremony.

Growing rice requires endless manual labor: transplanting the seedlings, weeding the flooded fields, and harvesting and drying the mature plants. Here, a group of Ainu have enlisted the help of a simple mechanical thresher.

Ainu men lead a ritual procession, displaying *marimo*, spherical algae up to 15 centimeters (6 inches) in diameter. The *marimo* festival is celebrated each autumn at Lake Akan, on Hokkaido Island. After the festival, the *marimo* are returned to the lake.

🔺 Burdened by a heavy net bag, an Ainu woman gathers sea urchins in the shallow coastal waters of Hokkaido. The tastiest tidbits, carefully picked out of the spiny shells, will most likely end up as garnish for *sushi* in an expensive Japanese restaurant.

◄ Ainu women carry their infants on their back as they go about their daily tasks. Tattooed lips are a traditional decoration for women.

🔺 An Ainu fisherman proudly displays his catch. Fishing and hunting are the traditional activities of Ainu men, but nowadays, farming is often a necessity.

◄ A full-bearded Ainu man and his wife grill fish over a wood fire in an old-fashioned sunken hearth. The tools, mats, and textiles on the wall behind them are a characteristic feature of Ainu houses.

⚱ For the Dong people of South China, the drum tower is the center of village life. Among its numerous functions, it provides a meeting place for the Council of Elders.

⚱ A crowd of Manchu people. The Manchu are descendants of an Altaic-speaking minority from the northeast who conquered China in 1644 and established the Qing dynasty, the last to rule over China before the revolution of 1911.

EAST ASIA

The nations that make up East Asia include the People's Republic of China, the Republic of China (Taiwan), the Republic of Mongolia, the People's Republic of Korea, the Republic of Korea, and Japan. As in the other regions, the traditional societies of East Asia are relatively few: the Ainu of northern Japan (see the feature *Worshipers of the Sacred Bear*); the remnants of a dozen tribes, known collectively as the Gaoshan, that used to inhabit the whole of Taiwan; the Mongols; and the numerous minorities of China. China maintains an official list of 55 minorities, but some of these are social categories rather than culturally distinct ethnic groups. For example, the Hui are merely Han Chinese who have adopted Islam, and the Hakka are a kind of caste grouping of people who follow certain occupations. The Zhuang, numbering 12 million, occupy a large area in South China, and the Miao and Yao are significant traditional societies. In northeastern China, there are groups such as the Daur, the Evenki, the Oroqen, and the Manchu. Like the Mongols, they have cousins who live in the taiga of Siberia.

The history of East Asia centers on the growth of Chinese civilization on a Neolithic base of village farming. At Banpo, near Xi'an, in China's Shaanxi province, archaeologists have found ingenious perforated pots dating from between 5000 BC and 4000 BC, which could have been used to steam rice, suggesting that the Chinese may have been eating steamed rice with chopsticks for 6,000 years. By the time the first documented emperor of all China, Qin Shi Huang (the First Qin Emperor, as he called himself), built his monumental tomb containing an army of life-sized terracotta warriors in the third century BC, Chinese culture encompassed irrigated agriculture, cities, metallurgy, writing, bureaucracy, standing armies, taxation, and many other features of a complex civilization.

For centuries thereafter, the spread of Chinese culture—and, in some cases, Chinese people—over much of East Asia was irresistible. Although the Koreans and the Japanese both adopted many features of Chinese culture, the Japanese were able to retain their political independence. The Mongols and Tibetans, on the other hand, although they eventually became vassals of China, managed to retain their distinct languages, customs, and religious beliefs. The Mongols, of course, like other northern peoples, such as the Kitai and the Jurchen, at one time conquered and ruled over China. It was precisely the constant threat of invasion from the north and west that led to the building of the extensive chain of fortifications known to the world as the Great Wall of China.

In the south, Han Chinese (a term that describes people speaking various dialects of the Chinese language who follow "orthodox" Chinese cultural patterns) spread along the coast and up the river valleys, gradually pushing the local peoples into ever smaller refuge areas. No Great Wall was needed here, since the process of settlement itself guaranteed that the indigenous population would be fragmented, and thus unable to organize resistance to Chinese expansion. Nevertheless, islands of traditional culture sometimes remained.

The typical traditional society of South China consists of people living by swidden (slash-and-burn) agriculture, although many people farm elaborately terraced irrigated slopes. Houses are made of wood or bamboo, and people wear distinctive, colorful costumes made of hand-woven textiles. Hunting and foraging in the rainforest, with the aid of handmade weapons, such as crossbows, and beautifully made carrying baskets, supplement the food supply.

The striking similarities in material culture evident from one tribe to another, not only within China but across adjoining countries in Southeast Asia, may be the result either of a substratum of pre-existing cultural patterns or of a process of diffusion across the region. Unlike the spread of Chinese culture, this diffusion is not well documented historically, but must be reconstructed from archaeological and ethnological evidence.

SOUTH ASIA

South Asia includes Afghanistan, Pakistan, India, Bangladesh, Nepal, Bhutan, Sikkim, and the island nation of Sri Lanka. In the absence of natural barriers to the movement of peoples, the region has been subject to numerous invasions and cultural diffusions over the millennia. The persisting traditional societies usually represent survivals of earlier peoples not completely absorbed by the newcomers, although in some cases they are the remnants of intrusive groups.

The Indo-European-speaking Aryans, who invaded from the northwest more than 3,000 years ago, laid the foundations for Indic culture. Later invasions, such as that led by Alexander the Great in the fourth century BC, had only a minor impact by contrast with later Islamic conquests, which made much of India Muslim and laid the foundation for its partition into separate Muslim and Hindu nations in the twentieth century, after India had become industrialized.

In the wake of the Aryan invasion, a complex social system was established, whereby the population was divided into broad social classes, which were further subdivided into a large number of castes. Members of a caste could have only limited social interaction with members of other castes, had to marry within their own caste, and were often guaranteed the right to practice a certain occupation, such as that of goldsmith, barber, or carpenter. The caste system provided a framework for giving surviving tribal groups a niche in the larger society, and at the same time protected them from being assimilated. Thus, it could be said that India institutionalized ethnic differences—in contrast to China, where the policy was to urge Chinese culture on everyone.

From early times, then, a number of formally recognized tribal peoples inhabited South Asia. In India, such peoples as the Bhil, the Toda, the

🔱 The great Bhosh Mosque in Lahore, Pakistan. South Asia's population is mostly Muslim or Hindu, but other religions, including Buddhism and Christianity, are also represented.

Oraon, the Santal, the Khasi, and the Naga have long been recognized as distinct social entities. (See the feature *The Naga: Headhunters of the Assam Highlands*.) In Pakistan, there are the isolated mountain peoples of the north, such as the Hunzakuts and the Nagar, some of whom remained independent until the coming of the British. In Sri Lanka, the Vedda are the remnants of a population that once occupied the whole island.

The ethnic groups of South Asia vary greatly in terms of population size, linguistic affiliation, technology, and social organization. The Toda of southern India, for example, once famous for their ritualized tending of water buffalo, on whose milk they relied for most of their food, now number only about 700. The Bhil, Gond, and Santal groups, on the other hand, each have populations of more than three million. Most of the tribes in India speak languages classified as Dravidian, while those in the northeast, such as the Naga and the Mizo, speak Sino-Tibetan languages, and the Munda tribes of eastern India speak languages that may be related to the Mon–Khmer group of Southeast Asia.

While a few tribes still live by hunting and gathering, most either herd livestock or have adopted a form of settled agriculture similar to that practiced by other Indian villagers. Yet differences in values, belief systems, and social organization continue to set the tribal peoples off from the dominant population—and frequently from each other. One of their persistent problems is poverty, caused in part by their lack of title to land. International funding for the Sardar Sarovar dam project, in southwestern India, was withdrawn in 1993, because the plans for resettling the tribal population did not include giving them land to replace that to be flooded.

🔱 These girls belong to the Kafir Kalash tribe, which inhabits the Hindu Kush mountains of northern Pakistan. "Kafir" originally meant unbeliever, and was a term used by the dominant Muslim populations of Afghanistan and Pakistan to describe the indigenous societies they encountered in remote areas.

🔱 Until recently, the Vedda hunted game with bows and arrows. Men's only clothing was a loin-cloth. Their physical type and way of life contrast strongly with those of most other Sri Lankans.

↬ A millet crop drying on posts in the Hunza Valley. Since the opening of the Karakoram Highway, the Hunzakuts have no longer been forced to be self-sufficient, but they still produce much of their own food.

♀ The mud-walled castle known as the Baltit Fort was once the seat of the Mir of Hunza. A British-led force of the Indian Army captured the fort in 1891, bringing the Hunzakuts' independence to an end.

The Hunzakuts: Farmers of the Karakoram Mountains

With the building of the Karakoram Highway, which was completed in 1978 and opened to foreigners in 1986, many travelers have been able to visit the remote Hunza Valley, in northern Pakistan, the home of the Hunzakuts. Here, they are greeted by small fields of grain and orchards of apricot trees clinging to a mountainside. At the top of the slope is an impressive castle, the Baltit Fort, once the palace of the Mir of Hunza. In the old days, the mir dominated the neighboring kingdoms, and his people made a profession of robbing the caravans that toiled through the mountains between India and China. In 1891, the British sent a military force to Hunza and took control of the kingdom, but for a long time, the people continued to follow their traditional way of life (with the exception of robbery).

CHRISTINE OSBORNE/CHRISTINE OSBORNE PICTURES

NIK WHEELER

The majority language of Hunza, known as Burushaski, has no known relationship to any other language in the world, suggesting that the Hunzakuts have formed a distinct society for a very long time. The Karakoram Mountains and neighboring chains have sheltered many small, isolated societies, but most have been found to have linguistic cousins within the Indo-European family.

Traditionally, the Hunzakuts were governed by the mir, who levied taxes in kind and, according to early travelers, lived well. The people often had a hard life, especially when cold weather in the spring reduced the supply of irrigation water. Since the government of Pakistan abolished the

NIK WHEELER

NIK WHEELER

NIK WHEELER

◄○ A village school holds a session in the open air. Islam brought literacy to Hunza, and the benefactions of the Aga Khan have improved educational opportunities.

◄○ The Hunzakuts use the flat roofs of their houses for drying apricots and storing hay, and children find they make excellent playgrounds.

↕ The village of Altit, like all Hunza settlements, sprawls at the base of a rugged mountain range.

Hunza monarchy in 1974, life has improved. People grow more vegetables and fruits, and have a better diet. A legend has grown up, without much evidence, that these people, living in a healthy climate and eating fruits such as apricots, have found the secret of longevity. In fact, like the people of many traditional societies, they lack adequate health care and suffer from such poverty-related diseases as tuberculosis.

Little is known about the aboriginal religion of the Hunzakuts. Nowadays, they are Muslims, belonging to the Ismaili sect identified with the Aga Khan, and in recent years, they have been the beneficiaries of his generosity. Schools, clinics,

and experimental agricultural stations have been built under the auspices of the Aga Khan Development Project (AKDP). Islam has brought male dominance and the seclusion of women; for example, only men dance in public. A shaman's dance is still performed, acting out the traditional method of healing by massage and incantation.

Hunza is in an area that was awarded to India at the time of partition, in 1948, but it has been occupied and governed by Pakistan since that time. The intermittent war between Pakistan and India, as well as skirmishing between Sunni and Shia Muslims in the vicinity, gives the Hunzakuts an uncertain future.

THE NAGA: HEADHUNTERS OF THE ASSAM HIGHLANDS

E. PENDLETON BANKS

THE MOUNTAINS ALONG THE BORDER between Assam, the extreme eastern province of India, and Myanmar (formerly Burma) have long sheltered a group of tribes that have resisted subjugation by the kingdoms or empires that have ruled over those areas, including the British Empire in the nineteenth and twentieth centuries. Of these peoples, perhaps the most intriguing are the Naga. They were described by the explorers and colonial administrators who first came in contact with them as naked savages (*The Naked Nagas* was the title of one of the best books about them), who lived in independent villages almost perpetually at war with one other.

☝ Human heads taken by headhunters, along with heads carved from wood, decorate the front post of a *morung* (young men's dormitory) of the Chang Naga. The *mithan* horns attached to some of the skulls suggest a connection between headhunting and *mithan* sacrifice.

☝ A Konyak Naga man wears an impressive headdress for a dance formerly performed when a head was brought to the village. The decorations of hornbill beaks and feathers, *mithan* horns, and goat's-hair tassels indicate his high status.

ALL PHOTOGRAPHS BY CHRISTOPH VON FÜRER-HAIMENDORF (EXCEPT BOTTOM LEFT, PHOTOGRAPHER UNKNOWN)/HADDON COLLECTION, MUSEUM OF ARCHAEOLOGY AND ANTHROPOLOGY, CAMBRIDGE UNIVERSITY

◄ Steeply thatched roofs give these Angami Naga houses an appearance that is at once rakish and imposing. The wooden "horns" denote the status of men who have given a certain number of Feasts of Merit.

⚲ The Naga are most ingenious at making baskets and other containers from cane and bamboo. Here, a Konyak Naga girl and her friend, adorned with silver jewelry, drink water from a bamboo container.

◄ Members of the Angami Naga tribe transplanting rice seedlings in a flooded terraced field. The monsoon climate dictates a rigid cycle of planting and harvest, but leaves time for other activities during the long dry season.

A Tradition of Warfare

As ethnologists gained more information about the Naga, outsiders came to see them less as "savages" and more as human beings. Warfare and headhunting were certainly an integral part of their culture. Naga villages were built on mountaintops and fortified against attack, and the central feature of each village was the *morung*, or young men's dormitory, where racks of human skulls were kept as trophies. But as in most societies, life was centered around making a living, building a house, getting married, and bringing up children. Crops were grown in swiddens (slash-and-burn clearings in the forest) or in beautifully terraced fields.

The dry season was a time for hunting, and small bovine animals called *mithans* were kept almost entirely to be consumed in Feasts of Merit, a complicated series of rituals in which great quantities of *zu*, or millet beer, were consumed. Men who attained high rank through Feasts of Merit were entitled to display huge wooden horns on the gable end of their house, whereas most houses were adorned by the skulls of *mithans*, or of wild prey.

The Naga were divided into a large number of tribes, including the Khota, the Ao, the Sema, the Angami, the Rengma, the Kacha, the Chang, and the Konyak, each with its own language and set of customs. Each tribe also had its own distinctive style of headdress and ornamentation; for the rest, most men wore only a short kilt or a loincloth. Having neither language nor political institutions in common, the Naga were frequently at war with other villages and tribes, even as they resisted assimilation by their neighbors.

The Push for Independence

During the Second World War, the Naga were caught up in bloody battles between Japanese and British military forces. Just as they were becoming reconciled to British rule, Indian independence sent them into defiant mode. They struggled against subjugation by the Indian government, and succeeded in establishing the quasi-independent state of Nagaland. But there was no going back to the traditional way of life. Missionaries had converted most of the Naga to Christianity, and intervillage warfare and headhunting had become counterproductive.

Today, the Naga still live in mountaintop villages and cultivate traditional crops. A few communities still hold the traditional Feasts of Merit and decorate their house-fronts with animal skulls, but human skulls are no longer displayed as trophies. Political campaigns have taken the place of warfare, and modern schools have replaced the *morungs* for young people. By a curious twist of fate, English has become the official language of Nagaland. Since no single Naga dialect was understood by all, it was necessary to find a common language, and that of the missionaries and the colonial rulers was chosen.

TRADITIONAL PEOPLES OF SOUTHEAST ASIA

A D   2 0 0   –   T H E   P R E S E N T

Farmers, Foragers, and Fisherfolk

MARY HAWKINS, P. BION GRIFFIN, AND THOMAS N. HEADLAND

SOUTHEAST ASIA includes 10 countries: Vietnam, Laos, Cambodia, Thailand, and Burma (Myanmar), on the mainland; and in the insular half, Malaysia, Singapore, Brunei, Indonesia, and the Philippines. Some 444 million culturally and linguistically diverse people occupy this region, the vast majority of whom live by farming, by fishing, and, especially in the more remote areas of Southeast Asia, from forests. Although Southeast Asia most often evokes images of people working wet-rice fields, the traditional societies of island Southeast Asia in particular draw much of their subsistence from forests and seas.

It is a mistake to think of traditional societies in Southeast Asia as isolated, primitive, and unchanging. Working within the constraints of climate and the physical environment, these societies have, on the contrary, been dynamic and continually changing. This chapter includes an account of two peoples, the Kenyah and the Banjar of Borneo, who exemplify the adaptive nature of many of Southeast Asia's traditional societies: peoples who have absorbed ideas and practices from others, and traded their products widely, while retaining their own cultural identity. At the other end of the spectrum, there is an account of the Negrito peoples of Southeast Asia—in particular, the Agta of the Philippines—whose way of life has been eroded and marginalized to the point that they now face almost certain extinction.

◄● Thatch is the most common roofing material in Southeast Asia, suitable grasses being both plentiful and cheap. Although households may individually repair their thatch, when a dwelling requires rethatching, neighbors will gather to help.

♦ An aboriginal ceremonial mask from the Malay Peninsula.
UNIVERSITY MUSEUM, MALAYSIA/TETTONI, CASSIO & ASSOCIATES/PHOTOBANK

Farming methods used in Southeast Asia vary greatly. In Borneo, the largest island, people commonly cultivate dry rice in swiddens—areas of forest cleared by the slash-and-burn technique. On the mainland, and on islands such as Java and Bali, "farmer" usually means "wet-rice cultivator". But even here, swiddens are used, and groups such as the Semang make their living by hunting game and gathering wild foods.

Continuity amidst Diversity

The historical, cultural, and linguistic map of Southeast Asia is bewilderingly diverse. Nevertheless, it shows marked continuities, irrespective of today's political boundaries. For example, the division of northern Borneo into Kalimantan (Indonesian Borneo) and Sabah and Sarawak (Malaysian Borneo), and the additional demarcation of the tiny, oil-rich state of Brunei, are not the product of agreement among the people who live there, but a decision by their former colonial masters. Borders determined by colonial powers, however, have limited meaning for the indigenous people of Borneo. The Kenyah, for example, are found on all sides of the Borneo borders, and it is not uncommon for some to live in Kalimantan and periodically to work in Sarawak.

Continuity is marked not by borders but by cultural factors, such as the universal practice of betel chewing, the use of a brass gong in music, and the prominence of women in ritual and trade. These practices link otherwise disparate groups, and point to an interchange of ideas and customs that has been taking place in Southeast Asia for centuries.

Climate and Agriculture

Southeast Asia lies within the humid tropics. High temperatures and monsoonal rainfall, in excess of 2,000 millimeters (80 inches) annually, are common to the entire region. Close to the equator, rainfall is evenly distributed throughout the year, but to the south and north, the months from June to September are usually dry. There are, however, significant local variations, depending on topography. Climatic unpredictability poses a great challenge to farmers. As a wet-rice farmer of southern Borneo remarked to the author while surveying his inundated field, "This is my problem: not water itself, but how to control it."

The peoples of Southeast Asia have been grappling with water control for centuries, and have developed elaborate irrigation systems, primarily for rice. Irrigation is most highly developed on the mainland, in Java and Bali, and in parts of the Philippines. In other areas, rain-fed wet rice and dry-field rice are more common. The marvel of wet rice is that it

⬤ Wet-rice fields glistening in the sun are a common feature of the Southeast Asian landscape. They testify to the central importance of rice in the diet, as well as to the local people's considerable engineering skills.

SOUTHEAST ASIA
From the hill farmers of northern Thailand to the sea peoples of Sulawesi, traditional peoples in Southeast Asia inhabit areas as diverse as their cultures.
CARTOGRAPHY: RAY SIM

HMONG

SHAN

YAO, LISU, AKHA

MLABRI

KHMU

Gulf of Tonkin

MON

KAREN

NEGRITO (ANDAMANESE)

Andaman Islands

Gulf of Thailand

NEGRITO (SEMANG)

ACEHMESE

SENOI

JAKUN

BATAK

Singapore

Sumatra

MINANGKABAU

KUBU

BADUI

Java

Bali

IBAN

Borneo

KENYAH

PUNAN

BANJAR

NEGRITO (ATTA)

Luzon

NEGRITO (AGTA)

South China Sea

NEGRITO (AYTA)

Philippine Sea

NEGRITO (ATI)

NEGRITO (BATAK)

Palawan

NEGRITO (Negros Island)

NEGRITO (Cebu Island)

NEGRITO (MAMANWA)

Mindanao

TASADAY

MINAHASA

TOALA

Sulawesi

TORAJA

BUGIS

Seram

Irian Jaya

Tanimbar

ATONI

Timor

draws most of its nutrients not from the soil but from the water that passes through the field. A single plot can be used year after year, for more than one crop a year, and may well improve through use. The output of most irrigated fields can also be increased by cultivation techniques. It is therefore not surprising that wet rice is most often associated with large, densely concentrated populations and the development of state societies, such as the historical kingdoms of the Philippines, Thailand, Malaysia, and Indonesia.

Swidden and rain-fed rice cultivation is obviously more vulnerable to climatic vagaries. An early, hot start to the dry season may ruin the crop, while an extended wet may flood cultivated fields and render them useless. A newly cleared swidden may give a handsome yield, but within a year or two, this will decline and the farmers will be forced to relocate. As an abandoned swidden takes years to regain its fertility, and yields just one rice crop a year, swidden societies are usually small and remote from centers of power, occupying land unsuited to wet-rice cultivation.

☛ Southeast Asian peoples have traditionally used wooden carts and animals to transport goods, but they have also developed the capacity to carry heavy and cumbersome loads on their shoulders—and even, as shown here, on their head.

DAVID WITTS/WILDLIGHT

VOJA MILADINOVIC/SIPA-PRESS/AUSTRAL INTERNATIONAL

⬆ At some point in their life, most Buddhist men will enter a monastery, where they will study and teach, and in so doing, bring great honor to their family. For most men, the stay is temporary; for others, the monkhood is a lifelong vocation.

Many of Southeast Asia's traditional peoples, whether living on the mainland or the islands, are swidden farmers. Although rice is central to their subsistence, corn, cassava, taro, sweet potatoes, yams, and fruit and other tree crops may also be grown. Rice was first domesticated in Southeast Asia, and by the fifteenth century, when Europeans arrived in the region, it was the pre-eminent staple crop and already the subject of myth and ritual. In contemporary as in historical Southeast Asia, "rice" and a meal are synonymous: one has not eaten until one has eaten rice.

Religion and Government: Legacies of Early Traders

Europeans were neither the first nor the most influential foreign group to arrive in Southeast Asia. Chinese peoples had been trading and settling there for centuries, and now make up about a third of Malaysia's population alone. Around the first century AD, Indian traders brought Hinduism and Buddhism to the region—not only their morality and religious customs, but also their notions of kingship and government. Local lords styled themselves as Hindu kings and built great monuments to Hindu gods, including the temple complexes of Angkor, in Cambodia, and Borobodur, in central Java. Sanskrit words have survived in the national languages of Malaysia and Indonesia, as well as in those of remoter island groups. Islam, however, had greater impact throughout Southeast Asia.

Islam was carried to Southeast Asia by Arab and Indian traders, taking hold both on the mainland and in the island outposts. The ruler of Melaka (present-day Malacca), the great trading port of precolonial Malaysia, converted to Islam in the late fifteenth century. Another early Islamic kingdom was that of the Banjar people of Banjarmasin, southern Borneo: to this day, the region is a center of Islamic orthodoxy. Islam today remains the major religion of the Indonesian archipelago, Peninsular Malaysia, and parts of the southern Philippines.

Christianity, brought to eastern Indonesia and Sulawesi by the Dutch, and to Borneo by the British and the Dutch, prevails among many indigenous Borneo peoples, as well as among groups in Indonesia's eastern islands, where it competes with local animistic beliefs. Although all major world religions have adherents in Southeast Asia, the local forms of Hinduism, Buddhism, Christianity, and Islam are not slavish copies. While the Balinese profess to Hinduism, and in Java's eastern mountains a small group of Tengger similarly identify themselves, their Hinduism is shorn of ideas of caste, and many of the purification rituals of Indian Hinduism are absent. Christianity in the Philippines, Buddhism among the Thais, and Islam among Malays all incorporate elements unique to these peoples. The way in which these societies have adapted ideas, technologies, beliefs, and rituals from state societies, infusing them with their own beliefs and practices, is typical of traditional societies throughout Southeast Asia.

⬇ From the summit of Java's ancient Buddhist temple of Borobodur, stone Buddha figures serenely survey the lands below.

GERALD CUBITT

THE BADUI OF WEST JAVA

BOEDHIHARTONO, BOEDHISANTOSA, AND MARY HAWKINS

WITH THE COMING OF ISLAM in the sixteenth century, most Javanese, elite and commoners alike, converted from Hindu-Buddhism to Islam. One group, however, which numbered about 800 and whose lineage can probably be traced back to the fifteenth-century West Javanese Hindu kingdom of Pajajaran, rejected conversion and fled to the hills, taking with them their religion, based on ancestor worship, and their way of life. To the present day, and despite the relative proximity of their homeland to the Indonesian capital of Jakarta, the Badui of West Java have preserved their isolation. In this, they are very much the exception among traditional societies in Southeast Asia, which are notable for their dynamism.

DESI HARAHAP

🔥 Dense forest conceals the Badui homeland from the eyes of the outside world. Within the forest, all forms of modernity, including vehicles, are forbidden. This man will always travel on foot.

Inner and Outer Society

Badui society is made up of two independent communities: an inner, exclusive, and strict group, which today numbers some 600 people, and an outer, more accessible population of some 5,000. Each group wears distinctive clothing, the people of the inner group wearing a short, dark sarong with a white blouse and white head cover, while those of the outer group dress all in black. Badui territory—in the highland of Kanekes, at the western tip of Java—is similarly divided into a sacred inner core and an outer fringe.

In the inner core are three villages, each with its own *pu'un*, or sacred chief. Here, there are no schools, no shops, nor any places of worship. For Badui of the inner zone, certain activities are *buyut*—taboo. These include reading and writing; the use of irrigation in agriculture; the rearing of cattle, pigs, goats, or horses; the use of a steel saw or an iron plow; smoking; drinking; and riding in vehicles. Any Badui who breaks a taboo will be exiled to the fringe of the Badui zone. Moreover, whenever the number of families living in the inner zone exceeds 40, one of them must leave. The *pu'un* decides the matter, and there is no dispute.

The Badui of the outer zone, around the sacred inner core, are found today in 24 villages. These people do not observe all the taboos, but the *pu'un* and other officers of the inner group visit them from time to time to see that they have not succumbed to foreign goods and customs. Many, however, readily accept education and modern health care.

The Badui of the inner core prefer isolation. When President Suharto of Indonesia offered government assistance to them, the *pu'un* came to the outer zone to meet him. In breaking the taboo on leaving the inner core, he expressed his respect for the president, but the meeting brought no changes to the 40 families of his tight-knit community. The Badui did not wish it, and the Republic of Indonesia did not care to interfere with their preferred way of life.

Religion and Customs

The Badui cultivate dry rice and other garden produce in swiddens. Contrary to general Javanese practice, they do not use hoes for cultivation, which has the benefit of limiting soil erosion in the hilly limestone country. Their agricultural practices are governed by rituals corresponding to the Javanese lunar calendar. They no longer hunt, and their belief forbids them to raise any four-legged animal. Fowl, fish, and various plant foods of the forest form the basis of their diet.

The Badui religion, like their dialect, is believed to derive from the Sunda, the ancestral people of West Java. Individuals do not perform acts of worship but rely on the *pu'un* and the council of elders to worship their ancestral spirits and gods at certain sacred places. One of these, consisting of megalithic remains known as the "Sasaka Domas", is the site of regular but highly secret rituals related to the agricultural cycle.

Marriage among the Badui is usually arranged by the parents. Although young people may choose their partner, they must marry within the group. Divorce is not permitted in the inner community, but it does occur among the outer group. If newlyweds need their own house, rather than living with parents, it is erected by the community. Dwellings are simple, built on poles about a meter (3 feet) from the ground, with walls of woven bamboo. There is a single entrance and no window. Inside, there is a sleeping area, a fireplace, and a few simple utensils.

Among the small traditional communities of Southeast Asia, the Badui are remarkable primarily for their strict rejection of the outside world—but also for having enjoyed an almost fivefold increase in population during the twentieth century.

TETTONI, CASSIO & ASSOCIATES/PHOTOBANK

TRADITIONAL PEOPLES OF MAINLAND SOUTHEAST ASIA

During the first and second centuries AD, state societies began to develop in the fertile lowlands of mainland Southeast Asia. At first, the differences between "state" peoples and those living in the surrounding hill areas were probably not great, but over time, as the lowland wet-rice economy flourished, the swidden-cultivating hill peoples were increasingly drawn into social and economic systems dominated by the lowland peoples. In this relationship, the hill people were not entirely subordinate. Rather, they were recognized as the guardians of the wild, who rendered periodic obeisance to the lowland rulers in return for acknowledgment of their status as the first inhabitants of the land.

A symbolic expression of this relationship is found in the exchange of gifts between the Khmer ruler of Cambodia and the Lords of Fire and Water of the Jarai tribe, a ritual that took place every three years between AD 1600 and AD 1860, when King Norodom of Cambodia brought the practice to an end. Another example, from Laos, continues to this day. Here, ceremonies are held twice yearly in which hill peoples make offerings to the lowland ruler. The very inclusion of hill peoples in the royal Lao ritual testifies to the fact that the Lao recognize their place and significance, yet the ritual ends with the symbolic assertion of lowland supremacy—the hill people are chased back to their villages.

Such symbolic relationships were underpinned by economic ties. The hill peoples provided the lowlanders with forest products, such as animal hides, tusks, and horns, and obtained from them in return metal, salt, and ritual objects. Occasionally, the hill people were captured by the lowlanders and used as slave laborers, usually on the construction of monuments, but also in war.

Although there are broad similarities in the structure of hill–lowland relations throughout Southeast Asia, the "hill peoples" themselves are strikingly diverse. Their languages, for example, do not belong to any single language group but include Austroasiatic, Austronesian, Hmong-Mien, Tai, and Tibeto-Burman.

Three million of Burma's population, and about 200,000 of Thailand's, speak the Tibeto-Burman language known as Karen. Before the middle of the eighteenth century, Karen peoples were confined to the hills of eastern Burma, where they cultivated swiddens and developed relations with the lowland Burmese state. The village was the center of social and political life, but sometimes, several villages were grouped together under a single chief. Such chieftainships rarely endured for more than one generation.

☝ The elaborate headdress of this Akha woman of northern Thailand indicates her high status within her village, as well as her advanced age.

JACQUES BRUN/EXPLORER/AUSCAPE

☞ As children, the hill peoples of northern Thailand and Burma learn to cultivate the land, to forage, and also to dance. Dressed in her ceremonial dance costume, this girl of the Lisu tribe enjoys a break from her everyday routine.

Traditional Societies of Borneo

The people of Borneo include Chinese, Malays, and Dayaks. Chinese migrated to Borneo over centuries, initially in search of gold, and they are presently an economically powerful group, particularly in the coastal towns. Any visitor to Pontianak or Banjarmasin, in Indonesian Borneo, or Kuching, in Sarawak, will notice that most trade stores are owned and operated by Chinese. Chinese companies are also prominent in Borneo's lucrative timber industry. Ethnically, however, Chinese make up only 4 percent of the population. Dayak peoples represent 45 percent, and Malays account for the remainder. (The term "Dayak" was first used by Dutch colonists to refer to all the non-Muslim indigenous groups of Borneo. Beyond this, "Dayak" is about as racially specific as the American "Indian", including peoples of diverse languages and cultures.)

While the Kenyah and other groups of interior Borneo are termed Dayak, the Banjar are usually called Malay. Nevertheless, Banjar peoples trace their descent to the home of the Dayaks, and to mixed marriages between southern Dayaks, Malays, and even Javanese. Although their language is closest to an archaic form of Malay, it is peppered with words, phrases, and concepts drawn from Dayak languages and overlaid with some Javanese. Perhaps the main reason for regarding the Banjar as Malay is their adherence to Islam.

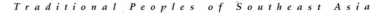

An elongated neck, supported by heavy metal rings, is considered a sign of great beauty in Burmese society.

Tobacco is one of the many crops grown by the hill peoples of mainland Southeast Asia. Horn pipes, such as the one this Lahu man is smoking, are common throughout the hill region.

Unity and continuity in Karen society were provided not by political groupings but by ritual structures based on households and small kin networks. In Karen cosmology, the ancestral spirit (*bgha*) is of supreme importance, and the most important *bgha* is that worshipped by a group of kinsmen living in different households, and often in different villages, who are related matrilineally. At least once a year, all members of the matrilineal cult group must come together and stage a sacrificial feast for their *bgha*. The leader at this feast is the eldest woman of the senior line. All group members must attend, lest the spirit be offended and cause some of them to fall ill.

During the eighteenth and nineteenth centuries, Karen moved into lowland Burma and to Thailand. With the arrival of missionaries, shortly after the British annexed lower Burma in 1826, many Karen converted to Christianity. Missionaries also set up schools, where Karen were taught Burmese and English, and the British government of Burma accorded special recognition to the Karen. When Burma became independent, a region was set aside as the Karen state of Kantharawadi, but many Karen despaired of working out a satisfactory relationship with the dominant Burmese. In 1948, just a few months before Burma became independent, the Karen rebelled, taking the town of Moulmein and threatening Burma's capital of Rangoon. The rebellion failed, and the Karen made their peace with the Burmese, but tension remains to this day. Like other hill peoples, the Karen are somewhat resentful of the political dominance of the lowlanders.

LIFE AND DEATH AMONG THE TORAJA

GÖRAN BURENHULT

For the Toraja, in the highlands of Sulawesi, in Indonesia, life is just a long preparation for death. Almost no distinction is made between life and death—most aspects of living are interwoven with and controlled by liturgies that have been memorized through time and are passed on by the priests. The tradition of ancestor worship remains strong.

The disposal of the dead is a drawn-out process, which, in fact, never ends. It consists of a series of regularized stages in the relationship between the living and the dead. To the Toraja, the water buffalo is the most sacred of all animals, and it is also the principal symbol of wealth. Buffaloes are bred and carefully tended for one single purpose: to be sacrificed during grand funerary ceremonies.

❧ *Opposite page:* Like the people of many other cultures in the Indonesian archipelago, notably on the Lesser Sunda Islands, the Toraja are masters of a complex weaving technique called *ikat.* This exquisite example is from the village of Palawa.

♀ In Toraja communities, megalithic traditions still form part of religious ceremonies, and the erection of stones is intimately linked to ancestor worship, as well as to mythological and cosmological concepts. The bones of the deceased are wrapped in *ikat* textiles and placed in rock-cut tombs on rock walls. Wooden sculptures depicting the dead, called *tau-tau,* are placed on the outside. The *tau-tau* at Suaya, southeast of Rantepao, such as those shown here, are among the most spectacular in the region.

🏠 The characteristic houses of the Toraja, with their conspicuous pointed gables (*tongkonan*), reflect a unique combination of mythology, cosmology, and everyday life. *Tongkonan* literally means "the place where you sit". A house forms a miniature cosmos, and all houses are divided into three sections, representing the Upper, Middle, and Lower worlds. In the upper section, the family regalia are kept in painted coffins of red sandalwood; the middle section is where the family members live and eat; and in the lower section, domestic animals are kept.

❧ The most sacred of offerings has just been made in the village of Sadang. The ancestor spirits have received the blood offering, and the soul of the deceased can now enter the realm of death, *Puya.* The carotid artery of the buffalo is cut with a long knife, and the animal bleeds to death within a few minutes, after which a liturgy called *Passomba Tedong* is read. At the funerals of important people, the offerings sometimes include as many as 250 buffaloes.

THE KENYAH

RIO HELMI/SIPA-PRESS/AUSTRAL INTERNATIONAL

⚧ All Kenyah women carry their babies in wooden baskets strapped to their back, but only women of high status may use elaborately designed and beaded baby carriers such as this.

⚧ In past times, Kenyah men hunted heads as well as wild game. Ceremonial hunting dances have survived into modern times.

The Kenyah consist of some 40,000 "Dayaks" who live along the major rivers of eastern Kalimantan (Indonesian Borneo) and Sarawak (Malaysian Borneo). Kenyah cultivate dry rice in swiddens, and they also fish and forage. All their settlement names are prefixed by the word "long", which is often taken to refer to the longhouses they live in. In the local languages, however, "long" means the confluence of two rivers, which is where the Kenyah like to locate their villages.

Stories of Kenyah origins place them around the headwaters of eastern Kalimantan's major river systems. From there, they have spread into Sarawak. The reasons for migration are numerous: the need to find new land to replace exhausted swiddens; political leadership struggles leading to groups breaking away and forming new villages; and the desire to escape warfare and slave raiding. Today, most Kenyah are nominal Christians, but pre-Christian beliefs and rituals have not disappeared.

RIO HELMI/SIPA-PRESS/AUSTRAL INTERNATIONAL

High Chiefs and Village Chiefs

In Kenyah society, no one individual ruler has authority over all others. Instead, authority is vested in high chiefs, who rule over particular river segments. Before European colonization, the position of high chief was not a formal office; his authority rested on strength, descent, and alliances with chiefly families in other river valleys. One of the effects of colonization was to formalize the high chief's position. From the middle of this century, national governments have continued the process, slotting the high chiefs into their formal government structure. In eastern Kalimantan (Indonesian Borneo), for instance, high chiefs are known in the national language as *kepala adat-istiadat besar* (great chief of custom and tradition), and are subject to the *camat*, the Indonesian government's district officer. In Sarawak (Malaysian Borneo), high chiefs are known as *penghulu* (a Malay word), or *temenggong*, and are likewise responsible to the district officer.

A high chief has authority over several villages, each of which has its own chief. These village chiefs, now most commonly known by their Malay or Indonesian name rather than their Kenyah name, are responsible to both the high chief and the district officer. Chiefs are usually of high social rank, and should be good orators and responsible representatives of their community. Ideally, they should rule by consensus.

The Kenyah, like the neighboring Kayan, are a society of aristocrats, commoners, and slaves. In the past, when the Kenyah were headhunters, aristocrats and commoners were divided into four ranks, two of aristocrats and two of commoners, and slaves (captives taken in battle) were owned only by the first rank of aristocrats. Today, slaves are not distinguished from commoners, and the four ranks have become two, one of commoners and one of aristocrats. The division between aristocrat and commoner remains significant: aristocrats are still prominent in leadership, and special agricultural rituals are performed for them. Rank is also expressed in body decoration and personal garments. High-ranking Kenyah wear more elaborate tattoos than commoners, and only they may use highly decorated baby carriers.

Marriage and Kinship

Ideally, marriage takes place between individuals of the same rank, and kinship is reckoned bilaterally, through both male and female lines. Following marriage, there is no fixed rule of residence. The couple and both sets of parents meet before the marriage and decide where the couple will live. The decision depends on various factors, including the age of the parents and the resources of each household. Emphasis on bilaterality and the sharing of authority between men and women is not only a feature of Dayak groups but is common to many societies throughout Southeast Asia.

The Kenyah naming system is patrilineal to the extent that a child has a name of its own and also carries that of the father; but when the child is named, the parents' names are altered to indicate their relationship to the child. When grandchildren are born, the parents revert to their personal names, adding the prefix *Pe*, indicating their respected grandparent status. The practice of naming individuals in relation to their children is called teknonymy, and it is common to Kenyah, Kayan, Banjar, Balinese, and many other Southeast Asian societies. In the midst of such diversity, this common practice is striking. It is perhaps best explained by the fact that, for most Southeast Asians, to be an adult is to be a parent. Childless people, be they married or not, are both pitied and of low status.

A Village Life

The Kenyah live in villages consisting of several longhouses, which each have 10 to 15 apartments, opening onto a communal verandah. Longhouses are usually placed parallel to the river, where the bank is steep, and are connected to it by notched logs. Sacred poles mark the upriver end of the village. Downriver, and separated from the village by water, is the cemetery.

Within a typical longhouse, the central apartment is occupied by the leader of the longhouse; on either side are the apartments of lesser aristocrats; and next to them, those of the commoners. Rank may be expressed in the roof height. The roofs of aristocrats in a particular longhouse are often higher than those of commoners, and the roof of the longhouse leader may be a meter or so (several feet) higher than his neighbors' roofs. Throughout island Southeast Asia, in various societies, the roofs of high-ranking families tower over the rest.

Land is owned by the village, which acts collectively in both ritual and agriculture. Each stage of the agricultural cycle is marked by a rite, performed by the villager in charge of farming ritual (the *laki malan*). On these days, a group made up of a member of each household gathers at the sacred poles, and no one may leave the village, nor may strangers enter it. This state of affairs, called *malan*, also prevails when a villager dies or a member of the community has transgressed traditional laws.

The Kenyah Household

The unit of production and consumption among the Kenyah is the *amin*, the household. The size of Kenyah households varies, members being related by either blood or marriage. Aristocratic *amin* tend to be slightly larger, in one community averaging

☞ Her elongated earlobes, lengthened through years of wearing heavy brass globes, identify this woman as Kenyah. The heavy beading of her costume and the design of her tattoos further identify her as a woman of high status.

CHARLES LENARS/EXPLORER/AUSCAPE

↪ The hornbill bird is indigenous to Borneo, where it symbolizes strength and virility. Hornbill feathers are an essential part of a Kenyah man's ceremonial dress.

⚲ Beads from places as far away as Venice have long been traded in Borneo, where they are prized heirloom items. This young woman's necklace probably contains beads passed on to her by her mother and grandmothers.

some 10 members as against about 7 for commoners. Each married couple within the household is expected to make their own rice fields, as is any young adult member, so most *amin* make several fields per year. The produce from the fields goes into a common store, as do the products of fishing, hunting, and gathering, and household members cook and eat as a unit. The introduction of cash cropping, mainly for rubber and pepper, and of wage labor, has brought new complications to the communal household. While the cash earned by individual men or women belongs to them and their spouse and children, they cannot refuse to use it for general household items, such as salt and kerosene.

Kenyah men and women are equally involved in cultivating the rice fields. Most work is done by the nuclear family, but for clearing, planting, and harvesting, exchange labor groups are often formed. Groups are also formed to cultivate the fields of the village chief and the *laki malan*, who, in addition to making their own personal fields, each control a field as part of their office. All households

CHARLES LENARS/EXPLORER/AUSCAPE

must contribute labor to cultivate the "official" fields, or otherwise pay a fine. The harvest from the chief's field is used in village rituals, but the harvest from the *laki malan*'s field is his own.

Community Life

Because a household's fields are often some distance from the village, the Kenyah build longhouses in the fields as well. These field houses are solid structures, built to last years rather than a season, and are usually smaller than the village longhouse. Members of the field longhouse may be drawn from several village longhouses, and each apartment houses a single nuclear family. Each field longhouse has an elected leader, most often an aristocrat, but the position is temporary. For rituals that are vital to the entire village, members must return to the village and join their village longhouses.

In the fields surrounding the longhouse and those close to the village, there are also field huts, which are used for shelter and rest, and often for courtship.

In terms of their social, ritual, and economic structure, the Kenyah are representative of many Dayak groups and also have much in common with other traditional societies of island Southeast Asia. This is most noticeable in the concept of *adat*. *Adat*, a Malay word, is usually translated as "custom", but its meaning is broader. When everything and everyone act according to *adat*, there is harmony and balance in the world. Wrongdoing, be it adultery, theft, or a ritual offense, leads to imbalance and sickness. When the wrongdoing is individual, a fine is imposed, the amount being decided at a village meeting. This notion of *adat* pertaining to custom, law, and religion is found among many island Southeast Asian societies. With the move towards state societies, and the spread of Islam and Christianity, however, the unitary force of *adat* has been considerably weakened.

C. AND J. LENARS/EXPLORER/AUSCAPE

INDONESIAN WOVEN TEXTILES: TRADITION IN A CHANGING WORLD

CHRISTINA SUMNER

The woven textiles produced in Indonesia today are heir to a tradition of exceptional variety and beauty. These textiles serve a range of practical purposes, and have traditionally played a significant role in Indonesian ceremonial and ritual life. Whether in the form of special clothing, temple hangings, or precious fragments, many textiles have symbolic power. Their presence and exchange during ceremonies affirm relationships; they delineate the sacred, and hallow the important rituals surrounding birth, circumcision, marriage, succession, and death.

The outstanding variety of materials, techniques, and motifs is a reflection of Indonesia's indigenous diversity as well as of the long-term impact of foreign influences—particularly from China, India, the Islamic world, and Europe. Over many centuries, new ideas from these sources have been assimilated into the many different regional weaving styles that have grown up, and into the region's cultural matrix generally. This cultural complexity is still very apparent in contemporary woven textiles, although, in a rapidly changing world, the traditional forms have been much altered.

The Pressures of a Modern Economy

Many factors have contributed to the changes that are taking place. During the twentieth century, the political and economic face of Indonesia has altered profoundly. Political events and new belief systems have brought about social changes, and the role and form of textiles have changed accordingly, for better and for worse.

Commercial cloth in good colors is now widely available throughout Southeast Asia, and this poses a serious threat to hand-made textiles. With the development of a uniform style of dress as an expression of Indonesian nationalism, batik has come to prominence, and regional weaving styles have been largely relegated to the realm of folk art.

⚤A Batak woman weaving an *ulos*, or blanket, on a traditional backstrap loom in Labuhan Galaga, northern Sumatra.

⚥This warp *ikat hinggi* (a man's shoulder or waist cloth), with a nontraditional design, was woven in East Sumba in 1964.

Education and tourism have helped to distance young Indonesians from their traditional culture, encouraging them, particularly the men, to opt for ready-made Western-style clothes.

Traditionally, Indonesian women have monopolized the skills of textile production. Today, while some women still hand-spin their cotton on spindles (in Sawu and Flores, for example), most weavers use imported mercerized cotton yarn. The traditional horizontal backstrap loom, once used almost exclusively throughout the archipelago, has been replaced in the textile factories of Java by electrically driven floor looms. With modernization and mechanization, men have infiltrated what was formerly women's work, the products of their labor destined for the urban and tourist markets rather than for regional consumption. On the other hand, some contemporary designers are revitalizing the Indonesian texile industry by employing village artisans with traditional skills to produce a

sophisticated range of woven, and also batik, designs.

Traditional Techniques

With the widespread interregional migration that has taken place in recent times, and improved communications between formerly isolated textile-producing communities, the distinctions between the regional styles produced by different ethnic groups are breaking down.

By far the best-known forms of Indonesian woven textile art are the *ikat* and supplementary thread techniques. Traditional *ikat* skills are still strong in the more remote areas, such as the interior of the larger islands of Sulawesi and Kalimantan and the more isolated islands of Nusa Tenggara, in the east. Although cotton warp *ikat* is the most common traditional form, weft *ikats* in silk are produced in Bali and the southern regions of Sulawesi and Sumatra. In Bali, cotton weft *ikat* sarongs are handwoven in quantity for the tourist market from commercially produced cotton thread.

Silk and precious metal thread were brought to Indonesia by Islamic traders during the sixteenth century, and were rapidly incorporated into local textile traditions. Natural silk has now given way to synthetic thread; and while gold and silver thread are still used to create supplementary thread patterns, they are no longer metallic but synthetic.

The Future

Traditional textiles are still woven in many areas of Indonesia, but they rarely approach the standard of earlier products, and their ritual meaning has also been greatly diminished. In this age of international tourism, much of Indonesia's weaving industry is geared to mass production of "traditional" souvenir textiles, which usually bear only a passing resemblance to the beautiful art works of past times.

At the same time, however, traditional textile production is being revived. Following extensive research, ancient designs and methods have been reintroduced to village artisans by contemporary entrepreneurs. Encouraged by an assured market, these skilled workers are now producing a new and different range of superb-quality textiles that are nonetheless deeply rooted in tradition and actively promote its continuance.

THE BANJAR

Coastal Southeast Asians have a long history of contact with the world outside their own communities. The Bugis people of Sulawesi, famed throughout the region as sailors and pirates, have for centuries played a major role in interisland trade. A visitor to Jakarta may still see many Bugis ships there, taking on all sorts of cargo, from motorbikes to sacks of sugar, for distribution throughout the islands. Similarly, coastal villagers from southern Borneo frequently cross the Java Sea, exporting dried fish and forest products and bringing home fine woodwork, cloth, and other manufactured goods.

The great majority of southern Kalimantan's people refer to themselves as *urang Banjar*, Banjar people. The Banjar sultanate, based in the main port of Banjarmasin and the nearby town of Martapura, is well documented in the historical literature of the region, but less is known about the Banjar themselves.

Although anthropologists have referred to the Banjar as a Malay people, the description is not wholly accurate. A Malay kingdom of inland Borneo probably gave rise to the Martapura kingdom, yet allowance must also be made for both Dayaks from southern Borneo and eastern Javanese migrating to the region centuries ago and marrying into the proto-Banjar group. When

questioned about their origins, Banjar mention Dayaks, Javanese, Malay, and even Chinese, but invariably conclude with *"Sudah lawas banar urang Banjar aja gin"* ("We have been Banjar and Banjar only for a long time"). Often, they will add: "The Banjar are Muslims", and Islam is certainly central to their identity.

Islam and Local Beliefs

The Banjar were probably introduced to Islam by traders visiting coastal settlements in the sixteenth century. (The oldest known copy of the Koran in Kalimantan has been dated to the early sixteenth century.) For nearly all Banjar, Islam regulates marriage, divorce, and inheritance. Wealthy men are polygamous, and children are taught to read the Koran and perform the daily prayers.

The adoption of Islam did not extinguish the Banjar notion of *adat*. The Banjar see the cosmos as co-inhabited by spirits, both malevolent and benevolent, to be propitiated through ritual. During childbirth, for example, they light a small fire of scented oil and leaves in a corner of the room to keep malevolent spirits at bay, and at night they cover their windows with wooden shutters to prevent ghosts from entering the house. Like many traditional societies of Southeast Asia, the Banjar are syncretists, borrowing and adapting from others in the process of evolving their own distinct traditions. This is particularly evident in their approach to marriage.

☿ Among the Banjar, tropical hardwood is the most prized building material, and was once considered essential to the construction of a traditional Banjar house. Large houses such as this one, with hardwood walls, floors, and roof, are now rare, owing to the high cost of the wood. This man is doubtless the envy of his neighbors.

RIO HELMI/SIPA-PRESS/AUSTRAL INTERNATIONAL

Marriage and Kinship

Marriage among the Banjar always involves the payment of a bride price. This is presented by the groom's female kin to the bride's mother and her female kin, and commonly consists of cash, clothing, and some furniture. The presentation is accompanied by a ritual meal. After the money has been counted, displayed, and blessed, and the gifts examined, a wedding date is set. The groom is absent from these negotiations, and the bride, although present, should remain silent while her female kin choose the date. The entire process is organized by older women: no men are present. That women should fulfill such an important role, and exercise the greatest authority, is not unusual for island Southeast Asia, although it is unusual for a society that so strongly identifies itself with Islam.

An emphasis on seniority and sexual equality is also evident in the Banjar kinship system. Banjar kinship is based on generation, birth order within generation, and, to a much lesser extent, gender. The critical feature of kinship terminology is its stress on seniority. Although the Banjar commonly extend kin names to close friends and neighbors, they are referred to only by generalized kin terms, such as *acil* (mother's or father's sister) or *kai* (mother's or father's father). Within the family, however, the parents' siblings and the grandparents' generation are always distinguished by birth order, without distinction of gender. The eldest of the parents' sibling group is called *julak*, the second sibling *gulu*, the third *angah*, and the fourth *amak*, but the fifth and subsequent are known by general kin terms that do differentiate between male and female.

The Banjar have terms for 11 generations, but only 8 are commonly used. Most Banjar do not know the names of their *angah* (great-great-grandparent) or *datu* (great-grandparent), but use these terms to mean "some time in the distant past". This has the effect of personalizing the passage of time. Similarly, the extension of kinship terms for nephew, niece, and grandchild to all those of appropriate age has the effect of personalizing the social world. The Banjar thus live in a world of kin.

Farmers, Fisherfolk, and Traders

The Banjar's economic activities are diverse, but are dominated by agriculture and fishing for subsistence and sale. While land is owned individually and inherited bilaterally, fishing boats are usually owned by groups of villagers and inherited patrilineally. Particular stretches of water may, in some sense, belong to particular villages, but there is no developed idea of ownership of the sea. Inland waterways are open to all, and it is common for women to fish for shrimp before washing their family's clothes in

the river. For the Banjar, the right to fish is embodied in the act of fishing, not in the more abstract idea of ownership of a fishing ground. In general, a person who expends labor is considered to be entitled to the products of that labor.

A similar notion applies to ownership of land. For most of Banjar history, land has been both plentiful and freely available. Individual households thus claim land in much the same way as the Kenyah do: by clearing and planting it. Fruit trees, coffee, and rubber are the most common dry-land crops, while rice is cultivated on both dry and flooded land. Banjar occasionally make swiddens to grow dry rice, but the most prized rice land is a flooded field. As these are in relatively short supply, ownership of them is fixed and jealously guarded. Even so, this does not guarantee an annual crop.

⬆ In the Banjar village of Tabanio, freshly caught fish are cleaned, split, salted, and left to dry in the sun on bamboo racks. Some will end up on tables in places as far away as Thailand and Japan.

⏣ Famous as pirates and fisherfolk, the Bugis of Sulawesi are at home with, and in, the water. The people of this village live in houses supported by stilts set in shallow waters.

Much Banjar rice land is not irrigated but fed by rain, making crops dependent on the vagaries of climate. It is not uncommon for a household to own 5 hectares (12 acres) or so of wet land—an amount that would be considered a king's ransom in mainland Southeast Asia, Java, or Bali, where nearly all wet lands are irrigated. But in southern Kalimantan, only half, or less, of that area may be cultivated within any one year, the remainder being too dry or too wet. Moreover, the land may drain or flood unevenly, and part of the crop is often destroyed by water or drought before harvest. Despite the risks, Banjar with access to wet land will almost always cultivate it, growing a local, long-stemmed variety of rice that stands up well to flooding. This yields a grain they claim is tastier than any of the quick-growing varieties now dominant in Java or Bali, or on the mainland.

Although the Banjar live very much in settled agricultural and fishing communities, they still forage in the forest for edible leafy plants, mushrooms, and timber.

The Banjar distinguish themselves from other Borneo groups, taking great pride in their reputation as traders. The Bugis of neighboring Sulawesi similarly see themselves as traders first and fisherfolk second. For centuries, the Banjar have transported products of the southern interior to the coast by riverboat, and then shipped them to other places in the Indonesian archipelago. Despite the access to the interior afforded by new roads, they still largely control trade in southern and central Borneo.

Mary Hawkins

THE NEGRITOS: DISAPPEARING HUNTER-GATHERERS OF SOUTHEAST ASIA

RAGHUBIR SINGH/ANA PRESS

A number of small Negrito populations are found in Southeast Asia, most of them mobile hunter-gatherers. With their dark skin, curly hair, and small body size, they could be referred to as Pygmies, but today that term is best restricted to the peoples of the African rainforests.

Negrito populations are now rapidly disappearing. Only four groups survive in the Andaman Islands—one of which, the Onge, dwindled in number from 1,000 to 96 between 1901 and 1988. There are also 10 groups in Peninsular Malaysia, totaling 1800, and about 300 Negritos live in Thailand. Most of the surviving Asian Negritos are found in the Philippines, where 29 ethnolinguistic groups, numbering 30,000 people, live on six of the major islands. The population decline is due to high death rates, resulting from a range of factors: encroachment by outsiders; deforestation; depletion of traditional game and plant resources; new economic forces, which have resulted in general poverty and previously unknown diseases; and cases of outright land-grabbing, murder, and kidnapping. The already precarious situation of the Philippine Negritos was worsened by the eruption of Mount Pinatubo in June 1991, which displaced at least three-quarters of the 15,000 Negritos in western Luzon (known as the Ayta).

It is now accepted that the Negritos are descendants of groups of *Homo sapiens* who migrated from mainland Southeast Asia into their present areas perhaps 25,000 years ago, during the Late Pleistocene era, subsequently developing their distinctive physical characteristics. They are assumed to be the aboriginal inhabitants of the Philippines.

All the Asian Negrito groups are, or were, hunter-gatherers. Today, they are found in various stages of deculturation, several groups having become extinct. With the sole exception of the Andaman Negritos, all engage in some marginal cultivation, and exchange and trade goods and their labor with neighboring non-Negrito peoples.

♠ An Onge mother and child from Little Andaman. A carrying basket and simple household equipment make up the belongings of these islanders, with their mobile way of life. The ocher is both a decoration and an insect repellant.

♀ Agta men in the remoter areas of eastern Luzon pride themselves on being capable hunters of wild pigs and deer. Bows and arrows are often still used, and in the dry season, dogs assist in the pursuit of game. In the wet season, the Agta favor stalking. Among some Agta groups, women also hunt and fish.

P. BION GRIFFIN

THE AGTA OF THE PHILIPPINES

O f the 29 groups of Negritos living in the Philippines, there are 10 groups, numbering about 9,000, who identify themselves as Agta. They are found throughout several thousand square kilometers of dense tropical forest along the eastern side of Luzon Island. The area is true rainforest, with copious rainfall distributed throughout the year, and is generally hot and humid. In the nineteenth century, 80 percent of the whole lowland area was covered by old-growth rainforest; by 1990, this had been reduced to about 9 percent, as a result of logging and clearing for farmers coming in from other areas of Luzon. Most of the Agta forest is now honeycombed with logging roads.

⚥ Although child-care is primarily the responsibility of Agta women, fathers of several children are also expected to show affection and to help with such tasks as babysitting and carrying children during family travels. Here, a mother is carrying her baby in the traditional way as she goes about her work. The house in the background, built for the rainy season, is of a recent style, influenced by farmers' architecture.

THOMAS N. HEADLAND

For thousands of years, the Agta have lived a relatively stable and adaptive life in the rainforest. Today, their culture and their very survival are under great stress, as thousands of colonists migrate into their areas, the forest is cut back, government soldiers battle guerrilla forces in Agta hunting grounds, game and fish resources are depleted to extinction, new diseases are introduced, and the people are moved onto small government reservations.

The social organization of the Agta is almost exclusively kin-based, and descent is traced through both parents. Most marriages are monogamous, taking place between unrelated people from different bands.

They live in small, widely scattered camps, mostly in open areas in the forest, but also on the coastal beaches of the Pacific Ocean, in open brushland, or in coconut groves. Camps are small, averaging about six nuclear households, and are moved every few weeks.

Agta houses are either simple lean-tos, where people sleep on mats on the ground, or small huts on stilts, with a bamboo or palm-wood floor about a meter (3 feet) above the ground and a thatched roof. Usually, there are no walls. Houses are very small, and mostly inhabited by a single, nuclear family.

The Agta have no chiefs or formal group leaders of any kind outside the nuclear household. Social life is controlled primarily by the parents, and women participate equally with men in decision-making. Individuals tend to do as they wish, and if they go against the norms of the camp, they will first be subjected to criticism, and then ostracism. If that does not work, families will simply move away from the offender.

A Subsistence Economy

Until the 1960s, the Agta's main economic activity was hunting. Men spent most of their time hunting wild pigs, deer, and monkeys with bows and arrows and, sometimes, crude shotguns. In some camp groups, Agta women also hunt large game. Their economy has long revolved around exchange with non-Agta farmers of wild meat for other foods. As game declined during the 1970s, however, the Agta gave more and more of their time to working as unskilled laborers for the growing populations of farmers.

The Agta have seasonally helped non-Agta farmers since prehistoric times, and they were also cultivating their own small slash-and-burn fields when they were first observed by Spaniards in the eighteenth century. Today, with so many having to work for wages, this form of cultivation is a very minor activity.

Nowadays, the Agta's main economic activity is collecting forest products for trade. The wild meat that was the main trade item of former times was supplanted in the 1980s by rattan. In 1992, the Agta had switched to collecting orchids, firewood, poles for housebuilding, medicinal plants, and riverine shellfish, all for trade for rice or cash. Increasingly, they also work as forest guides for loggers and as night guards of logging trucks and bulldozers. In general, there is little division of labor between the sexes.

Agta Religion

The Agta are animists, but their beliefs have been modified by Christianity. In contrast to other tribal peoples, they do not take their religion very seriously. They do, however, hold to a strong belief in a spirit world containing many classes of supernatural beings. The ghosts of recently deceased adult relatives are especially feared, as they are prone to return to the abode of their family during the night, causing sickness and death. Agta people sometimes offer small gifts to the spirits if they are taking something from the forest or clearing a garden. Both men and women may be spirit mediums, diagnosing and treating disease with herbal medicines and simple prayers to their spirit "friends". In difficult cases, they may conduct séances, chanting prayers over the patient until, in a trance, they are possessed by their familiar spirits.

♀ Boys and girls take part in hunting even before their teenage years. Here, a young Agta boy backpacks an immature wild pig (*Sus barbatus*) home from the hunt. The Agta mostly kill immature and old pigs and deer. The strongest adult animals usually evade them.

The Future

Demographic studies have shown that Agta populations are in severe decline. Their death rate exceeds the birth rate, and life expectancy is only about 21 years. Infant mortality is high. The high death rate results mainly from tuberculosis, pneumonia, and gastrointestinal illnesses. The people also suffer from chronic malnutrition, malaria, intestinal parasites, alcoholism, and unsanitary living conditions. Homicide is frequent, especially among males.

It is predicted that by the year 2005, the tropical forests of the Philippines will be gone. Perhaps the most tragic aspect of this loss is that by that time the unique and ancient Agta culture will be extinct as well.

P. Bion Griffin and Thomas N. Headland

🍯 The seasonal collection of honey is extremely important to the Agta, as it is to all hunter-gatherers of the tropical forest. Liquid honey is eaten and traded, and bee larvae are eaten dipped in liquid. This young Agta man is preparing a bundle of dry and wet leaves to smoke a honeybee cluster. He will climb up the tree to reach the comb, cut the honeycomb out, and lower it to less agile companions below.

THE TASADAY: STONE AGE CAVE DWELLERS OR THE MOST ELABORATE HOAX IN SCIENTIFIC HISTORY?

Thomas N. Headland

In 1971, NEWS FLASHED AROUND THE WORLD of a band of cave-dwelling people living deep in the Philippine rainforest. The discovery was made by Manuel Elizalde, Jr, the head of Panamin, the government agency in charge of tribal groups. A group of 26 people, the Tasaday, were reportedly following a Stone Age way of life, surviving solely on wild foods and wearing leaves for clothing. They knew nothing of the outside world, not even that there was a large agricultural village just 4 kilometers (less than 3 miles) away. They neither hunted nor grew food, but ate only what they could forage: wild bananas, roots, berries, grubs, and crabs and frogs fished by hand from small streams. They had no pottery, cloth, metal, houses, weapons, dogs, or domestic plants. Their cave was in dense rainforest in South Cotabato province, southern Mindanao, at an elevation of 1,200 meters (4,000 feet).

The National Geographic Society brought worldwide attention to the discovery through articles in *National Geographic Magazine* in December 1971 and August 1972, and its television film on the Tasaday was shown repeatedly in Europe and America in the course of 1972 and 1973. News reporter John Nance's bestseller, *The Gentle Tasaday: A Stone Age People in the Philippine Rain Forest*, spread their fame further in 1975. Journalists, film makers, and nine scientists were flown in by Panamin to visit the site, although only one, ethnobotanist Douglas Yen, was able to stay for more than a few days. (Yen was there for 38 days.) Then, in 1973, the authorities stopped all contact with the Tasaday, and nothing further was heard of them for 13 years.

The 1986 Hoax Claim?

In 1986, immediately following the overthrow of Philippine President Ferdinand Marcos, came reports that the original Tasaday story was a complete hoax. On 18 March, after an easy hike from a major airport, Swiss journalist Oswald Iten reached the Tasaday unannounced. He found them living in houses, growing crops, and wearing clothes. An hour's walk away, he found their cave, abandoned and overgrown. When, a week later,

ALL PHOTOGRAPHS BY JOHN LAUNOIS/BLACK STAR

reporters from the German magazine *Stern* flew to the area, their arrival was notified ahead of time. These reporters filmed the same Tasaday individuals that Iten had photographed, but now they were living in the cave and wearing leaves—several with colored underpants showing underneath. In the following months, hundreds of news articles argued the case for and against Elizalde having fabricated the whole event.

By the end of the 1980s, the controversy had been reduced to a single question: were the Tasaday a group of primitive, isolated foragers and a major anthropological discovery, or simply a giant hoax?

The Current Consensus

In fact, neither view is correct. By the early 1990s, a general consensus had emerged. Most scientists had moved away from the opinion that the Tasaday were totally isolated, offering a genuine glimpse of Stone Age life. Some of the skeptics had similarly moved from their position that the Tasaday were simply "paid performers", faking a primitive way of life for scientists and the media.

Although the 30 scholars actually involved in the controversy in the 1980s still disagree on many details, all recognize that the Tasaday were not living as Stone Age foragers. They still disagree as to whether they were living without iron tools or cultivated foods, and as to what, if any, contact they had with nearby farming villages. All agree that they are a genuine minority tribal people who have always lived in the general area where they were found in 1971.

◄ The Tasaday, "discovered" during the height of the war in Vietnam, represented a new, or old and lost, peaceful way of life for humans. Portrayed as the true "noble savages in the Garden of Eden", the peaceful Tasaday were poorly understood, and still are, even today.

⚱ The overt affection observed among the Tasaday captivated the hearts and minds of media audiences around the world. Instead of warriors, fathers were seen to be loving, demonstrative care-givers.

⬤ The nature of the Tasaday's "pre-metal" technology, if one existed, is conjectural, and may be resolved only through archaeological research.

Disagreement continues, however, as to whether the 26 people (the community had increased to about 70 in 1986) were a separate ethnic population, or merely a group from a nearby village of Manobo tribal farmers who were asked by Panamin officials to dress in leaves and live at the cave site whenever visitors were flown in.

It now seems likely that the Tasaday were indeed foragers, living similarly to other hunter-gatherers in Southeast Asia, such as the Negritos. Linguistic analysis of Tasaday speech suggests that they separated off from a Cotabato Manobo agricultural group relatively recently—some time in the last century—and moved deeper into the rainforest to near where they live today, abandoning farming for a semimobile, foraging way of life. They were probably in contact, for trade and other purposes, with the people in the agricultural village of Blit, which at the time was just a three-hour walk southwest from the Tasaday cave.

Eight Facts

Certain evidence that has recently emerged concerning the Tasaday's way of life before 1970 supports this hypothesis, indicating that journalists and some scientists

exaggerated the Tasaday's primitiveness and led the public to assume that they were more isolated than they actually were. The American Anthropological Association's *The Tasaday Controversy: Assessing the Evidence*, published in 1992, documents the following eight facts.

The Tasaday were not wearing leaves when they were first encountered in 1971 but commercially manufactured cloth, and it was Elizalde who asked them to wear leaf G-strings and skirts. They had trade goods before they were discovered, indicating that they were not out of contact with the modern world. Before 1971, people in nearby towns were eating meat from wild game the Tasaday had killed and smoke-dried. The South Cotabato rainforest lacks sufficient wild plant foods to sustain a foraging group living solely on wild foods. No one ever observed the Tasaday subsisting from wild foods. Their bamboo utensils were of cultivated, not wild, bamboo. The stone tools they were photographed with were fakes. The Tasaday do not speak a separate language or an unintelligible dialect, but a dialect of the nearby Cotabato Manobo language.

The story that the Tasaday were a Paleolithic cave people living in cultural and linguistic isolation from surrounding communities for hundreds of years is patently false, but it has been established that there was a small community called the Tasaday who were living as a separate—but not isolated—group of rainforest hunter-gatherers. Whatever skepticism we may feel today concerning the early claims of their "primitiveness" and extreme isolation, they are an indigenous minority people whose lands and rights should be protected.

⬤ Beyond the writings of journalist John Nance, the research of ethnobotanist Douglas Yen has provided most of our information about the Tasaday. Yen identified a wide range of forest plants eaten by the Tasaday. He questioned the adequacy of their observed diet, suggesting a need for long-term research, which has not eventuated.

ABORIGINAL AUSTRALIA

A D   1   7   8   8   –   T H E   P R E S E N T

Dreamings and Nightmares

L EE S ACKETT

D ESPITE BEING THE DRIEST continent, Australia offers a surprising range of environments. Stretches of the western and southern seaboards receive little rain, and some two-thirds of the interior are desert or semidesert. Vast grasslands bound the arid region in the east and north.

There are also expanses of wetlands, rainforests, and timbered mountains. Before European settlement, Aboriginal peoples occupied all these zones, from the richest to the seemingly most impoverished.

In coastal Arnhem Land, the downpours of a tropical wet season fed major river systems, ensuring the Burrara of a profuse supply of land and sea resources. The sweeping ranges of central Australia channeled and trapped water, supporting an abundance of plant and animal life and providing the Western Aranda with one of the more secure of desert environments. The Ngarigo, who inhabited the cool, lush southeastern highlands, moved further up country during the short summers to exploit the normally snowlocked uplands of the Australian Alps. In southern Australia, the Ngarrindjeri enjoyed bountiful inland, riverine, and marine resources along the lower Murray River, while the Peerapper exploited the rookeries and sea mammal colonies along Tasmania's cold, windy, and rainswept beaches and on the offshore islands.

◄ Gagudju country, in north-central Arnhem Land, is well watered and rich in resources. It is also spectacularly beautiful. Land rights legislation has enabled the Gagudju to win legal title to their land, which they have leased back to the government for use as a national park.

◓ The people of the King Sound area of the Kimberley region, in northwestern Australia, are famous for their baobab nut carvings. Carving baobab nuts, like carving emu eggs, involves scraping away layers of shell to produce a multicolored design.
ROSALIE POTTER

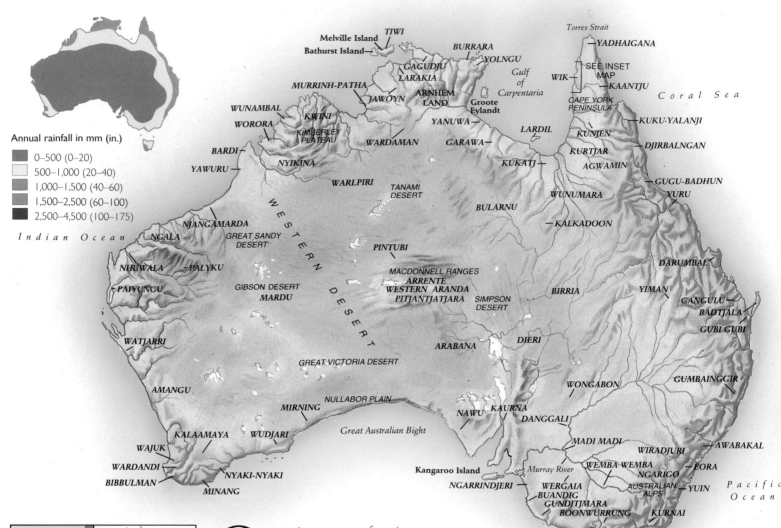

Annual rainfall in mm (in.)

0–500 (0–20)
500–1,000 (20–40)
1,000–1,500 (40–60)
1,500–2,500 (60–100)
2,500–4,500 (100–175)

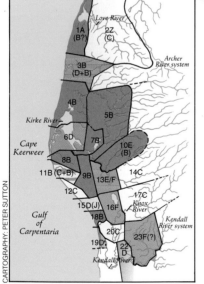

CARTOGRAPHY: PETER SUTTON

CLAN ESTATES AND LANGUAGES

▮ etc.	Distinct language varieties in 1977
1, 2, etc.	Clan estates (schematic only)
A, B, etc.	Languages owned by clans in early 1900s
( )	Languages owned by clans in 1977, where different from early 1900s
- - -	Research incomplete in 1977
/	Alternative names
(?)	Ownership unresolved in 1977

O ccupying a range of environments, Aborigines were also culturally diverse. For example, before colonization, the Kuku-Yalanji, of Cape York Peninsula, were virtually sedentary, whereas the Dieri, of the Simpson Desert, were highly mobile. But even peoples living in environmentally comparable areas had quite different cultures. The maritime Nuenonne, of Tasmania, did not eat fish, whereas the Gagudju, of north-central Arnhem Land, fished keenly for barramundi. The Warlpiri, of the Tanami Desert, had a complex system of social categories based on crisscrossing lines of patrilineal and matrilineal descent, while the Mirning, of the western Nullabor Plain, were loosely organized. The Yolngu, of eastern Arnhem Land, practiced circumcision as part of the male initiation rite, yet off the coast of western Arnhem Land, on Bathurst and Melville islands, the Tiwi practiced depilation.

Although life in different areas permitted, promoted, or necessitated different cultural practices and institutions, Aborigines throughout Australia had much in common. They all subsisted by hunting and gathering, the men mostly being responsible for the former and the women— usually the principal providers—for the latter. There was much emphasis on sharing. People normally lived in small family groups, on or near patches of country with which, as the place

ABORIGINAL AUSTRALIA

Aboriginal people today distinguish between at least 600 tribal groups, based primarily on land ownership but also on language, religion, history, and marriage. Some of these groups (spelled as the present-day communities prefer) are shown here. Territories vary in size with rainfall, so the distribution of names gives some idea of the distribution of people before the arrival of Europeans. The inset map, of an area in northwestern Queensland occupied by the Wik community, shows the complexity of local clan estates and languages. Clans share a common male ancestor, totems, ceremonies, and country; languages are related but different.
CARTOGRAPHY: RAY SIM

of their conception or birth, some of them had special affiliations. Through kinship and marriage, they were linked to numerous other groups in their region. Men and women took part in certain rituals, but there were also separate male and female rites. Men were responsible for rituals believed to be vital to the ongoing well-being of the entire society. This fostered male chauvinism.

THE MARDU

One of the very few Aboriginal peoples to have survived into quite recent times with their culture relatively intact is the Mardu, of the Western Desert. Mardu country, comprising the western part of this vast desert, was one of the last areas to be penetrated by Europeans, and a number of Mardu were pursuing a traditional way of life as late as the 1960s. This allowed anthropologists to build up quite a comprehensive picture of their precolonial world, giving us an invaluable insight into traditional Aboriginal life.

Mardu (meaning "people") is something of a term of convenience. It is a term used today by speakers of a number of desert dialects, including Giyadjarra, Mandjildjarra, and Budidjarra, when talking about themselves collectively. Members of some neighboring groups also use it to refer to these desert peoples.

The Western Desert

On first impressions, the Western Desert seems to be one of the harshest habitats on Earth. Annual rainfall averages less than 200 millimeters (8 inches), summer shade temperatures regularly top 45 degrees Celsius (113 degrees Fahrenheit), and yet it freezes on midwinter nights. This is a landscape devoid of permanent streams or lakes—even springs and rockholes are scarce. Few species of plants and animals survive here, and human population densities were traditionally low, averaging one person per 200 square kilometers (75 square miles).

In the eyes of early observers, the Mardu led a very precarious life. Equipped only with tools of stone, bone, and wood, and with a limited capacity to store food, they seemed to these outsiders to be condemned to a life of constant toil, haunted by the "specter of starvation". In fact, living in small, sustainable groups and moving about the landscape to take advantage of favorable local conditions, the Mardu—like most hunter-gatherers—were secure in their ability to provide for themselves.

ROBERT TONKINSON

Mardu children began acquiring adult skills at an early age. Mardu boys used toy spears and spear-throwers to develop the hunting techniques they would need later in life.

Westerners view deserts with foreboding. The Mardu, by contrast, were confident that their Western Desert homelands would provide for their needs. For them, the desert abounded with life and meaning.

JEAN-PAUL FERRERO/AUSCAPE

The people of the Lake Eyre area, in South Australia, carved small, physical images, called toas, of places and things of mythical importance. This toa depicts a grave—now a waterhole—dug by an ancestral being.
SOUTH AUSTRALIAN MUSEUM

ROBERT TONKINSON

🔸 Using digging sticks and wooden carrying bowls, Mardu women gathered as much as 70 to 80 percent of their families' daily food.

STANLEY BREEDEN

🔸 Late in the dry season, the fruit of the pandanus trees ripens and drops to the ground. The nuts, though small and difficult to extract, are highly prized.

➔ Aboriginal Australians held that the features of their environment were created by the actions of ancestral heroes. The Gagudju, of north-central Arnhem Land, believe that the creator being Indjuwanydjuwa turned to stone. For them, the existence of the formation they know by this name (shown here) proves that this happened.

A Day in the Desert

In *Yiwara*, American ethnoarchaeologist Richard Gould describes the activities of a group of 13 Mardu on a typical midsummer's day in 1966. Rising at dawn, the group breakfasted on the remains of the previous evening's meal and discussed what they intended to do. The two men chose to hunt emus at a nearby spot where they had previously been successful. Arriving there, they fashioned a screen of brush to conceal them from view and settled down to wait. After some five hours, an emu appeared, but when one of the hunters stood to launch his spear, it snapped, frightening the bird away. The men decided that more emus were unlikely to come their way and headed back to camp, tracking and killing a small goanna along the way.

After the men had left, the rest of the group, consisting of three adult women, a teenage girl, and seven young children, set off in the opposite direction in quest of plant foods. They had to walk further than the men, about 8 kilometers

(5 miles), but in less than an hour, the four women had harvested some 18 kilograms (40 pounds) of staples. They arrived back at camp shortly after the men, who already had the goanna roasting in the coals of a fire. When it was cooked, the meat was divided among the group. Later in the afternoon, the women husked and ground the foods they had collected, using the coarse "flour" to make dampers —a kind of flat cake about 20 centimeters (8 inches) in diameter—which they cooked in the coals. When night fell, adults and children alike settled down to sleep.

The little group of Mardu spent less time locating, obtaining, and preparing food than modern Western workers spend earning their income. They were then left with quite a few hours free to engage in other pursuits. On this particular day, the women spent the period between returning to camp and preparing the evening meal in relaxing, napping, chatting, and looking after the youngest children. The men, meanwhile, withdrew to a secluded location,

BELINDA WRIGHT

where they incised designs on a secret ritual object. This was a very important task, for, like most hunter-gatherers, the Mardu believed that their livelihood—and, indeed, every aspect of their lives, including the very existence of the world around them—depended on their relationship with powerful supernatural beings.

Mardu Dreaming

The Mardu believed that they, their culture, and the world they inhabited were the products of the events of the *jugurrba*—the Dreaming. Before the *jugurrba*, the land was flat, featureless, and lifeless. Then, marvelous creatures with uncanny magical abilities emerged from where they had been locked in sleep beneath the Earth's surface. They could alter their shape and size, and take the form of humans or animals or any kind of natural object. Through their actions and interactions, they molded the landscape—indeed, the landscape was an enduring testimony to the events of the Dreaming.

Near Jiluguru, in the Durba Hills, the beards of the Wadi Gujarra, the Two Lizard-men, became part of the environment when they metamorphosed into stone. They can be seen as dark piping against an ocher-colored rockface. To the southwest, at Wambin, in the Carnarvon Ranges, the dragging tail of Marlu, the Kangaroo-man, created a break in a line of hills the Wadi Gujarra had formed earlier. At Maburi, to the east, a scatter of stones and boulders are the petrified bones of animals caught in a blaze when a large assembly of Dingarri people—male and female beings, who usually traveled separately—fired the countryside.

As the spirit beings created and became the features of the desert, they imbued all they touched and every place they dwelled in with vital essence of themselves. It was from this life force that all future, earthly life sprang. In *The Mardu Aborigines*, Australian anthropologist Robert Tonkinson tells how a man named Marnagal became a descendant of the Wadi Gujarra. One day, Marnagal's father, Jadurda, killed a wallaby that had approached him and seemingly allowed itself to be speared. When Marnagal's mother, Minu, later discovered she was pregnant with him, she was certain he had come to her through the wallaby. This was confirmed when Marnagal was born with the mark of his father's spear on his shoulder. Marnagal was said to have been left by the Two Lizard-men when they threw a club at a kangaroo near the place where Jadurda had killed the wallaby. The club had turned into the wallaby, which, when eaten by Minu, had quickened Marnagal.

⬧ Mardu camps were usually little more than quickly and easily fashioned brush windbreaks. On cold winter nights, people kept a number of fires burning.

⚲ Arnhem Landers wove baskets from such things as pandanus leaves and waterlily fiber. Designs were painted on. Women used the baskets to carry the foods they gathered, and men used them to store sacred objects.
OLIVER STREWE/AUSTRALIAN PICTURE LIBRARY

⚖ These dogs were made of spinifex resin by the Lake Eyre people, of South Australia. They are models of dogs that belong to ancestral beings.

As the beings shaped and enlivened the countryside, they set in place a way of life that humans were to follow for all time, encompassing everything from technology to social and religious practices. Mardu men hunted with spears and spear-throwers, and Mardu women gathered with digging sticks and wooden bowls, because those were the tools given to them by the Dreaming ancestors. Distant cousins—people from different groups—married one another, and sons-in-law and mothers-in-law avoided all contact with each other, in accordance with Dreaming Law, and males were circumcised and subincised in emulation of the beings who first performed these rites.

When their creative deeds were done, the ancestors returned to their slumber. This did not end the *jugurrba*, however, for it was perpetuated in the very act of people living their daily lives. Furthermore, the Dreaming ancestors, now discernible only by their imprints on the natural world, continued to take an interest in human affairs, and from time to time, the Mardu communicated with them directly through the medium of ritual.

Invoking the Power of the Dreaming

The spirit places spawned by the ancestral beings, called *jabiya*, were the sites of regular rituals. Initiated custodians—the men responsible for looking after a particular place, who possessed the secret knowledge of it and, in some cases, were animated by its associated spirits—would be joined by other men who happened to be in the area in performing songs and dances believed to have been first performed by the founding ancestor or ancestors. This placed them in contact with the spirit entity, which they then tried to cajole into releasing more of its associated animal species. Tonkinson tells how a senior guardian of an emu *jabiya*, for example, said to the emu ancestor, "We want emu eggs. Make plenty. Give us lots. We want some for eating, some for emus—for meat! Keep them coming! You will do it because we all came to see you and to start you."

Land Rights and Duties

Just as *jabiya* were scattered across the landscape, so groups of Mardu were distributed throughout the desert. Single young men traveled widely, seeing and learning about other areas and their associated Dreamings. Young women ultimately left their own countries for those of their husband. Married couples, accompanied by their children, attended rituals in nearby areas and sometimes made longer journeys, perhaps to escape drought conditions, or simply to visit relatives. But a man's ritual duties compelled him to return to the territory of his father and his father's father, and to follow them in caring for the land and its Dreamings.

Not just for the Mardu, but for Aborigines throughout Australia, the land rights of particular groups, the different technologies in use, and the kinship and marriage systems that linked people from different groups and areas were given special significance and purpose by the belief that they emanated from the actions of the Dreaming beings. With the coming of Europeans, Aboriginal life was totally disrupted. People were summarily dislocated from their land and livelihood, and Aboriginal social and economic practices, ritual performances, and ideology all came under attack.

⚖ Rituals, as here in Arnhem Land, are times of high excitement. People today speak of performing rituals as both "doing business" and "having fun". Everyone is expected to attend and is encouraged to participate.

➔ Early researchers largely overlooked the role of women in Aboriginal society, some even suggesting that women had no ritual life. In reality, women had a robust religious life. These Warlpiri women, in central Australia, like women in many other groups, continue to tap the power of the Dreaming.

COLONIZATION AND DISPOSSESSION

Although cut off by sea from the rest of the world for the past 8,000 years, Australia was not wholly isolated. Artifacts such as plumed headdresses and such practices as the smoking of corpses testify to contact between the peoples of Cape York and Papua New Guinea. For centuries before the arrival of Europeans, Indonesian fisherfolk had visited Australia's northern shores, and from the early 1600s, a succession of Spanish, Dutch, English, and French navigators had charted parts of the continent's coastline and touched land at numerous points.

As significant as these influences and encounters must have been for Aboriginal people, the establishment of a British settlement at Sydney Cove in 1788 marked a fundamental turning point in Aboriginal history. Before 1788, outsiders had come and gone, but now they had come to stay. The colony's first governor, Arthur Phillip, was commanded to "endeavour by every possible means to open

an intercourse with the natives ... enjoining all ... to live in amity and kindness with them. And if any of our subjects shall wantonly destroy them, or give them unnecessary interruption in the exercise of their several occupations, it is our will ... that ... such offenders ... be brought to punishment ... "

Even as it enjoined a policy of peaceful coexistence, the Crown acted as if Australia were *terra nullius*, an unowned land, because the Aborigines were not sedentary agriculturalists, who could be seen to hold exclusive rights to particular areas of land. The unquestioned assumption was that the Aborigines could move aside, and hunt and gather elsewhere, opening up desirable countryside to settlement, farming, and herding.

But Aborigines were not able to move aside, precisely because of their traditional ties and obligations to particular sites and regions, and this put them on a collision course with the settlers. Indications are that the Aborigines initially assumed that the colonists would simply stay a while, as kinspeople had in the past, and then return to their own areas. When it became clear that they would not move on, Aborigines began to attack settlers and to prey on their livestock.

People in Arnhem Land covered the walls of rock shelters with paintings of objects from their environment they found significant. Here, a major item of food, a barramundi, shares space with a European sailing vessel.

The rich resources of the Bathurst Islands allowed the more sedentary Tiwi to develop a form of fixed statuary. Some intricately carved Tiwi grave posts stood more than 4 meters (14 feet) tall.
OLIVER STREWE/AUSTRALIAN PICTURE LIBRARY

With the coming of Europeans and European material culture, rifles were painted alongside spears and spear-throwers on rock shelter walls.

Depopulation

Some of the newcomers, like Lachlan Macquarie, who as governor of the colony of New South Wales established a school for Aboriginal children in 1814, argued that it required "only … the fostering Hand of Time, gentle Means and Conciliatory Manners" to halt the Aborigines' depredations and move them into European society. Many colonists, however, sought to resolve their problems with the indigenous Australians by more immediate, physical means, using force of arms to secure their land and property.

While in theory whites and blacks alike were to be punished for harming each other, it was invariably blacks whose rights were abused and ignored. Indeed, Aborigines came to be deemed pests, to be eliminated along with dingoes,

This sketch, published in 1853, depicts the threat Aborigines were perceived as constituting to early white settlers. It also sharply captures the European response to that threat. As a contemporary onlooker said of the situation in central Australia, the settlers "allow themselves to become involved in major outrages. They carry on manhunt as a kind of sport."

kangaroos, and other vermin. Poisoned meat was placed where unsuspecting foragers might find and eat it. Punitive expeditions were launched to track down and annihilate whole groups allegedly guilty of trespass, theft, or murder. In Tasmania, settlers literally formed a "Black Line" in an attempt to drive the original inhabitants from the island.

As well as being driven from their homelands and cut down in violent clashes, Aborigines were devastated by introduced diseases. Influenza, measles, whooping cough, and, above all, small-pox ravaged populations far beyond the frontier. Syphilis and gonorrhea compounded the destruction by their adverse effect on fecundity.

Conservative estimates suggest that a precolonial Aboriginal population of more than 300,000 was reduced to 60,000 by 1930, a period of 140 years. A more radical view claims that the population of the area that is now the states of New South Wales and Victoria numbered 250,000 before contact, and that this had fallen to a mere 15,000 by 1850—in less than 70 years. Perhaps most dramatic of all, the Aboriginal population of Tasmania declined from somewhere between 5,000 and 10,000 in 1803, when the first European settlers arrived, to a reported figure of nil in 1835. Those who had not succumbed to illness had been killed or deported. The last of the so-called full-blood Tasmanians had died before the centenary of Australia's colonization.

THE PALAWA OF TASMANIA

Greg Lehman

In Tasmania more than anywhere else in Australia, the British focused on an ultimate solution to their most frustrating problem. The indigenous people (or Palawa) stood between them and an empty land. The administration deported Aboriginal families from their homelands and allowed disease and lawless extermination to do the rest. Tasmanian Aborigines today see this as an attempt at genocide.

While the Governor and the Colonial Office were opposed to such killing, the everyday reality was more like that described by Tasmanian senior civil servant H.M. Hull. In a paper published in 1859, *Experience of Forty Years in Tasmania*, Hull reported: " … it was a favourite amusement to hunt the Aborigines; that a day would be selected and the neighbouring settlers invited, with their families, to a pic-nic … After dinner all would be gaiety and merriment, whilst the gentlemen of the party would take their guns and dogs, and accompanied by two or three convict servants, wander through the bush in search of blackfellows. Sometimes they would return without sport; at others they would succeed in killing a woman, or, if lucky, a man or two."

But the best efforts of the British achieved very little. While the killing continued, Aboriginal women were bearing the invaders' children. Almost forgotten in the mountainous bushland, or on smaller islands such as Cape Barren, these women taught their sons and daughters the importance of their native heritage and the strength of Palawa spirit.

Today, while Tasmania's history books boast of a hard-won land and view the death of so many Aborigines as a sad necessity, Palawa people use their kinship, oral histories, and traditions to keep an ancient culture alive.

Contrary to popular belief, Tasmanian Aborigines have survived. They have entered universities and legal practices and been active in the contemporary arts. An Aboriginal school has opened, and the old languages are again being spoken. In a land rights campaign that began in the 1840s, the Aborigines of Tasmania have today reclaimed their sacred sites in defiance of continuing pressures to assimilate into white Australian culture.

The Franklin River valley, in Tasmania's Southwest wilderness, contains important cultural sites. In 1981, the Aboriginal community joined with conservation groups to prevent the construction of a dam here.

The Governor's proclamation of equity in law never became reality for the tribes of Tasmania. The 1992 Royal Commission into Aboriginal Deaths in Custody detailed how such injustice continues today.

Relearning the "old ways" is a vital part of Palawa children's education. The value of storytelling and song is emphasized at the Aboriginal Children's Center and Kindergarten.

Aunty Ida West, an Aboriginal Elder.

⚱ This photograph of an Aboriginal maid ironing at Kaleno station, in Bourke, New South Wales, was taken in 1912. The assimilation era saw concerted efforts made to move Aborigines into the wider society. But at what level were they to be incorporated? For the most part, Aborigines were trained for what was seen as their lowly station in life.
MITCHELL LIBRARY, STATE LIBRARY OF NEW SOUTH WALES

♀ Newly subdued Aborigines were curiosities. But even where photographers sought to present them as they "really were", as in this photograph taken in northern Queensland about 1917, the reality was a constructed one. The formal poses in such photographs serve to underline this artificiality.

A Doomed Race?

Survivors of the undeclared war gathered at the fringes of towns and at special missions and reserves. Here, they were made dependent on handouts and payments in kind in return for performing menial tasks. This did not arrest the drastic population decline. On the contrary, the meager rations, squalor, and overcrowding that many Aborigines had to endure exacerbated their plight.

By the 1840s, even the most compassionate colonists were conceding that the Aborigines were "a doomed race", and by the late 1860s, their fate seemed to confirm emerging social Darwinian notions of evolution through struggle and "the survival of the fittest". Just as more efficient species displaced less efficient ones, so, it was argued, more efficient cultures displaced less efficient ones. Aborigines were not dying because of things settlers had or had not done—their passing, it was claimed, was a working out of a law of nature. Western civilization was merely supplanting Aboriginal savagery. The most anyone could do was "smooth the dying pillow" of the condemned with various welfare measures.

It was not until the early part of the twentieth century that European Australians began to accept that Aboriginal people were not conveniently going to disappear. Despite the concerted efforts of some whites and the total indifference of most others, Aboriginal numbers were beginning to increase in certain areas.

The Policy of Assimilation

In 1937, representatives of state and territory Native Welfare Departments met in the first of a series of sessions that generated the policy of assimilation. In the words of a policy statement issued by a later conference of delegates, it was agreed that measures must be taken to enable Aborigines "to attain the same manner of living as other Australians and to live as members of a single Australian community enjoying the same rights and privileges, accepting the same responsibilities, observing the same customs and influenced by the same beliefs, as other Australians".

Seeing this policy as a long-overdue offer of Aboriginal equality with Europeans, black activists and liberal whites immediately threw their support behind it. For many policy-makers and members of the wider community, however, assimilation was but a more benign way of getting rid of Aborigines and the "Aboriginal problem". Aboriginal culture would vanish as Aborigines rejected it in favor of European culture. Aborigines would fade away through miscegenation. A.O. Neville, Chief Protector of Aborigines in Western Australia, stated in 1933: "The blacks will have to go white. [This] is exemplified in the quarter castes, by the gradual absorption of the native Australian black race by [the] white. I have noticed no throw-backs in such cases … "

Since the double-barreled process of cultural and biological genocide was going to take

COO-EE HISTORICAL PICTURE LIBRARY

generations, Aborigines would need protection in the meantime from corrupting influences and unscrupulous elements. To this end, laws were enacted that gave designated non-Aborigines the power to prohibit the movement of Aborigines in their charge from one place to another; to determine whom they could work for; to tell them whom they could marry; to administer corporal punishment to perceived wrongdoers; and even to remove children from the care of their parents. Protective legislation was so comprehensive that one jurisdiction went so far as to decree how many dogs an Aborigine might own—one.

The only prospect of escape from the racist legislation, although not from racism itself, was through formal exemption. Under the Western Australia Native (Citizen Rights) Act of 1944, for instance, an Aborigine who won a certificate of citizenship was "no longer a native" and enjoyed "all the rights ... of a natural born or naturalized subject of His Majesty". Merely to qualify for citizenship, however, applicants had to demonstrate, among other things, that they could "speak and understand the English language"; had "dissolved tribal and native association except with respect to lineal descendants or native relations of the first degree"; had "adopted the manner and habits of civilised life"; were "of industrious habits and ... good behaviour and reputation"; were not "suffering from active leprosy, syphilis, granuloma or yaws"; and would benefit from their new status.

Mardu on the Margins

During the assimilation era, many Mardu left their homelands for towns, settlements, and missions on the edge of the desert. Some did so voluntarily. Others were relocated by patrols charged with clearing a strip of land for a missile-testing range or moving "nomads" suspected of suffering from malnutrition and other serious diseases to areas where they could receive treatment. Either way, the formerly autonomous Mardu fell subject to administrative control.

⚓ Photographs of Aborigines in Western-style clothing arrayed before houses and churches illustrate what earlier audiences saw as the unquestionable benefits of civilization. But peoples' shabby, hand-me-down clothing points to the true poverty of their condition. This photograph was taken about 1880, possibly at Lake Tyers Mission, in Victoria.

⚓ This Pitjantjatjara family were photographed outside their home in central Australia in 1963. Some people have lived, and still live, this way by choice; others, because they have no other choice.

➤ As poignantly illlustrated by this photograph taken about 1894, the constraints of classroom education have often contrasted sharply with the less structured education of traditional Aboriginal culture.

➤ The boomerang has become something of an icon of the Australian Aborigine. Few boomerangs were of the returning variety. Most were marvelously crafted throwing sticks, the largest measuring up to 2 meters (6 feet, 6 inches) in length. The hooked, or "number seven", boomerang was made to catch on and swing around a defender's shield.
ROSALIE POTTER

By the late 1960s, more than 300 Mardu were more or less settled in and around the tiny township of Wiluna, on the western side of the desert. Some lived in crude shacks on a small reserve or nearby mission; others, in equally primitive conditions on surrounding pastoral stations.

As there were only about 25 full-time jobs for Aborigines, most Aborigines were looked upon as a labor pool from which employers could draw as and when necessary. During their frequent and often lengthy periods of unemployment, the Mardu were denied the social service benefits granted to most other Australians, to ensure that they would learn the value of work. This not only kept them eager to accept work when it was offered, but also kept their annual per capita disposable income woefully low— less than a quarter of the national average.

Mardu and Missionaries

Mardu parents, to their dismay, lost their children to the mission school and dormitory system, whereby children were separated from their parents and closely monitored by whites. In these institutions, the emphasis was on Bible study and training young people for what was considered to be their station in life. The teachers belittled Aboriginal culture, encouraging children to break rules their parents held dear and generally to behave in ways that offended their elders.

The missionaries also struck directly at Aboriginal religious beliefs and practices. Knowledge that had been exclusive to initiated males was made public. Aborigines were banned from performing traditional rites or wearing ritual body paint on mission land. Mission residents who broke these rules were summarily evicted.

Off the mission, the lowly status and powerlessness of the Wiluna Mardu were even more starkly defined. A de facto "sundown law" barred Aborigines from the town after nightfall. Aborigines addressed whites as "mister" or "missus" or "boss", whereas whites addressed Aborigines by their given name. Whites automatically went to the head of queues. Audiences attending concerts and other entertainments were segregated, and segregation extended into death, with separate sections in the cemetery for whites and Aborigines.

Assimilation

There was, in fact, no assimilation—at Wiluna or anywhere else. On the contrary, instead of edging the Mardu and other Aborigines towards European society, the oppressive laws kept them apart and simply formalized their marginal status. The assimilation laws also provoked both latent and manifest opposition among Aborigines. They protested about their exclusion from the provisions of national wage agreements. They agitated for equal access to welfare services. They got drunk despite the laws denying them access to alcohol. They took their rituals underground.

SELF-DETERMINATION AND SELF-MANAGEMENT

Assimilation, the policy that was supposed to run its course for generations, was virtually abandoned in less than 30 years. In 1967, the people of Australia overwhelmingly supported a referendum that gave the federal government the right to legislate on behalf of Aboriginal people—a right that formerly had been the prerogative of the states. The outcome has been a dual policy of self-determination and self-management, aimed at enabling Aborigines and Torres Strait Islanders, in the words of a 1983 Department of Aboriginal Affairs background paper, to "as individuals and as communities be able to make the kinds of decisions about their future as other Australians make and to accept responsibility for the results".

To this end, the federal government has channeled substantial funding into the area of Aboriginal affairs: rising from $97 million in 1973–74, to $162 million in 1983–84, to $951 million in 1993–94. Some of this money has been used to buy supplies and property from non-Aborigines and to pay the salaries and fees of non-Aboriginal bureaucrats, lawyers, consultants, and so on. Other funds have been spent on underwriting a host of economic ventures, housing initiatives, and health, education, legal, and social programs.

Being Black

The Australian government's official definition of an Aborigine is one who has Aboriginal ancestry, identifies as an Aborigine, and is known as such in the community in which he or she lives. However, this only recognizes our relationship to the welfare state.

Our suffering is often used to characterize our Aboriginality. Certainly, the pain of loss and disempowerment give us common cause with the indigenous nations of the world. These things make us recognizable to the historian and the politician.

But our real identity lives in our words and actions. The sacred sites that we live to protect, the stories, songs, and poems that capture our passion—these are the true account of us as a people. The politics of survival are not our culture. They are a measure of the days we live in. Our true culture is where we stand—on our land.

Greg Lehman

In addition, some Aborigines and Torres Strait Islanders have won title to their traditional lands. Aborigines and Islanders now elect representatives to a specially formed Commission, which has a certain amount of autonomy in planning and budgeting for community development programs. Anti-discrimination legislation now combats the more blatant acts of racism. But as Aboriginal people are quick, and right, to point out, racism is still rampant. They are still called disparaging and insulting names, turned away from discos, and refused service in hotel bars. They still miss out on jobs, and find that someone else has already rented accommodation they are interested in.

A number of Aborigines have won widespread recognition for their view and depiction of the world around them. But at what price? In the process, their culture has become a commodity.

BARK PAINTING IN ARNHEM LAND

WALLY CARUANA

ABORIGINAL IMAGES on flattened sheets of bark were first observed by Europeans in Tasmania in 1807, although the earliest surviving barks, found in Victoria and on Essington Island, in the Northern Territory, date from the mid-nineteenth century. The tradition of bark painting still flourishes across tropical northern Australia, including Queensland and the Kimberleys, but it is now strongest in Arnhem Land.

Bark painting is part of the Aboriginal tradition of painting on ritual objects, people's bodies, rock shelters, and the inner walls of bark huts. The interest in the art of Arnhem Land shown by researchers and collectors from the early years of the twentieth century, and by museums and the art market since the 1960s, has encouraged the production of bark paintings in greater numbers than ever before.

Traditional Materials

Bark is easily removed from stringy-bark trees (*Eucalyptus tetradonta*) in the monsoon season when the sap is rising. The sheet of bark is first cured over a fire, the rough outer bark is then removed, and the inner surface is rubbed smooth in readiness for painting. The sheet is then weighted down to make it completely flat.

The bark painter's palette consists of four basic colors: red and yellow in the form of ochers of various qualities of luster, white from pipe-clay or kaolin, and black, usually made from charcoal. These pigments are mixed with any of a variety of natural binders, such as egg yolks, orchid juice, or wax, although these have largely been replaced by commercial synthetic glues in recent times.

Brushes are made from palm leaves, feathers, and the chewed ends of twigs. Today, commercial paintbrushes are often adapted to the artist's needs. The extremely delicate lines found in Arnhem Land barks are produced by using a thin brush made from a few hairs attached to a short stick. The brush is dragged repeatedly across the surface of the bark to produce the fine lines that make up the dazzling patterns of hatching and cross-hatching for which this art form is renowned.

Clan Patterns and Totemic Designs

Patterns of hatched lines, which identify clans and countries, and nonfigurative or conventional designs representing totemic entities, are common features of bark paintings. They are used to impart a visual excitement, which embodies the presence of supernatural forces. From central Arnhem Land, Tony Dhanyula's (born c. 1935) *Waterholes made by the Djang'kawu Sisters at Garuyak* of 1984 depicts the conventional design of circular freshwater springs joined by lines indicating the paths taken by the Djang'kawu ancestors. The image is decorated with the cross-hatched designs of his clan, the Mayarr Mayarr, which refer to the spiritual forces infused by the Sisters into the land.

Clan patterns and totemic designs vary across Arnhem Land, as do styles of bark painting. In western Arnhem Land, clearly recognizable figurative images are painted against a monochromatic ground, usually red. Artists

↪ Tony Dhanyula (born c. 1935)
Buyuyukulmirri/Liyagawumirri language, Mayarr Mayarr clan, central Arnhem Land, Northern Territory
Waterholes made by the Djang'kawu Sisters at Garuyak, 1984
natural pigments on eucalyptus bark; 133.5 cm x 75 cm
COLLECTION: NATIONAL GALLERY OF AUSTRALIA, CANBERRA.

acknowledge the relationship between bark paintings and ancient rock art in the region, using some of the same techniques found in rock paintings. So-called X-ray paintings show the internal organs and skeletal structure of figures, while *mimi*, or dynamic, art incorporates images of the spirit figures who inhabit the rocky country. In *Animals and mimi figures* of 1985, Robin Nganjmira (1951 to 1991) uses both conventions.

In central Arnhem Land, bark paintings feature formal compositions of conventional designs, often including figures, while in northeastern Arnhem Land, paintings are usually composed within a grid structure. Here, the use of conventional patterns reaches its zenith, although naturalistic images also appear, as in *Ancestors of the Yirritja* of c. 1979 by Yanggarriny Wunungmurra (born 1932). Nandabitta's (1911 to 1981) *The Angurugu River* of 1970 is characteristic of bark paintings on Groote Eylandt, with its black ground (the color made from manganese), against which are set figurative images decorated with patterns of dashes, dots, and lines.

This broad classification of painting styles serves as a useful general guide to bark paintings in Arnhem Land, but a number of other factors, such as the ritual context of the painting and the nature of the subject itself, have a bearing on style. A dynamic tradition that reflects the essential nature of Arnhem Land culture, bark painting is now recognized as one of the major painting idioms in modern Australian art.

Nandabitta (1911 to 1981)
Anindilyakwa people, Groote Eylandt
The Angurugu River, 1970
natural pigments on eucalyptus bark; 64.9 cm x 35.6 cm
COLLECTION: NATIONAL GALLERY OF AUSTRALIA, CANBERRA.

Robin Nganjmira (1951 to 1991)
Kunwinjku people, western Arnhem Land
Animals and mimi figures, 1985
natural pigments on eucalyptus bark; 39 cm x 177.5 cm
COLLECTION: NATIONAL GALLERY OF AUSTRALIA, CANBERRA/ ABORIGINAL ARTISTS AGENCY

Yanggarriny Wunungmurra (born 1932)
Dhalwangu people, northeastern Arnhem Land
Ancestors of the Yirritja, c. 1979
natural pigments on eucalyptus bark; 155.5 cm x 56 cm
COLLECTION: NATIONAL GALLERY OF AUSTRALIA, CANBERRA.

☞ Making string-figures was a popular pastime in Aboriginal society. Men, women, and children all delighted in creating complex webs and figures.

BELINDA WRIGHT

⚲ Tiwi poles, fashioned to commemorate deceased kinspeople, were traditionally decorated only with symbolic designs. In more recent times, anthropomorphic images have been introduced.

OLIVER STREWE/AUSTRALIAN PICTURE LIBRARY

The Conditions of Poverty

Despite the funds going into Aboriginal affairs, the hoped-for transformations still seem a long way off. Aborigines continue to live, figuratively and often literally, on the margins of Australian society. They suffer the highest rates of unemployment, and are among the poorest Australians. Their average annual individual and family incomes are only about half those of non-Aborigines.

Aborigines also face appalling educational disadvantages. Whereas virtually all non-Aboriginal children aged between 5 and 15 attend school, only about 85 percent of Aboriginal children do so. In the older age groups, the disparity is even more marked. Whereas about three-quarters of non-Aboriginal Australians aged between 16 and 17 attend school, less than a third of Aborigines do, and only 7 percent of Aborigines aged between 18 and 20 pursue some form of tertiary studies, in comparison with 40 percent of non-Aboriginal Australians.

Like poor and poorly educated people elsewhere in the world, indigenous Australians have a sorry health record. Infant mortality rates are three to four times greater than the national level. The children who do survive are prey to diseases, such as trachoma, that could have been eradicated long ago. Aborigines' life expectancy is only 50 to 60 years, compared with 70 to 80 years for other Australians.

Again like poor people elsewhere, Aborigines are subject to above-average rates of arrest and imprisonment. A Royal Commission into Aboriginal Deaths in Custody held between 1987 and 1991 found that, proportionally, Aborigines and Torres Strait Islanders were far and away the most frequently jailed people in Australia. Although collectively they now number only about 227,000, or just

under 1.5 percent of the nation's population, they constitute a staggering 25 to 30 percent of the prison population. This statistic led William Clifford, a former Director of the Australian Institute of Criminology, to suggest that Aborigines may well be the most jailed people in the world.

Under the policy of self-determination and self-management, the more the Aboriginal situation changes, the more it remains the same.

Development at Wiluna

A person who had passed through Wiluna during the assimilation era (from the 1930s to the 1960s) and returned today would see many obvious changes. The shire council, once firmly controlled by local pastoralists, is now dominated by Mardu, and it is acknowledged that the township must answer the economic and social needs of its large Aboriginal population, and not just those of the minority white population.

The Wiluna Mardu are today registered as a company, which allows them formal access to government funds. This money is intended to assist community development, which, in turn, is intended to improve the Mardu's economic and social circumstances. Reserve and mission areas have become part of a state-run Aboriginal Lands Trust, and the Mardu jointly hold and operate an emu farm, a citrus orchard, and Wiluna's only store. An elected council nominally determines the specific directions any new initiatives will take, and through the council, the community employs nine or ten non-Aborigines to advise on and oversee the various enterprises.

Although a few shacks remain, most Mardu live in modern houses, some of which are dispersed among white people's homes. Community jobs

AUSCAPE

♦ By removing eggs from the nest, workers at the Wiluna Emu Farm prompt the female emus to lay more. The eggs are then incubated under controlled conditions.

are available for all who wish to work. Higher and more certain incomes have enabled some of Wiluna's Mardu to buy such things as cars, furniture, television sets, video and hi-fi equipment, toys, bicycles, and motorbikes.

Wiluna has a special Aboriginal school, with a large staff and a number of Aboriginal teacher aides. The Mardu also run an after-school program to involve young people in healthy, productive extracurricular activities. A well-appointed clinic, staffed by trained nurses and Aboriginal medical workers, offers treatment for many common infant and adult health complaints.

Mardu Developments

But these and other changes mask as much as they reveal. Where once the Mardu (and other Aborigines) were kept dependent on charity and rations and controlled by missionaries and other "protectors", today they rely on government grants and loans and social service payments, and are controlled by advisors and administrators. Their special school and after-hours programs are entirely government-funded. Many of the houses they live in are owned by the state, and the community jobs they have come to count on are federally funded.

While community development has overtaken the township of Wiluna, increased mechanization has greatly reduced the number of jobs available in the pastoral industry. None of the new community projects is anywhere near being self-supporting. Most are (somewhat paradoxically) overly labor-intensive, having been set up specifically to create jobs, and have a history of inconsistent and inefficient management. All salaries are paid out of Community Development Employment Project allocations—funds that community members would otherwise receive as unemployment payments. Formerly, the Mardu were denied the dole to make them work—now, they must work to receive it.

Rather than promoting self-determination and self-management among the Mardu, so-called community development gives the whites who

supervise most of the projects tremendous power. The Mardu remain a captive workforce, attending to the wishes of non-Mardu bosses, who tend to dominate the projects and to structure them in such a way that they function smoothly and become testaments to their own organizational prowess.

Furthermore, the Wiluna Mardus' dependence on development projects exposes them to criticism and constraint from distant administrators. Having had nonprofitable projects and work arrangements foisted on them, the Mardu are attacked for being unproductive and for failing to run commercially viable schemes, and threatened with a cut in funds unless improvements are made.

The Mardus are also castigated for not becoming as "socially responsible" as planners and policy-makers expect them to be. About the time the development initiative began, the House of Representatives Standing Committee on Aboriginal Affairs reported that, with a single exception, all Wiluna men and most Wiluna women were heavy drinkers, and that at least 55 percent of the community's income was spent on alcohol. It was assumed (in social engineering fashion) that the provision of work and pay would have alleviated this problem. In fact, now that people have access to a regular and substantial income instead of relying on relatively few pay packets and social welfare checks, the level of alcohol consumption has risen. Again, perplexed officials have reacted by threatening to cut funds if the Mardu do not begin spending their money in a more fruitful way.

Just as it was once widely accepted that Aborigines were fated to disappear, and then assumed that assimilation was the most desirable course, few in Australia today question the notion that the future of Aboriginal people lies in self-determination and self-management through development. While

AUSCAPE

♦ The Wiluna Emu Farm was the first of its kind, and a number of similar ventures have since been started. A market is starting to develop for emu steak and emu pâté.

♀ Aborigines have worked in the cattle industry almost from its earliest days. Pastor Friedrich Albrecht, a missionary at Hermannsburg, in central Australia, from 1926 to 1962, claimed that "without the assistance of the Aborigines, the cattle industry could never have been developed".

DAVID HANCOCK/SKYSCANS

☛ Yothu Yindi is an Arnhem Land band, founded in 1986 by Mandawuy Yunupingu. The group uses music and songwriting as a vehicle for conveying important Aboriginal political messages about such things as land rights and education. In 1992, Yothu Yindi were featured at the launch of the United Nations' Year of Indigenous People in New York.

☛ Toas were fashioned as religious objects, giving concrete expression to mythic references and allusions. Today, many people appreciate them in a new way, as delicately sculptured works of art.
SOUTH AUSTRALIAN MUSEUM

☛ *Opposite page*: In Western Desert art, each painting tells a story. Men and women artists use a dot-technique to build up highly symbolic representations of Dreaming happenings.

☛ Students of Sydney's National Aboriginal and Islander Skills Development Association (NAISDA) College in rehearsal. NAISDA became incorporated in May 1988, and students attending NAISDA College have performed nationally and internationally in works that blend elements of traditional Aboriginal/Torres Strait Islander and Western dance forms. Graduates of NAISDA College have the opportunity of auditioning to join the Aboriginal Islander Dance Theater or non-Aboriginal dance companies.

some politicians and related officials see the current policy and practices as representing good, radical advances, the Mardu situation suggests that in certain respects Aborigines have merely swapped one form of dependence and domination for another. The policy remains essentially assimilationist. Not only are the Mardu, and Aborigines and Torres Strait Islanders in general, expected to embrace Western work and business practices, they are expected to conform socially as well.

Surviving in Their Own Land

During the 1988 Bicentenary celebration of the colonizing of Australia, an occasion Aborigines chose to remember with a year of mourning, 30,000 blacks and whites gathered in Sydney to protest against the celebration of 200 years of occupation. Opening the proceedings, Aboriginal actor and activist Gary Foley announced "What we're saying here today, and what's very clear, and what will be very clear to [then Prime Minister] Bob Hawke and to people all over the world when they see their television screens tonight and tomorrow, is that we have survived."

The theme of Aboriginal survival is present in the songs of Aboriginal bands such as No Fixed Address and Yothu Yindi, in the poetry of Oodgeroo Noonuccal and Jack Davis, and in the prose of Ruby Langford and Mudrooroo Narogin. Consistently, the message is that Aboriginal people and Aboriginal culture have survived in spite of, rather than because of, white people and white institutions.

Prominent Aborigines, from Patricia O'Shane, the country's first indigenous magistrate, to Galarrwuy Yunupingu, Australian of the Year in 1978, and Charles Perkins, the first Aborigine to gain a university degree and the first to head a federal government department, are justifiably scathing

DAVID HANCOCK/SKYSCANS

in their assessments of many aspects of policy and practice in the area of Aboriginal affairs. While they acknowledge that the material conditions under which most Aborigines live have improved in the years since the 1967 referendum, they stress that much remains to be done. They demand that it be done on Aborigines' terms. As Gary Foley went on to say at the Bicentennial demonstration, "We have survived, and we are here today to call on the Australian Government to give us justice, to give us the opportunity to attain our economic independence so that we can be free and dignified as people in our own land, and decide for ourselves our own future in this country."

PETER SOLNESS/WILDLIGHT

THE ART OF URBAN AND RURAL ABORIGINES

Wally Caruana

THE ART OF ABORIGINAL and Torres Strait Islander people living in both urban and rural areas of Australia came to the fore during the 1980s. Previously, such artists seldom had opportunities to practice their art. What work they did was usually dismissed as a trivialization of the ancient traditions of Aboriginal art, generally perceived to be embodied in the bark paintings and sculptures of Arnhem Land and, since the early 1970s, in the canvases of the desert regions.

The art of urban Aboriginal people is not confined to a single style, but is influenced by the links people have with their often distant traditional base, as well as by European techniques and their own social milieu. Its origins stretch back to the nineteenth century, when Tommy McRae (1836 to 1901), in northern Victoria, William Barak (c. 1824 to 1903), at Coranderrk, near Melbourne, and other Aboriginal artists at the frontiers of colonial expansion were commissioned by the new settlers to produce sketches in ink, paint, and ocher. These drawings are mostly naturalistic renditions of traditional life, hunting and ceremonies being favored subjects, but also include commentaries on contemporary life seen from an Aboriginal perspective.

A Twentieth-century Resurgence

Although Aboriginal artists continued to practice throughout urban and rural Australia, the emergence of urban art in the latter half of the twentieth century is linked to the social and political advances made by Aboriginal people in the late 1960s. It accelerated in the 1970s, when there was a general proliferation of the so-called minor art forms. Photography and print-making, in particular, were

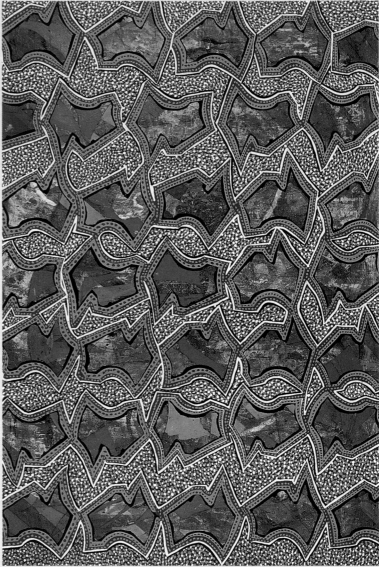

convenient vehicles for carrying Aboriginal messages far and wide. The first Aboriginal print-maker was Kevin Gilbert (1933 to 1993), who started work in 1965.

Among the pioneers of the movement are Thancoupie (born 1937), a ceramicist from Weipa, in northern Queensland, and Trevor Nickolls (born 1949), a painter from Adelaide. Both were trained at art school, but their work is informed

🔊 Jeffrey Samuels (born 1956)
New South Wales
This changing continent of Australia, 1984
oil on composition board;
187 cm x 124 cm

as much by traditional concepts as by personal experience.

The exhibition "Koori Art '84", in Sydney, heralded the arrival of urban and rural artists. It brought together painters such as Nickolls and Jeffrey Samuels (born 1956); the photographers Brenda Croft (born 1964) and Michael Riley (born 1960); and the sculptor and print-maker Fiona Foley (born 1964). These and many other

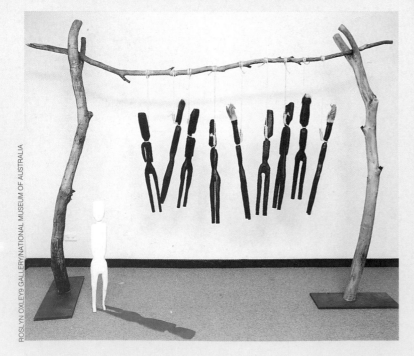

◄● Fiona Foley (born 1964)
Badtjala people, Queensland
The annihilation of the blacks, 1986
wood, synthetic polymer, feathers,
hair rope; height 210 cm

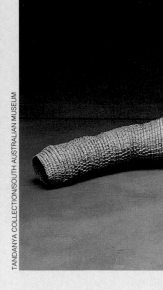

TANDANYA COLLECTION/SOUTH AUSTRALIAN MUSEUM

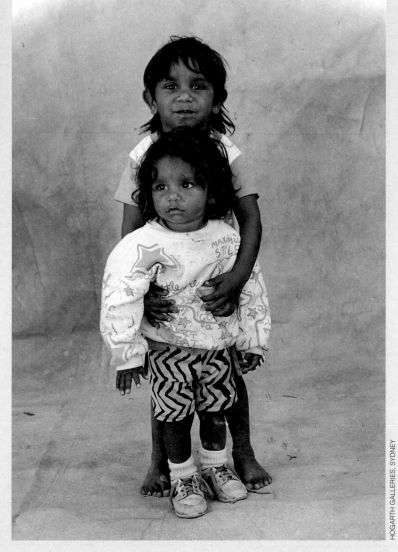

HOGARTH GALLERIES, SYDNEY

artists had previously worked in relative isolation, but they shared similar goals. This common ground led to the establishment of cooperatives to provide opportunities for artists to work and exhibit. The first was Boomali, established in Sydney in 1987.

Artists emerged from other urban areas as the movement

Yvonne Koolmatree (born 1945)
Ngarrindjeri people, South Australia
Eel trap, 1990
sedge grass; length 275 cm

Kevin Gilbert (1933 to 1993)
Wiradjuri language, New South Wales
Lineal legends, matrix 1967, printed 1990
linocut; 62 cm x 50 cm
COLLECTION: NATIONAL GALLERY OF AUSTRALIA
GORDON DARLING FUND

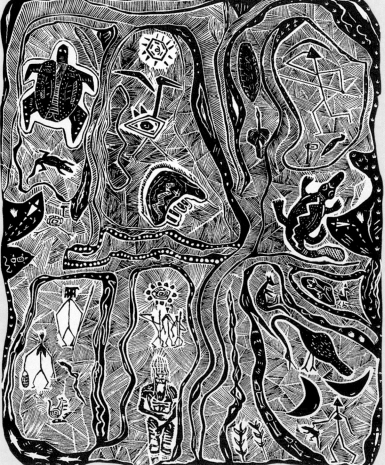

gained momentum, including Lin Onus (born 1948), in Melbourne, and Sally Morgan (born 1959), in Perth, whose work reflected the experience of growing up Aboriginal in a predominantly European society.

The New Wave

The late 1980s saw a new wave of artists make their mark. They include Robert Campbell Jnr (1944 to 1993), from northern New South Wales, who painted his Aboriginal perspective of Australian history; Gordon Bennett (born 1955), Richard Bell (born 1953), and Judy Watson (born 1959), from Queensland; Yvonne Koolmatree (born 1945) and Ian W. Abdulla (born 1947), from the Coorong, near Adelaide; and Karen Casey (1956), from Tasmania, all offering commentaries on Australian society,

Michael Riley (born 1960)
New South Wales
Moree kids, 1990
editions of 10 silver gelatin prints;
56 cm x 39 cm

their personal experiences, and traditional values.

Today, urban Aboriginal artists have succeeded in entering the mainstream of art, and their work, born of their cultural and social backgrounds, represents a recent evolution in the artistic traditions of Aboriginal and Torres Strait Islander Australians.

Note: Urban and rural Aboriginal people are often referred to by the local generic terms for Aboriginal people: among the most commonly used names are Koori, in the southeastern corner ōf the continent; Murri, in Queensland; Nyoongah, in southwestern Australia; and Nunga, in South Australia.

PACIFIC PEOPLES IN THE MODERN WORLD

A D   1   7   5   0   –   T H E   P R E S E N T

A Diversity of Islands and Cultures

DAN JORGENSEN

S CATTERED ACROSS THOUSANDS of kilometers of ocean, the peoples of the Pacific first became known to Europeans after Ferdinand Magellan's circumnavigation of the Earth in the sixteenth century. The eighteenth-century voyages of Louis Antoine de Bougainville, James Cook, and their contemporaries brought the South Seas into the Western imagination as the home of noble peoples whose lands resembled European visions of arcadia. These explorers were followed by beachcombers, adventurers, and castaways, and in the following century, the painter Paul Gauguin and such writers as Herman Melville and Robert Louis Stevenson helped create a popular vision of a tropical paradise of clear lagoons, palm-studded beaches, and forest-clad valleys. While these images continue to exert a fascination that attracts tourists to the Pacific from all over the world, the cultures of Pacific islanders, and the environments people inhabit, are considerably more diverse than any such stereotypes allow.

◀ Although apparently traditional in forms of dress, Papua New Guinea's Trobriand Islanders have long been enthusiastic about literacy and formal education. Educated Trobrianders are prominent among Papua New Guinea's academics, writers, and government officials.

⚭ In many parts of island Melanesia, masks are often used to represent the presence of spirits at mortuary rituals. The distinctive *malanggan* masks of New Ireland, such as this example, collected in 1888, were traditionally destroyed at the end of such ceremonies.
HILLEL BURGER/PEABODY MUSEUM, HARVARD UNIVERSITY

🔔 Paul Gauguin's evocative Tahitian paintings portrayed Polynesia as a pagan garden of innocent and unspoiled beauty, a view that had a powerful appeal for Europeans at the height of the Industrial Revolution. In his paintings, Gauguin carefully omitted any reference to the influence of missions and the violence of French colonial rule, and thus helped to create the myth of Pacific islanders as "untouched" and outside the currents of world history.

Scholars conventionally divide the Pacific into three major areas—Melanesia, Micronesia, and Polynesia—each of which is distinguished by a particular combination of geographical, cultural, and linguistic features.

Melanesian societies are usually small, communities rarely numbering more than a thousand or so. Warfare was widespread in precolonial times. Although male and female roles were sharply defined, these societies were in other respects egalitarian, only rarely recognizing the principle of hereditary rank. Political leadership was for the most part achieved by men who became prominent in exchanges of various kinds that formed a framework of alliances between autonomous local communities. By contrast, Micronesian society is strongly hierarchical, entire descent groups being ranked in relation to each other and titles often being tied to land. But while land was important, seafaring traditionally played a crucial role in Micronesia, where complex interisland relations were sustained by means of long-distance canoe travel. Traditional Polynesian societies were different again, having elaborate institutions of chieftainship, with some chiefs exercising authority over as many as several

thousand people. Such societies often resembled small states, a development that was intensified in the early stages of European contact, when some chiefs aligned themselves with colonial powers to extend their sphere of influence.

The contact history of the Pacific is varied. Some parts of Micronesia, such as Guam, came under Spanish rule as early as the seventeenth century, whereas parts of Melanesia, such as the interior of New Guinea, were not brought under colonial administration until the twentieth century. No Pacific culture has entirely escaped exposure to the wider world, but different cultures have been affected to greatly varying degrees.

The Earliest Settlers

The archaeological record shows that the Pacific was settled from the west to the east. Melanesia was settled considerably earlier than either Micronesia or Polynesia, recent research suggesting that the western islands—New Guinea, New Britain, New Ireland, and the Admiralties—have been inhabited for more than 30,000 years. This antiquity of settlement is reflected in the extremely complex linguistic and cultural picture Melanesia presents: the island of New Guinea alone is estimated to have 750 languages, belonging to more than 60 distinct language families. Collectively classified as Papuan languages, they form a distinct group that is not related to the languages spoken in many other parts of the Pacific, which fall within the Austronesian family.

Austronesian languages originated in Southeast Asia, and were brought to

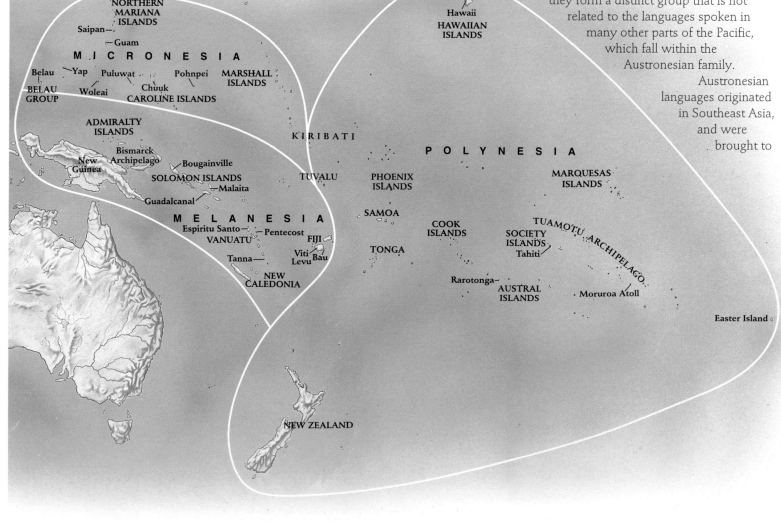

HANS J. BURKARD/BILDERBERG

the Pacific about 3,500 years ago via two routes: from eastern Indonesia into coastal Melanesia, and from Sulawesi or the Philippines to Belau (formerly Palau), Yap, and the Marianas, in western Micronesia. Within western Melanesia, Austronesian speakers are found mainly along the New Guinea coastline and on the adjacent islands of New Britain, New Ireland, and the Admiralties. With the exception of a few groups in the Solomons, all other Pacific islanders speak one of the Austronesian languages, and this is consistent with archaeological findings suggesting that eastern Micronesia and Polynesia were settled by people from eastern Melanesia more than 3,000 years ago. The last parts of the Pacific to be settled were Hawaii, New Zealand, and Easter Island, all of which were colonized from eastern Polynesia within the last 2,000 years.

Pacific environments can be broadly characterized in terms of island types. The islands of Melanesia are mostly continental islands, as are the North and South islands of New Zealand. Apart from New Zealand, Polynesia consists of high volcanic islands and a few coral atolls, while Micronesia has a few high islands and many atolls.

The Islands of Melanesia

Continental islands have complex landforms, including mountains, rivers, and alluvial basins, and relatively varied flora and fauna. In this region, New Guinea is the most ecologically diverse of these islands.

⬧ An aerial view of Bora Bora, one of the Society Islands (French Polynesia). A high island typical of Polynesia, Bora Bora has a central volcanic core and a fringing reef. Now a popular tourist destination, Bora Bora was one of many staging areas for Allied troops during the Second World War, when it served as the inspiration for Bali Hai in James Michener's *South Pacific*.

NEW GUINEA
⚲ Settled more than 35,000 years ago, New Guinea is now politically divided between the Indonesian province of Irian Jaya and the independent state of Papua New Guinea.
CARTOGRAPHY: RAY SIM

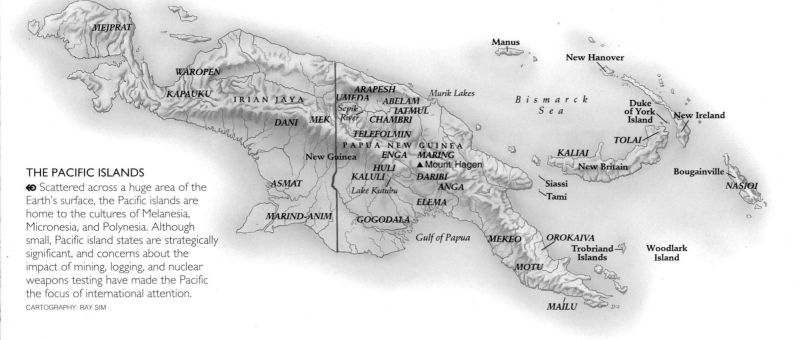

THE PACIFIC ISLANDS
⬤ Scattered across a huge area of the Earth's surface, the Pacific islands are home to the cultures of Melanesia, Micronesia, and Polynesia. Although small, Pacific island states are strategically significant, and concerns about the impact of mining, logging, and nuclear weapons testing have made the Pacific the focus of international attention.
CARTOGRAPHY: RAY SIM

These dancers from Papua New Guinea's Southern Highlands Province have donned wigs, feathers, and face-paint in a display of masculine beauty that some local people liken to that of the male bird of paradise, whose plumes are ubiquitous items of adornment in the highlands. Such dances not only show off individual performers to good effect, but also demonstrate the strength and vitality of their clan.

ROBERT MITCHELL/ASPECT PICTURE LIBRARY

More than a matter of stocking the larder, occasions such as this display of yams in the Trobriand Islands provide the setting in which individual worth is publicly evaluated and reputations rise or fall.

JUTTA MALNIC

The backbone of New Guinea is formed by parallel mountain ranges rising to 3,500 meters (11,500 feet) above sea level. When the first Europeans crossed the ranges early in the twentieth century, they were astonished to find a series of broad intermontane valleys whose floors resembled parkland rather than jungle. This landscape is largely man-made, the result of repeated forest clearance over several thousand years. Consisting primarily of grassland, with some secondary forest, these valleys are the home of the Pacific's largest indigenous population, New Guinea's central highlanders.

Many highlanders are accomplished agriculturalists, employing a range of techniques—from complex systems of ditches, mounds, and mulching to the use of bamboo irrigation channels—to sustain high yields from semipermanent plots. It was once thought that intensive agriculture developed here only after the sweet potato had arrived from the New World, but remnants of gardens excavated at Kuk, near Mount Hagen, have revealed that such practices are part of a tradition going back 9,000 years—making New Guinea one of the oldest regions of settled agriculture in the world.

Along New Guinea's north coast and on adjacent islands, offshore fishing is often combined with the cultivation of coconut, breadfruit, yams, sweet potato, and taro in a system of shifting forest gardens. This pattern is common throughout Melanesia. The people of the Murik Lakes, near the mouth of the Sepik, for example, inhabit an area rich in fish and shellfish, building their settlements on sandbanks. Having virtually no land for gardens, they specialize in fishing, trading part of their catch with neighboring peoples for pigs and garden produce. A similar situation is found on Siassi and Manus islands, and in parts of the Solomons.

Polynesia: A Volcanic Landscape

The characteristic landforms of Polynesia are high islands, which are, in fact, the summits of volcanic seamounts rising above the ocean surface. In most cases, the central peaks rise high enough to create a local microclimate, forcing humid air masses upwards until they cool sufficiently to produce rainfall. Rainforest is the most common vegetation, although some very large islands, such as Hawaii, have extensive dry zones on their leeward sides.

Traditionally, Polynesians have built their livelihood around a combination of horticulture, animal husbandry, and fishing. Their fishing techniques are elaborate, including the use of hooks, lures, nets, and traps, and the most sought-after sites are sheltered, reef-fringed lagoons. Settlements are usually situated near the shore, while gardens and plantations are located inland. On Rarotonga, for instance, each family has its own permanent house, built on the narrow coastal plain; lays claim to a stretch of beach and lagoon for fishing purposes; and cultivates patches of taro in the interior. Although different crops dominate in different areas—sweet potato on Easter Island and in New Zealand, breadfruit in the Marquesas, for example—most Polynesians depend on horticulture for their livelihood, supplementing this with fishing, using a repertoire of techniques that go back at least as far as the early settlement of the eastern Pacific.

Micronesia: High Islands and Coral Atolls

High islands are also found in Micronesia, notable among them being Yap, Pohnpei (formerly Ponape), Chuuk (formerly Truk), Guam, and Belau. Here, too, horticulture and fishing predominate. But the characteristic island form of Micronesia is the coral atoll, usually consisting of a series of small islets formed along the rim of a circular or semicircular reef enclosing a large, central lagoon. Atolls are generally only a few meters above sea level, and their low elevation and small land area make them risky environments. Much of the central Pacific is swept by seasonal typhoons, and some atolls, particularly in the Carolines, have been repeatedly hit by storm-driven waves that have wrought destruction on houses and crops. Moreover, because of their low elevation, atolls are unable to intercept moisture-laden winds, making them susceptible to drought. This applies particularly to Kiribati and parts of the Marshall Islands. With their lack of streams and their porous coral soils, atolls retain very little fresh water, and their inhabitants must therefore rely largely on the brackish water from man-made wells.

In the face of these difficulties, the people who live on Micronesia's atolls subsist predominantly by deep-sea fishing and by reaping the rich harvest of the lagoons, supplementing these resources by growing coconuts, breadfruit, and swamp taro. Coconut palms are resistant to salt water, and the green nuts also provide drinking liquid, while breadfruit, although seasonal, can be stored in pits. Swamp taro is grown either in naturally occurring depressions or in pits dug for the purpose by taking advantage of the freshwater "lens" that floats above the level of the salt water. These atoll gardens have to be heavily mulched, but the huge investment of labor they represent is warranted by the fact that, even in this difficult environment, swamp taro grows all year round and is also able to withstand periods of drought.

This man on Saipan is using a throw net, a common technique of inshore fishing found throughout the Pacific. Beyond the reefs, islanders use ocean-going canoes and fishing lines to catch larger fish.

M.P. WARNER/PACIFIC STOCK

Fishing is crucial to the livelihood of all the coastal peoples of the Pacific. In Tahiti, as elsewhere, a day's catch provides a pleasurable diversion as well as food for the table.

HANS J. BURKARD/BILDERBERG

THE IATMUL OF THE SEPIK RIVER BASIN

Brigitta Hauser-Schäublin

EVEN TODAY, THE SEPIK RIVER BASIN is an untamed and primeval tract of country. From their mountain source near the Irian Jayan border, the sluggish waters of the mighty Sepik River roll down between the spurs of the coastal range and the highlands to empty into the sea. In the process, they endlessly remodel the features of the broad alluvial plain where the Iatmul live—a people many have come to know through the pioneering studies of Gregory Bateson and Margaret Mead.

In the middle course of the river, every flood creates new meanders and seals off old ones, tearing away huge masses of soil, along with living trees and bushes. Former stretches of the riverbed silt up with time, turning first into swamps and then into solid earth. This continual cycle of creation and destruction is characteristic of the Sepik basin. With its alternating wet and dry seasons, this region demands the highest degree of adaptability from plants, animals, and humans alike.

Indigenous People

The people of the Sepik basin speak a Papuan language—a family of a stock of languages that predates the Austronesian languages spoken throughout most of the Pacific—and are thus to be numbered among the aboriginal inhabitants of the island of New Guinea. The Iatmul live along the middle course of the Sepik River, which extends for 1,000 kilometers (about 700 miles). Living in a region where fluctuations in the water level of up to 8 meters (26 feet) are part of everyday life, they have long depended on canoes for travel and transport.

The Iatmul build their villages along naturally elevated river banks. Their sturdy dwellings, raised on stilts, are often hidden behind coconut and sago palms. The staple diet in this region consists of fish and sago. Despite the exceptional fertility of the soil, tuberous plants are grown only as a secondary activity, as the dry season is often too short to allow such crops to ripen.

Iatmul settlements consist of villages made up of several separate hamlets. These hamlets are subdivided locally into two moieties (or social units) on the principle of

A woodcarver working on a large, anthropomorphic figure. Nowadays, most carvings are produced for the international art market.

The canoe is the major means of transport in an area dominated by the meandering Sepik River. The people of this region have long adapted their way of life to the river's unpredictable ways.

opposed pairs, such as river–forest, heaven–earth, man–woman. Clans are also subordinated to this principle of moieties, and house sites are determined according to clan membership. While hamlets may disband, the village is the largest permanent unit found in this region, serving the purposes of communal life, ritual, and defense.

Each settlement is dominated by one or more imposing men's houses: communal buildings rising to 12 meters (40 feet), with soaring gables, decorated facades, and richly carved house posts. These houses are the focus of the Iatmul's political and religious life, which is the province of men. In the past, it was to these houses that Iatmul warriors brought the heads they took in raids on neighboring tribes—trophies of successful male aggression and symbols of the eternal cycle of life and death. Today, they are the site of male initiation rites and meetings between clan representatives.

Division of Labor

In this male-dominated society, it is the women who are responsible for providing their families with their daily food. Setting out in their canoes, they go fishing (usually every morning) and also travel to markets, where they barter sago and fish for vegetables, fruit, and earthenware cooking utensils. Iatmul women also have their own cooperative systems, which strengthen their social cohesion in everyday life and in times of crisis.

While men occasionally go hunting for pigs or crocodiles, or for smaller animals, such as marsupials, they have no day-to-day responsibility for the group's subsistence. In the past, their energies were focused on fighting, and warlike activities and rituals dominated their sociopolitical, religious, and emotional life. Today, for those men who have not migrated to the towns in search of work but stayed behind in the village, certain rituals are still an important part of life.

Art and Myth

The carvings and paintings for which Iatmul men are renowned all over the world are primarily cult objects, material symbols of a highly developed religious world of ideas. Of paramount importance in this world is the relationship of the Iatmul with their ever-changing environment. This is perhaps most dramatically symbolized in myth by the great crocodile, which silently rose to the surface of the floodwaters and created land, only to vanish again the next moment back into the flood—an admired and dreaded lord of life on land and water.

This father and his small son are decorated with body paint, which is worn mainly on ceremonial occasions.

Women prepare sago pancakes. Each day, one or two pancakes are cooked for each family member, and then stored in his or her own plaited basket, suspended from the roof.

The starch of the sago palm has to be extracted by a laborious process of pounding, washing, and settling.

Men's houses are still built today, although they are much smaller than in previous times. They are used for male initiation rites and meetings between clan representatives. In the past, it was to these houses, too, that warriors brought the heads they took in raids on neighboring tribes.

BRYAN AND CHERRY ALEXANDER

⚓ A smaller cousin of the seagoing *wa*, this outrigger canoe on Woleai can be used inside the lagoon and on short hops from one islet to the next.

⚲ In past times, Micronesia's Marshall Islanders used navigational aids such as this wickerwork chart to find their way to distant islands by tracking the complex interaction of currents. The shells mark the location of islands.

OLIVER STREWE/WAVE PRODUCTIONS

LONG-DISTANCE VOYAGING IN MICRONESIA

With the precariousness of atoll environments, it is not surprising that Micronesians are the Pacific's most accomplished seafarers. This has long allowed them to maintain links with far-flung communities, without which they would not have survived in times of hardship. Within Micronesia, the best sailors generally come from small islands, while those from large islands, such as Belau or Pohnpei, are regarded as landlubbers.

The characteristic ocean-going craft of Micronesia is a single-outrigger sailing canoe of modest dimensions, manned by a navigator and four to six crewmen. Perhaps the best example of the Micronesian boatbuilder's craft is to be found in the canoes of Puluwat, in the central Carolines. Known as *wa*, they consist of a keel carved from breadfruit wood to which planks are fastened with coconut fiber lashings, the seams being caulked with breadfruit sap. Equipped with an outrigger and a single mast, the *wa* is fast, seaworthy, and maneuverable, largely owing to two related features. First, the mast is able to pivot in such a way as to allow the sail to move from one end of the canoe to the other when sailing against the wind, so that the bow and stern become interchangeable. This technique, known as shunting, makes it possible to always keep the outrigger to windward, giving the canoe excellent balance and stability. Second, the hull of the canoe is asymmetrical, which has the effect of controlling water flow, thereby countering the outrigger's drag. The result is masterpiece of sophisticated design: a canoe that is steady but agile in almost all weather conditions.

The design of Micronesian canoes is matched by the navigational skills of Micronesian sailors. Not all men achieve the status of navigator. Those who do undergo instruction on land and at sea from early adolescence until well into adulthood. Micronesians routinely make voyages over hundreds of kilometers, out of sight of land. On Puluwat and throughout the Carolines, sailors rely on a range of information to find their way, including wind and wave patterns, the location of reefs, and sightings of birds, marine life, and stars. Stars are particularly important: sailors recognize, and have individual names for, the positions in which they rise and set, and also have names for the headings indicating the routes between islands. Although magnetic compasses are now commonly available, they have not replaced reliance on the stars and other signs. Elsewhere, particularly in eastern Micronesia, voyagers were guided by their knowledge of the wave patterns set up by a prevailing swell in the vicinity of a particular island. This knowledge was sometimes formalized in elegant wickerwork charts, with shells marking the location of islands.

ornaments to new dances and rituals. Trading partners offered each other hospitality, treating one another almost as kin, and partnerships were kept in the family, each man passing his partnership on to his sons when he died. There was a brisk traffic in imported valuables, but also in grudges. The mountain people regarded the plains people as notorious sorcerers, and enlisted their help to bring misfortune to their enemies. When someone fell ill, he or his kin would try to trace the enemy responsible and the sorcerer his enemy had employed, and would then try to buy the latter off with a payment of shells.

The Mountain Arapesh were an important link in a network of interregional trade that joined the Sepik basin to northern coastal areas. Similar exchange systems, involving even the remotest communities, were widespread throughout traditional Melanesia and did much to stimulate the production of goods and a diversity of cultural forms. Middle Sepik societies came to specialize exclusively in a particular craft or activity, bartering items as various as fish, sago, sacred flutes, and items of esoteric knowledge.

Perhaps the most famous Melanesian trading systems are those involving long sea voyages. In some areas, especially along New Guinea's northern coast, one could construct a map of a community's far-flung trade connections simply on the basis of the diversity of household and ritual goods to be found in its settlements. Along New Guinea's southern coast, the Motu people specialized in making pottery and undertook annual trading expeditions (known as *hiri*) to the Papuan Gulf. Traveling in fleets of large, multiple-hulled sailing canoes (called *lagatoi*), they exchanged their pots for sago and the hardwood logs they needed to build their canoes.

A Mailu net-maker from Papua New Guinea. The maritime orientation of coastal peoples depended on a relatively sophisticated technology, and fishing equipment required constant maintenance.

A Motu woman and her daughter making pottery, using the paddle-and-anvil method. This photograph was taken before the Second World War. Motu pottery was renowned along the Papuan coast, and served as one of the mainstays of the local economy.

FRANK HURLEY/AUSTRALIAN MUSEUM

MELANESIAN TRADING SYSTEMS

Margaret Mead and Reo Fortune began their field work among the Arapesh of New Guinea's Torricelli Mountains by accident. En route from the north coast to the Sepik plains, they found themselves stranded in the small village of Alitoa, unable to get carriers to go any further inland. In 1931, what struck them was Alitoa's extreme isolation. The only connection the Mountain Arapesh had with the outside world was through a network of narrow, muddy mountain trails, yet along these trails there flowed such a constant stream of goods, ideas, and influences that Mead was eventually to characterize the Mountain Arapesh as an "importing culture".

Self-sufficient in terms of food and life's necessities, they relied on their trading links with neighbors for such items as clay pots, stone tools, and ceremonial goods, the latter ranging from shell

FRANK HURLEY/AUSTRALIAN MUSEUM

This combination of craft specialization and seamanship was particularly striking among the peoples who lived on the small islands lying off the New Guinea mainland. The Mailu islanders, for example, similarly specialized in pottery, which they traded for food, and enjoyed a monopoly on sea travel over a long stretch of coast. An even more extensive trade system operated between the northeast coast of New Guinea and the western end of New Britain. Here, the Tami and Siassi islanders set out in their large, double-masted canoes from islands barely large enough to provide house sites to exchange their finely carved bowls for such commodities as obsidian, pottery, mats, pigs' tusks, and dogs' teeth.

Ceremonial Exchange

Melanesia is also remarkable for its elaborate systems of ceremonial exchange, which are a means by which people at once acquire prestige and establish ties. The best-known example is the *kula*, a system favored by the Trobriand Islanders and their neighbors in the Massim region, off New Guinea's east coast. *Kula* is a system of strategic gift-giving involving elements of cooperation and rivalry. Each gift must be repaid by an equivalent gift, and by accepting a gift, a person incurs ongoing obligations to the giver. This endless round of exchanges and the ties it creates link the people of a number of islands in what is known as the Kula Ring.

Setting off in elaborately carved and decorated canoes, *kula* voyagers sail to their partners' villages to exchange red shell necklaces (*soulava*) for white arm shells (*mwali*). The former travel clockwise, and the latter, anticlockwise. Each item has a personal name, and *kula* gifts are always accompanied by stories about their previous owners. Like family heirlooms, *kula* objects keep memories alive and derive their value from the ties they symbolize. By inducing his partner to give him a particularly renowned article, and thereby joining his name to those of the previous owners, a man is able to achieve a kind of fame and immortality. The recipient is obliged to provide a suitable *kula* object in return and also to hand on his gift to a partner in the other direction, for the general rule of *kula* is that valuables must continually be passed on.

Although a circular system of exchange in which nothing is bought or sold seems economically pointless, *kula* is a consuming passion and underpins relations between island communities scattered over a vast area. The practice of linking communities through ceremonial exchange is widespread in Melanesia, taking various forms, in which the politics of reputation seem always to play a role.

A further elaboration of this theme is to be seen in the *moka* system of Mount Hagen. Living in the central highlands of Papua New Guinea, the Hageners are skilled gardeners and also raise pigs, a valuable resource that plays a major role in Hagen politics. As in other parts of New Guinea, traditional warfare was frequent and destructive in Mount

Hagen in the precolonial period. *Moka* is a system of ceremonial exchange that links partners from a number of diverse groups, and paying death compensation to erstwhile enemies is one of the commonest ways of establishing *moka* relationships.

Moka transactions are festive affairs held at a clan's ceremonial ground, the focus of attention being a line of pigs tethered to stakes. The pigs will be given as gifts, and people come to see how many will be given and who the recipients will be. Wearing their finest decorations, men of the host clan dance in formation before the assembled visitors. The names of the *moka* recipients are called out, and formal speeches are made. Guests then depart for home, the fortunate ones taking their newly acquired pigs with them. Each recipient must provide a return gift at some future *moka* occasion, but it must be substantially larger than the original gift. This is the very essence of *moka*.

For Hageners, prestige and power are earned through giving, and making large *moka* gifts has long been the way men acquire a reputation and rise to the position of "big man". Although clansmen join together in making their *moka* presentations, each gift passes publicly from a specific donor to a specific recipient. In this way, personal reputations are made at the same time that the group gains in status.

Big men continually compete with one another, and exercise influence by virtue of their ability to juggle debts and credits within the network of mutual obligations in which all Hagen men are enmeshed. An ambitious man will help fellow clansmen to acquire pigs and shells for marriage payments and can generally be counted on in times of need, thereby cultivating a reputation for generosity while placing others in his debt.

🔥 Robesa, a *kula* master from Waviyai, on Woodlark Island, displays *soulava*, the red shell necklaces that circulate in the *kula*. These necklaces are signs of his standing among his partners, and in due course, he will pass them on.

🔥 An indication of this Hagen man's status is provided by his *omak*, a series of tally sticks adorning his chest. Each stick represents a major gift that he has given away in a *moka* exchange.

🔗 *Opposite page*: This Trobriand man is wearing an especially prized *kula* valuable —a *doga*, or circular boar's tusk. More than mere adornment, such decorations give a good indication of a person's "name" or reputation, since they can only be secured as gifts from previous owners.

THE KULA RING

GÖRAN BURENHULT

BRONISLAW MALINOWSKI

IN THE ARCHIPELAGO of coral and volcanic islands east of New Guinea, in Melanesia, there operates a unique system of ceremonial exchange known as the Kula Ring. This complex system, first studied by the Polish–British ethnographer Bronislaw Malinowski between 1915 and 1918, links a number of different island cultures. Among the most important are those of the Trobriand Islands, Woodlark Island, and the d'Entrecasteaux Islands, but other, more remote islands and island groups also form part of the *kula* system.

Only two kinds of ceremonial valuables, or *vegu'a*, are passed on in the Kula Ring: *soulava*, or *bagi*, long necklaces consisting of hundreds of pierced and polished *Spondylus* shells, which travel clockwise, and *mwali*, white armrings made of cone shells (*Conus millepunctatus*), which travel counterclockwise. Both kinds of objects are elaborately decorated with tiny cowrie shells and other types of ornaments. The objects are exchanged between different partners on different islands, *soulava* being traded for *mwali*, and vice versa, and will then continue to make their way round the ring as they are successively exchanged with partners in adjacent regions. Sometimes, after several decades of traveling, an object will return to its place of origin for a short while.

⌂ Nigada Bu'a, the seagoing *kula* canoe belonging to Omarakana village, in Kiriwina, in the Trobriand Islands. This photograph was taken by Bronislaw Malinowski, a Polish-born ethnographer, who worked in the Trobriand Islands between 1915 and 1918.

⚲ Chief Dauya, at Wawela, in Kiriwina, displays his collection of *soulava* (or *bagi*). His house, situated on the beach at Wawela, is richly adorned with *kula* symbols. In the *kula* system, each valuable is known individually and has its own name.

⚲ The decorated prow of a *kula* canoe from the island of Kitava. Every detail of the elaborately carved and painted prow board (*lagim*) has its own particular significance and magical importance. The prow, the *lagim*, the front tip of the outrigger, and the platform are all adorned with cowrie shells.

GÖRAN BURENHULT

GÖRAN BURENHULT

Kula objects are almost never worn by their owners; nor are they used on ceremonial occasions. Yet they are the most significant symbols of status and prestige in the area, and a successful *kula* partner usually grows in political influence. The objects cannot be kept for long, but must be circulated in certain patterns and directions. The longer an object has been in circulation, the more valuable it is, and the more respect its temporary owner enjoys.

Specially designed and elaborately decorated seagoing canoes, called *masawa*, are used for *kula* expeditions. The building, launching, and sailing of these canoes are surrounded by a great deal of magic, and a number of ceremonies and magic incantations are performed to protect canoes against bewitchment, harmful tree spirits, and the dangers of the open sea, and to bring good fortune on the next *kula* exchange. A typical *kula* canoe can accommodate a crew of between 7 and 14 men, who paddle and sail the vessel over long distances.

An extensive exchange network involving everyday commodities, including pottery, rock, shells, betel nuts, coconuts, and rattan, operates in tandem with the Kula Ring. It has been suggested that it was the need for these materials that spurred the development of a ritual system of exchange, in which the objects exchanged serve no other purpose than that of being tokens of friendship and status.

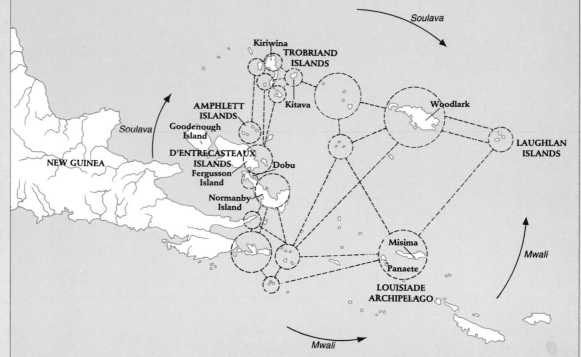

CARTOGRAPHY: RAY SIM

THE KULA RING

The system of ceremonial exchange known as the Kula Ring operates in the archipelago off the eastern tip of New Guinea, in Melanesia. The most important areas and routes are shown here. *Soulava* necklaces are traded clockwise, whereas *mwali* armrings travel counterclockwise. The routes were first mapped by Bronislaw Malinowski, in 1922.

➼ Villagers by their *kula* canoe at Wapaya, on the west coast of Kitava. A *soulava* is hanging from the long-itudinal stem decoration, or *tabuya*, which holds the *lagim* in place.

♀ A *kula* canoe at sea off the western coast of Kitava, in the Trobriand Islands.

GÖRAN BURENHULT

GÖRAN BURENHULT

CHIEFS AND STRANGERS IN POLYNESIA

One of the distinctive characteristics of traditional Polynesian societies was their emphasis on rank. Typically, the entire society was believed to be descended from ancestors who were gods, but some people were considered to be more closely related to the gods than others. Even within families, elder children and their descendants belonged to senior lines, while younger children and their descendants belonged to junior lines. Being the gods' nearest earthly relatives, chiefs were related to all members of the society as "fathers of the people". Their persons were sacred (*tapu*), and they were endowed with divine power (*mana*). In some societies, notably Tahiti and Hawaii, they wielded the power of life and death. In their dual role as political and religious leaders, chiefs received offerings that were at once tributes and sacrifices. In return, they were responsible for their people's welfare.

Although rigid in theory, Polynesian political systems were flexible in practice. While *mana* was usually conferred by birth, the gods could grant it to some individuals and withdraw it from others. *Mana* was demonstrable power, and a challenger who succeeded in overthrowing the incumbent chief established his *mana* at the same time that his rival lost his own. Similarly, a chief who became unpopular was held to be losing his *mana*. In Hawaii, such chiefs were often killed by lower-ranking opponents from within their own chiefdom. Because claims to rank could be traced both paternally and maternally, a new chief could strengthen his line by marrying a woman of the former chief's line, and legitimacy was conferred by genealogical chants that incorporated him into the ancestral pedigree.

Polynesian chieftainship thus involved a combination of rank, centralized political power, and competition, and these features came strongly into play when Europeans arrived in the eighteenth century. In Hawaii, for example, Kamehameha I cultivated a reputation for friendliness towards outsiders, which helped him to secure firearms. With these, he waged a series of successful campaigns against neighboring chiefdoms, which he incorporated into his own to form a small state. In the course of a succession dispute in 1819, his heir, Liholiho, publicly violated, and thus abandoned, the *tapu* tradition, and invited American missionaries to Hawaii. They were to have a major influence on local affairs, and from this time, Hawaiian royalty lost its aura of divinity and became increasingly identified with landownership. This process culminated in the 1840s with an event known as the Great Mahele, meaning land division, when Kamehameha III allocated individual land titles by royal decree. The aristocracy gained title to large blocks of land, which they could sell to foreigners for cash. In this way, aristocrats often became wealthy, while commoners who emulated their example became landless and drifted to towns.

Hawaiian society was rapidly transformed as chiefs took advantage of foreign technology and influence to defeat their rivals. The nineteenth century witnessed the rise to power of Pomare II in Tahiti, Cakobau in Fiji, and Taufa'ahau (later George Tupou I) in Tonga in similar fashion. In Tahiti, Pomare subdued his pagan rivals with help from the London Missionary Society (LMS) in 1815, but in the 1830s, one of his successors, Queen Pomare, became embroiled in rivalries between the LMS and French Catholic missionaries. She eventually appealed to Britain for protectorate status but was refused, and the French annexed Tahiti in 1842. In Fiji, the expanding chiefdom of Bau was able to extend its hold over Viti Levu with the aid of firearms, but was opposed by a rival chief on Lau, Ma'afu, who had Tongan support. Cakobau, the chief of Bau, converted to Christianity and courted the British, who pressured the Christian Tongans to transfer their support to him. Proclaiming himself *Tui Viti* (King of Fiji), Cakobau assumed sovereignty over the Fiji group and ceded it to Britain in 1874, an act in part intended to secure the position of Bau's chiefs by forestalling

♀ A village chief from Western Samoa. Western Samoa's constitution attempts to reconcile tradition, *faaSamoa*, with western legal concepts. One provision limits voting in parliamentary elections to title holders, or *matai*. While affirming traditional values of rank, the system is more democratic than it appears, since recent estimates suggest that as many as 75 percent of all adult males hold *matai* titles.

NIK WHEELER

THE BETTMAN ARCHIVE/AUSTRALIAN PICTURE LIBRARY

THE GRANGER COLLECTION

♦ Both a traditional chief and a political innovator, Kamehameha I (?1758 to 1819) consolidated Hawaii's independent chiefdoms and attempted to establish a modern state by joining Hawaiian notions of rank with Western ideas of monarchy.

◄● In this engraving, made about 1820, King Kamehameha I, founder of the Hawaiian kingdom, is portrayed with his subjects, whose apparently traditional attire contrasts with their king's European-style garb.

Cakobau's rivals and bringing resident foreigners under control.

The kingdom of Tonga emerged in the nineteenth century after a series of struggles for succession to various chiefly titles. Taufa'ahau converted to Methodism and subdued other high chiefs with the aid of Wesleyan missionaries, who provided him with firearms. Taking the name of George Tupou I, he promulgated a constitution under which he reigned as monarch and appointed the prime minister and cabinet, while the Free Wesleyan Church became the state church, with observance of the sabbath a provision of the constitution. Although any man over the age of 16 theoretically had the right to a land allotment, landownership was in practice vested in chiefs, who were appointed by the king in recognition of past service. This system differed from traditional Tongan land tenure, which was vested in kinship groups known as *ha'a*, and ignored customary rank.

J. LANGEVIN/SYGMA/AUSTRAL INTERNATIONAL

⚮ Originally brought to Fiji as indentured laborers to work in the canefields during the colonial period, Indo-Fijians now comprise roughly half of Fiji's population. Although ethnic Fijians control virtually all of the country's land, Indo-Fijians have been very active in commerce and are crucial to the national economy.

↪ One of the problems facing most rural peoples in the Pacific is finding a reliable source of cash income. This pearl farmer and his family in Samarai, Papua New Guinea, examine the results of their latest harvest, which will be graded and sold on the international market.

COLONIALISM IN THE PACIFIC

Commercial exploitation of the Pacific was sporadic in the early years of contact, the islands being mainly of interest as provisioning stations for whalers and merchant shipping. But by the mid-nineteenth century, the Pacific sugar industry had become established. In Hawaii, Asian laborers were imported to work in the canefields, while sugar producers in Queensland (in northern Australia) and Fiji sought workers elsewhere. Melanesians, who had largely been bypassed because of their hostility to outsiders, now began to attract attention as cheap labor. "Blackbirders", as labor recruiters came to be known, secured workers by inducement or force, particularly in the Solomons and the New Hebrides. Blackbirding practices verged on slavery, ceasing only when the Melanesian islands became protectorates of various European powers. The Fijian sugar industry then turned to India for laborers, and, as in Hawaii, local people were eventually outnumbered by immigrants. In other areas of the Pacific, foreign settlement was sparse, with the exception of New Caledonia and New Zealand, where fierce land wars were fought between settlers and local people. Elsewhere—in New Guinea, the Solomons, and Vanuatu, for example—copra plantations were established, becoming the mainstay of many colonial economies, while tropical products, such as bêche-de-mer, pearls, and sandalwood, provided ample scope for the often extravagant schemes of expatriate adventurers.

By 1900, most Pacific islands had been claimed by European powers, and the first half of the twentieth century saw several shifts in colonial alignments as a result of rivalries between the great powers. Global ambitions made Pacific bases strategically desirable, and after the Spanish-American War, the United States acquired Guam, while Spain sold its remaining Micronesian territories to Germany. Following the First World War, Japan and Australia assumed control over former German territories, and just two decades later, the Second World War plunged the region into turmoil again.

The Pacific was heavily affected by fighting between Allied and Japanese forces, and the war brought a number of unexpected developments in its wake. On Guadalcanal, for example, military authorities created the Solomon Islands Labour Corps, which brought together islanders from nearby Malaita to help in the campaign against the Japanese. Drawing on their experience of military discipline and community life, ex-Corps members later organized the movement known as Maasina Rule, after a local word for "brotherhood". Maasina Rule had strong Christian overtones and emphasized the unity of Malaitan peoples. Villages were organized into districts, with chiefs and councils; custom was codified; and taxes and fines were introduced. Members observed disciplines such as assembling for roll call, marching, and raising the flag. They were forbidden to work on plantations with low pay and encouraged to work on community projects instead. Although suppressed by the British administration, Maasina Rule provided a framework for Solomon islanders to assert their own form of political control. Similar movements grew up on Manus and Tanna islands and elsewhere, reflecting a deep dissatisfaction with colonial conditions as well as a desire for a new way of life.

JUTTA MALNIC

❧ Their strategic location made many Pacific islands battlegrounds between Japanese and Allied forces during the Second World War, often with a disastrous impact on islanders caught in the middle. Here, United States marines on Tarawa take part in the fighting that wiped out the Japanese garrison and devastated much of the atoll.

THE BETTMAN ARCHIVE/AUSTRALIAN PICTURE LIBRARY

Colonial administrative control in the Pacific was restored after the war, but by the 1950s, it had become clear that the colonial systems were destined for change. Indonesia claimed Dutch New Guinea in 1949, and although its claim went unrecognized, Indonesia persisted, attacking Dutch forces in New Guinea in 1961. Two years later, in 1963, the United Nations oversaw the incorporation of West New Guinea as the Indonesian province of Irian Jaya. In the meantime, decolonization in Asia and Africa was leading to demands for self-government in the Pacific. Between 1962 and 1980, most of the Pacific's colonial territories achieved independence, in each case without bloodshed. More recently, the Marshall Islands, the Northern Marianas, and the Federated States of Micronesia (FSM) became self-governing under the terms of compacts of free association with the United States.

At present, Indonesia, the United States, and France remain the Pacific's major colonial powers, and each faces resistance within its territories. The Free Papua Movement (Organisasi Papua Merdeka, or OPM) has operated sporadically against Indonesian authorities in Irian Jaya for some years. Although the OPM's prospects of success are slim, military operations against it have caused Irianese to flee across the border to Papua New Guinea, provoking a number of diplomatic incidents. In Belau, a series of court battles over a constitution spelling out Belau's relationship to the United States is still in progress, the storage of nuclear weapons on Belauan soil

OLIVER STREWE/WAVE PRODUCTIONS

being the main bone of contention. New Caledonia has long been the scene of discord between Kanaks and French settlers, and in 1987, French paratroopers killed a number of Kanak militants. Although an accord has been reached between French authorities and Kanak representatives, it is unclear how lasting the peace will be. French Polynesia has also seen agitation for independence, motivated in part by protests over nuclear testing on Moruroa Atoll.

🔸 In a ceremony of the waning days of colonial rule in the Pacific, the last governor of the British Solomon Islands Protectorate bestows an honor on a local dignitary. The Solomon Islands became an independent nation in 1978, and are organized as a parliamentary democracy.

JEAN-PAUL FERRERO/AUSCAPE

The Postcolonial Pacific

With independence, many Pacific countries faced issues different from those of the colonial era. While colonial regimes made little pretence of representing indigenous people, the legitimacy of postcolonial goverments is based in part on their claim to do exactly that. This has proved to be a problem in some of the new Melanesian states, such as Papua New Guinea and Vanuatu, which are culturally very diverse, in contrast to the more homogeneous Polynesian and Micronesian states. On the eve of Vanuatu's independence in 1980, secessionist revolts broke out on Santo and Tanna islands, and in both cases, a sense of cultural distinctiveness described as "custom" (*kastom*) played a conspicuous role. Although put down by government forces with the assistance of troops from Papua New Guinea, the Vanuatu rebellions highlighted some of the difficulties facing the Pacific's new multi-ethnic nations. An irony of the contemporary situation is that the same *kastom* once appealed to in the cause of national independence may now be threatening to the postcolonial state.

A second problem facing new Pacific nations is the need to finance government operations, which were previously funded by the colonial powers. For this reason, contemporary Pacific nations are preoccupied with plans for economic development, although Pacific countries are well off by Third World standards. Most people are self-sufficient in terms of food, and conditions of life are generally adequate, if not affluent. But this subsistence wealth goes hand in hand with monetary poverty. Throughout the Pacific, small-scale copra production is a source of income, but earnings from this are marginal. Some Pacific countries depend heavily on money sent home by islanders working abroad. This is especially true of Tonga, where remittances account for the greatest proportion of personal income. The Cook Islands and Western Samoa have very high rates of migration to New Zealand, where Pacific islanders form sizeable communities. The ability of islanders to find work overseas is crucial to these economies.

Of all Pacific countries, Papua New Guinea is the richest in natural resources. The centerpiece of the country's economy has been the huge copper mine on the island of Bougainville, which has contributed more to national revenues than any other source. In recent years, a number of other large-scale resource operations have been established, including the Ok Tedi and Porgera mines, the Lake Kutubu oil field, and massive

◀❍ A mother and daughter from Tanna Island, Vanuatu. The decorations and apparently "traditional" dress indicate that some special occasion is afoot. For everyday wear, cotton dresses and blouses are preferred.

🔫 In 1989, rebels of the Bougainville Revolutionary Army (BRA) seized control of the Panguna mine in what became a campaign of secession against the Papua New Guinea government. Although the BRA was clearly in disarray by the end of 1993, fighting on the island continued, often between BRA elements and local Bougainvillean "resistance groups" supported by the government.
DAVID ROBIE/CAMERA PRESS/AUSTRAL INTERNATIONAL

◀▶ The Panguna mine on Bougainville is one of the world's largest open-pit copper mines, and has provided Papua New Guinea's government with one of its chief sources of revenue since independence in 1975. More recently, however, control over the mine has been the major bone of contention between the Papua New Guinea government and Bougainvillean secessionists.

timber projects. Such projects are meant to finance government services, but they come at a considerable cost. Environmental damage has been extensive, and the social unrest resulting from mining operations has been very disruptive for the country as a whole. The Nasioi people, on whose land the Bougainville mine is built, have been dissatisfied for some time over the distribution of the project's costs and benefits.

Disputes surrounding the renewal of the mining lease erupted in violence in 1989, when local people dynamited some mine facilities. The ensuing fighting between government forces and the self-proclaimed Bougainville Revolutionary Army (BRA) left a number of people dead. Negotiations between the government and the BRA have repeatedly broken down. In 1992, the situation was at a stalemate, with the BRA claiming control over Bougainville, while the government maintained a blockade aimed at forcing a resolution. In the meantime, the closure of the mine has prompted a national financial crisis, and the BRA's secessionist claims have called the unity of the postcolonial state in question. In Papua New Guinea, at least, a way of reconciling local people's interests with the demands of financing the state has yet to be found.

◀▶ These Huli men in Papua New Guinea's Southern Highlands Province produce pit-sawn timber for use in local building projects. Timber is one of Papua New Guinea's major resources, and by the early 1990s, the country's extensive rainforests had come under increasing pressure from international logging interests.

117

☝ Photographed by anthropologist Paul Wirz in 1930, a Gogodala artist puts the finishing touches to the prow of a canoe. This is part of the carving tradition revived after A.L. Crawford visited the area in the 1970s.
PAUL WIRZ/MUSEUM OF VÖLKERKUNDE, BASEL/ CRAWFORD HOUSE PRESS

♀ A scene from the Gogodala Cultural Center, in Balimo, which was built with government support in 1974. In the opening ceremonies, attended by Papua New Guinea's first Prime Minister, Michael Somare, a new generation of Gogodala recreated rituals abandoned decades previously. Since that time, Gogodala performers have taken part in cultural shows and exhibitions as far away as Port Moresby.

Indigenous Culture in a Post-traditional World

Pacific cultures have always changed in response to new conditions, and this process was accelerated by European contact. The image of Stone Age peoples surviving into the twentieth century is largely mythical, and fantasies of tribes that have yet to encounter a European are precisely that. Anthropologist Roger Keesing has argued that even among such apparently "traditional" people as the Kwaio of Malaita, who observe taboos, sacrifice pigs to ancestors, and arrange marriages with transfers of shell wealth, the persistence of indigenous cultural practices can better be explained as a deliberate form of resistance to external domination than as a product of isolation. The Kwaio were key participants in the Maasina Rule movement of the 1940s, and their present way of life could more accurately be called neotraditionalist than culturally conservative.

The Gogodala of Papua New Guinea's south coast are another case in point. Frank Hurley visited the area in the 1920s in order to make a photographic record of Gogodala life and to document their rich carving traditions. But when A.L. Crawford went to collect examples of this art in the 1970s, he found Gogodala carving to be virtually extinct. In the 1930s, the Gogodala converted to Christianity, giving up their religious ceremonies and, with them, their art. By the 1970s, their pastors were renowned for their evangelical efforts throughout southwestern Papua New Guinea.

Crawford's search for traditional art, however, stimulated a renewed interest among the people themselves. Although the Gogodala had abandoned their traditional communal longhouses for single-family houses over the previous two generations, a group of people banded together to build a large longhouse at Balimo in 1974, with the support of Papua New Guinea's National Cultural Council. Christened the Gogodala Cultural Center, the house is part of a cultural renewal whereby local art forms are being revived and taught to young Gogodala artists.

While this development asserts the value of Gogodala tradition in the modern world, the situation is far more complex than simply bringing the past back to life. The cultural center is neither a dwelling nor the site of ceremonies. As Christians, the Gogodala have no desire to revive their traditional religion. Instead, the center serves as a local museum and a storehouse for artifacts made for the international art market. The center and the Gogodala revival are thus the product of several interactive forces: indigenous culture, emerging national pride, and the desire to bring business development to an otherwise impoverished area.

The revival of Gogodala tradition goes hand in hand with the production of art for sale, but the effects of marketing traditional culture can be mixed. Inexpensive air travel allows tourists to visit many areas that were largely inaccessible until a few years ago, and in countries such as Papua New Guinea, tour operators promote travel to areas advertised as "remote" and "untouched". Trips up the Sepik River, for example, offer the possibility of witnessing initiation ceremonies and buying artifacts made specifically for sale. While this provides welcome income and keeps carving skills alive, it seems inevitable that it will bring about a shift in the meaning of indigenous practices that local people may not be able to control. In Vanuatu, Pentecost islanders find that their celebrated "land dive" has become a prime attraction for tourists. A ritual intended to establish the fertility of crops and a young man's status within his community has become a paid performance staged for outsiders.

Contemporary Hawaiians find themselves a minority in their own land, and many are engaged in a continuous struggle to retain control over their cultural identity. Tourism has been a feature of life in Hawaii since the latter part of the nineteenth century, and while it has brought money to the islands, native Hawaiians have not been the main beneficiaries of tourist dollars. Displays of "traditional" Hawaiian culture staged for tourists have drawn sharp criticism from those who resent their culture being misrepresented in the pursuit of profit. Hula dancing, for example, has been exploited by the tourist industry for decades. In an attempt to reclaim their heritage, Hawaiians are now engaged in a hula revival, with competitions emphasizing the role of traditional chants.

This is part of a more general Hawaiian renaissance, in which, for example, Hawaiian language and culture courses are increasingly being encouraged within the educational system. Some rural communities continue to cultivate taro, the traditional staple, despite their dependence on the wage economy, and even those who no longer garden themselves set store by traditional foods as a symbol of their identity. There has also been renewed interest in the seafaring abilities of Polynesian ancestors, the much publicized voyage of the *Hokule'a*, from Hawaii to Tahiti, in 1976 serving as a focus for Hawaiian pride. But while tradition is unquestionably very important to Hawaiians, the value of Hawaiian identity has been enhanced by the challenges to it inherent in Hawaii's incorporation into the United States and the massive influx of alien populations into Hawaii.

The hula has become a symbol of resurgent Hawaiian identity. Here, dancers take part in the Halau o Kekuhi Kamokila Campbell Hula Festival, where chants and other more traditional aspects of the hula are highly prized.

The Hawaiian sovereignty movement dramatized its goals during the 1993 centenary of the overthrow of the Hawaiian kingdom by American business interests.

⮕ Fiji's Colonel Sitiveni Rabuka successfully staged two coups in 1987 aimed at preventing a multiracial coalition from coming to power. Claiming to represent the interests of ethnic Fijians, Rabuka has been active in parliamentary politics and held the office of Prime Minister for a number of years since the coups.

⚲ A highlands politician from Simbu Province, in Papua New Guinea, on the campaign trail. Although the juxtaposition of bullhorn and traditional dress may strike a seemingly incongruous note, highlands big men were always astute politicians, whose oratorical skills were an essential ingredient in mustering political support.

Elsewhere in the Pacific, self-conscious ideas of tradition often have frankly political aims. In New Zealand, Maori activists have argued for the creation of parallel Maori institutions to reflect the importance of their traditions in a bicultural state. In Tonga, the Tupou dynasty and the nobility justify their control over land and politics by an appeal to tradition, but they are now facing widespread, if quiet, opposition from commoners operating with church support who are increasingly dissatisfied with their landless status and have brought charges of corruption. The 1987 Fijian elections were over-turned in coups led by Colonel Rabuka, one of whose stated aims was to protect indigenous Fijians against the economically powerful Indo-Fijian community. Rabuka and his supporters in the military and the Taukei (Landowners) Movement argue that they are the defenders of Fijian traditions and emphasize

🔥 Blowing a conch trumpet on Viti Levu (Fiji) serves to mark the opening of various public occasions.

the cultural differences dividing them from Indo-Fijians. These are said to include placing a higher value on community and family relations than on money, observing the Christian sabbath, and, above all, respecting chiefly authority. Critics have pointed out that, although represented as indigenous cultural values, many of these traditions are scarcely older than Indian immigration. They argue that the true aim of the coups was to secure the interests of relatively wealthy chiefs (especially from Bau) at the expense of commoners and Indo-Fijians alike.

Among the Duke of York islanders, popular tradition credits the nineteenth-century missionary George Brown with originating several local customs, including the use of strings of shell disks as bride payment. Surprising as this may be to Westerners, such cases are an important reminder that it is becoming increasingly difficult to distinguish between indigenous and imported traditions. Pacific peoples are acutely aware that they are part of a larger world, and one of the challenges facing them is to define their place within it in a way that opens up possibilities for them while at the same time leaving room for them to be themselves—a process that is far from simple.

A SINGSING IN NEW IRELAND

J. PETER WHITE

SINGSING IS *TOK PISIN* for a festival that involves dancing, feasting, and, usually, singing. (*Tok pisin*, sometimes wrongly called pidgin English, is the national language of Papua New Guinea.)

In New Ireland today, singsings are held on important occasions. One I went to in 1985, for instance, was part of a final funeral ceremony for a man killed in the Pacific War in the 1940s. Other occasions have included the opening of a new church and the completion of a successful election campaign.

The singsing shown here was held at St Joseph's Vocational School, in Fissoa, on 2 June 1990. New buildings were opened by the Prime Minister of Papua New Guinea, the Honorable Rabbie Namaliu. The American Ambassador and many provincial politicians were present. Teams of singers and dancers came from all over the island, which extends for nearly 400 kilometers (250 miles). Dukduk dancers, with their distinctive conical headdresses, came from the neighboring island of New Britain. Food, consisting of vegetables and pork cooked in earth ovens, was provided for all the visiting groups.

🔥 Dukduks dance individually, leaping into the air. Their bodies are invisible under almost spherical bundles of leaves. In their home territory, dukduks often represent the spirits of dead persons. Here, they pause briefly for the opening ceremony.

🔥 Many singers come in village teams. They practice for weeks beforehand, singing in their local language or in the national language, *tok pisin*.

🔥 Headdresses like this are made of bamboo, grasses, feathers, and paint. Each is the individual creation of its owner, and if it is reused, it will be extensively modified.

🔥 Dukduks can take either male or female form. Even at a singsing, all other people must show them respect by keeping out of their way.

121

TRADITIONAL PEOPLES OF AFRICA

A D   1   5   0   0   –   T H E   P R E S E N T

Cultural Diversity and Enduring Values

M.C. JEDREJ

AFRICA IS THE MOST CULTURALLY DIVERSE of all the continents. Its indigenous cultures are so numerous as to almost defy description, and over large parts of the continent, especially around the coasts, there are also powerful and deep-seated cultural presences that have their origin on other continents.

But despite the turbulence of the past—and the equally turbulent forces of the present—in the vast interior of Africa, indigenous ways of life, bodies of practical knowledge, institutions, and systems of beliefs and values have persisted to the present day. This is not because of a blind adherence to habit and custom, but because, for what is still largely a rural population, traditional knowledge and ways of life are an immensely rich and developing resource, which is drawn upon not only to tackle the perennial problems of everyday life—of growing crops and herding livestock, of dealing with disease and illness, birth and death—but also when confronting and responding to unprecedented events and the challenges of historical change.

In this account, five broad and enduring African cultural groups are identified. These are the forest peoples of the Guinea Coast, the central Africans, the pastoralists, the hill tribes, and the hunters and gatherers. These groups are not a classification into which each and every African culture can neatly be slotted. Rather, they should be seen as prominent landmarks in a very complicated indigenous cultural landscape.

◄◙ In many East African societies, men of the same age belong to named groups called "age-sets". Here, Samburu men celebrate the ritual marking the promotion of their age-set to adulthood.

◙ Only Benin royals were permitted bronze heads. Terracotta heads such as this were made by the bronze casters for their own altars.

INDIGENOUS CULTURE AREAS OF AFRICA

The southern and western extent of pastoralism is limited by the presence in the forest and savanna woodlands of bloodsucking flies of the *Glossina* genus (commonly known as the tsetse fly), which transmit the fatal disease *trypanosomiasis* to cattle and horses. The disease also affects people, when it is known as "sleeping sickness". Although cattle cannot survive permanently in the forest zone, agriculture spreads beyond the forest into pastoral areas.

The Sahara is the great boundary between the Mediterranean world and tropical Africa, but to those people who have made it their home, it is a trade route. Almost all the gold circulating in Europe before the sixteenth century came from Africa, south of the Sahara. It was in order to find the source of this "golden trade of the Moors" that the Portuguese set out in their ships in the fifteenth century to explore Africa's west coast.

CARTOGRAPHY: RAY SIM

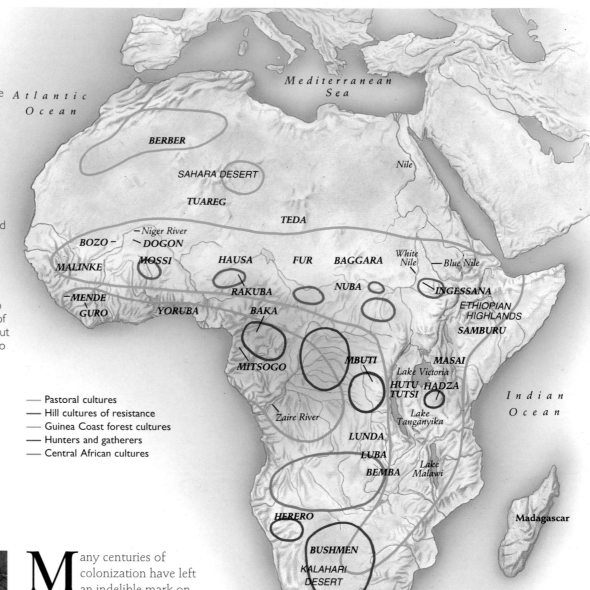

Pastoral cultures
Hill cultures of resistance
Guinea Coast forest cultures
Hunters and gatherers
Central African cultures

⚓ This eighteenth-century French engraving shows West African captives being taken aboard slave ships, to be transported across the Atlantic and sold to the owners of sugar plantations in the West Indies. The sugar was then exported to Europe.

M any centuries of colonization have left an indelible mark on large parts of modern-day Africa. (See the feature *Madagascar: Island of Mystery*.) The region north of the Sahara Desert has been virtual extension of Arabia for several hundred years. Today, the ancient indigenous peoples of North Africa and the Sahara are represented by the people who speak Berber and related languages such as Timasheq (Tuareg). Although Berber speakers have been Muslims for several hundred years, scarcely differing in their ways of life from the Arabic-speaking peasantry around them, their fragmented distribution in North Africa reflects their status as a people who have been displaced from the fertile lowlands to the highlands and the deserts. Now confined to the less accessible regions, they are a rural people with a strong tradition of resistance to the domination of the towns and the people of the richer plains.

Cultural features of the eastern coastline down to Kilwa, in southern Tanzania, are similarly reminiscent of Arabia and even India, while several hundred years of European colonization and settlement in southern Africa have overwhelmed the original indigenous cultures in that region. On the Atlantic coast of West Africa, European intervention was superficially limited to the coast, the site of the slave stations to which, over a period of 300 years, until the end of the nineteenth century, some 12 million manacled Africans were dispatched for shipment to the West Indies and South America. Today, the port of Freetown, in Sierra Leone, with its old Creole population, seems to have more in common with Kingston, Jamaica, than it does with African towns only a few kilometers inland.

HUTCHISON LIBRARY

THE FOREST CULTURES OF THE GUINEA COAST

The most conspicuous and persistent cultural feature of the peoples of the Guinea Coast forest is their preference for living in villages, large towns, or even cities, rather than in individual dwellings dispersed through the landscape. On the Guinea Coast, a village or town is not so much a concentration of dwellings or a settlement pattern as the outcome of the way the people have come to understand and appropriate space. This is reflected in their language. Whereas in English, the words "town" and "village" denote a collection of dwellings, in the local vernacular of the Guinea Coast, the equivalent word has the sense of "container", referring to the space carved out of the forest that contains the houses, rather than the houses themselves.

From the end of the rainy season in October until the beginning of the next rains in May, household members set out from the village each day to work on their farms in the forest. It is a time of plenty. Almost all food is cooked at the farmhouses, and craft work, such as woodworking, basketry, and rope making, is also done there. In the evening, they return to the village to eat in the chief's house or on a neighbor's verandah, shouting greetings to all who pass and inviting them to come and share the food. During the rains, they are confined to their cold, wet settlements, where they huddle around smoky fires to keep warm. Only occasionally do the men make trips into the forest to set traps, tap palm wine, cut firewood, and collect leaves and roots for medicinal and magical purposes. Sickness and fevers take hold among the old and weak. It is a season of deaths and burials.

◉ In the forest around some of the old towns of the Guinea Coast, there are more recently founded satellite villages that are subordinate to the original settlement. In the nineteenth century, towns were fortified, and the people in the villages took refuge in them.

Turning Bush to Town

While the forest is regarded as a vastly rich and diverse life-sustaining resource, it is also recognized as a dangerous place, where serious injuries and fatal accidents can happen. The settlement, in contrast, offers security and social order. Among Yoruba-speaking peoples, who are the dominant culture of southeastern Nigeria, a successful *oba*—a town chief or ruler—is described in honorific poems as one who: "Turns forest to settlement, turns bush to town/*Oba* who turns a rubbish heap into a market."

In Sierra Leone, a town's founding ancestor (from whom the present town chief traces his descent) is commonly recalled as a great hunter, and the site of the town as the place where he killed an elephant—the people who gathered to butcher and eat the animal (a procedure that takes several days) having decided to stay permanently. Sometimes, hunter and hunted are identified, and it is said that a town's founding ancestor was himself an elephant, who on his death returned to his elephant form. Most forest paths in this area are, in fact, elephant tracks, and so people feel that they are following, literally, in the paths of their ancestors.

Guinea Coast houses are sometimes of quite impressive proportions, with thatched, steeply pitched roofs and finely plastered walls, which are often whitewashed and decorated with paintings. But for all the reassurance offered by their creative ability to "turn bush to town", the people of this region remain deeply aware that, in the end, they are utterly dependent on the continuing fertility of the surrounding forest.

⚲ The sixteenth-century Portuguese explorer Valentim Fernandez wrote about the strength and size of Guinea Coast houses, qualities that persist to the present day.

CHARLES LENARS/EXPLORER/AUSCAPE

⚲ Independence Day is always a nationwide celebration in African countries. But independence from colonial rule did not mean that the indigenous states once again became sovereign. Rather, the colonial state was taken over by Africans. Here, in Nigeria, the Oba of Oshogbo and the State Governor walk together.

JAMES H. MORRIS

Setting Boundaries

The relationship between town and forest is, therefore, something to which people devote a great deal of attention. This relationship has a number of aspects, not the least of which is the townspeople's land rights to the forest. The borderline between town and forest is sometimes marked by a specially constructed boundary, and there are rules and prohibitions governing these different spaces. Many of these flow from the "magical medicines" the town chief buys, often from very distant sources, to promote the well-being of the forest and the vital relationship between it and the settlement—certain acts being held to render these medicines ineffective. For example, there is a rule restricting sexual intercourse to the settlement. Intercourse in the forest considered to be immoral: it is said to spoil the forest, endangering its fertility and offending the spirits who dwell there. Other prohibitions may be specific to a particular town (and have to be learned by newcomers), and the rules also change over time.

Where Two Worlds Meet

People's experience of the relationship between forest and settlement lies at the very heart of Guinea Coast cosmology and religion. At a deeper level, this relationship functions as a metaphor for the more abstract relationship between the visible world of mortal and frail humans and the invisible world of powerful spirit beings. A great many Guinea Coast rituals and ceremonies have the practical aim of manipulating this relationship for humans' benefit. Ceremonies are therefore held either on the boundary between settlement and forest (symbolic of the boundary between the human and spirit worlds) or in the forest itself (where the two worlds meet). The grotesque masquerades, elaborate costumes, and ritual paraphernalia of local secret societies and other cults all draw upon elements of both settlement and forest, giving rise to deliberately strange and confused images aimed at bringing these two worlds together even while they try to keep them apart. Some of these images, the people say, are beautiful and attractive; others are ugly and frightening. It is the attempt to reconcile these opposing forces that results in the magnificent ceremonial spectacles that are such a defining feature of Guinea Coast culture.

⊖ The ambiguities of the mask—its embodiment of the visible and the invisible, the nonhuman mask and the masked human—are brilliantly exploited in Guinea Coast cultures to represent the boundaries of this world and the world of spirits, the village and the forest. The metaphorical play with boundaries includes the boundary of time. The dye mask, for example, representing a forest spirit of the Guro people of the Ivory Coast, appears in the village at dawn, the boundary between night and day.

WETTSTEIN & KAUFRIETBERG MUSEUM, ZURICH

MADAGASCAR: ISLAND OF MYSTERY

M.E.F. BLOCH

MADAGASCAR IS A LARGE ISLAND, almost twice the size of Great Britain, which lies off the east coast of southern Africa. One would have thought that the cultural and linguistic affinities of its people would be with the nearby continent of Africa, but the truth is much stranger.

The people of Madagascar, the Malagasy, now numbering approximately 10 million, speak a language that is quite closely related to some of the languages spoken in Southeast Asia, in such places as Borneo and the Philippines—countries that lie thousands of kilometers away on the other side of the Indian Ocean. There are other signs, too, of contact with that part of the world: some of the Malagasy look much like some of the people of Asia, and they also cultivate irrigated rice on terraces far more reminiscent of Java than of anywhere in Africa.

Early Asian Voyagers

Clearly, people originating from Southeast Asia must have reached Madagascar at some time in the past, and recent archaeological finds suggest that such people were there from at least the seventh century AD. But if this is so, how did they get there? The truth is that we do not know. Perhaps they sailed across the Indian Ocean in outrigger canoes similar to those the coastal Malagasy use to this day; but then it seems strange that islands such as Mauritius, which lay in their path, remained uninhabited until relatively recent times. In any case, such a journey appears almost incredible. Perhaps some early Southeast Asian groups were once settled in colonies all around the Indian Ocean in places such as Sri Lanka, southern Arabia, and the East African coast, and then disappeared from all these places, remaining only in Madagascar—but if this is so, these people have

⬤ In the south of Madagascar, men commonly guard cattle with a spear. This man is holding the (probably fake) egg of an extinct bird, most likely to sell to tourists.

left no trace. The Southeast Asian origin of the people of Madagascar remains one of the great mysteries of human history.

A Mixed Heritage

The Malagasy are not descended solely from Southeast Asian peoples, however. It is clear from their appearance and many facets of their culture that many of their forebears must have been of African origin. The population of Madagascar is clearly the product of these two different origins, although the people living in the center of the island tend to look more Asian, while those living in the western and southern areas tend to look more African. Everywhere, however, the two elements are at present fused into a varied unity.

The African element would at first seem to be less problematic, but in fact it, too, is quite mysterious. It has not been possible to

⬤ The Malagasy of the central plateau are great traders, and selling small livestock is one of their major means of obtaining cash. This woman is probably on her way to market.

link the Malagasy with any specific African people, and, strangest of all, however African some of them appear, the Malagasy speak only Malagasy, which is clearly a Southeast Asian language. For the Malagasy to be so totally integrated, it would seem that their ancestors must have shared a common history from long ago. Again, it must be said that we know little of that distant history.

Madagascar has not, however, been immune to other, better documented, outside influences. From at least the twelfth century, Arabs and other Muslims established a network of trading posts along the East African coast, and this ultimately extended to Madagascar, so that some Malagasy are Muslims to this day. In the eighteenth century, European pirates of many nationalities, including the infamous Captain Kidd, set up small, independent states on the east coast. For a long time, slave traders operated on the coast, and then, in the nineteenth century, British missionaries came to the island. After a period of uneasy contact, the latter established a close alliance with some local rulers, so that by the time the French colonized the island at the beginning of the twentieth century, many people had become Christians.

☜ The Malagasy of the south concentrate much of their artistic creativity on tombs. These posts mark the cattle sacrifices made when the tombs were completed.

☝ A fisherman from the west coast steers his outrigger canoe as the boats return home with their catch.

☜ For the Malagasy, every occasion is a good one for trading. These people have come to attend a ritual, but that does not mean that a little business cannot be done.

The Island Today

Today, Madagascar is an independent country, and its people live in very varied ways. Some are highly educated, the level of literacy in Madagascar being among the highest in the Third World. Many live much as European or Asian peasants do, relying on irrigated agriculture and livestock. Some make a living in other ways: in the south, it is common to see cattle herders guarding their herds with spears; on the west coast, there are nomadic fishermen who go to sea in tiny outrigger canoes; in the eastern forest, people who live in small houses, often perched high on stilts, survive by creating fields by burning down a patch of forest.

Perhaps the most striking man-made features in Madagascar are tombs, which in many areas are much grander and more permanent than houses. In the south, these tombs are covered with the skulls of cattle sacrificed for the dead, and often they are surmounted by sculptures in wood and concrete, which may represent mythical birds or, more surprisingly, airplanes, buses, or policemen arresting cattle thieves.

THE MATRILINEAL PEOPLES OF CENTRAL AFRICA

S outh of the equatorial forest, in the upper reaches of the tributaries of the Kasai River, the landscape changes to grassland, with scattered patches of woodland. A number of ethnic groups live here, sharing a more or less common culture. Nearly all these societies are structured as chiefdoms or kingdoms, the best known being the Lunda, Luba, and Bemba peoples, whose kings ruled over powerful, centralized domains in the seventeenth and eighteenth centuries. Even though today some of these central African "kingdoms", especially in the north, close to the equatorial forest, consist of little more than a few villages, the idea of kingship is upheld. But the overriding characteristic of the peoples of this area, and one that has persisted to the present day, is their matrilineal social organization.

⚲ In the modern state, subjects are revealed to the rulers and thereby controlled through such surveillance techniques as identity cards, official records, and censuses. In the traditional African state, by contrast, rulers compelled the allegiance of their subjects by virtue of the dazzling image of power they embodied and projected.

DANIEL LAINE/ACTUEL

A rule of succession to a chieftainship, for example, is described as matrilineal when a male chief is succeeded by one of his sisters' sons rather than by one of his wives' sons. Likewise, in matrilineal societies, an ordinary man's personal property, his weapons and tools, will be shared out after his death among his sisters' sons rather than his wife's (or wives') sons. This does not, of course, disadvantage his sons, since they look to their mother's brothers to inherit titles and personal wealth. They also inherit their father's secret, magic knowledge (pertaining to such things as protection from sorcery and curing illnesses), something a man always passes on to his own sons. Women, in these societies, inherit from their mothers.

Clans and Lineages

Society is organized into clans, which are similarly matrilineal. All clans have their own name, and also their own myths, legends, and conventions, making clan membership an important part of each person's identity. People of the same clan are considered to be descended from the same ancestor and therefore cannot marry.

Perhaps more important than clan membership in terms of day-to-day life is membership of one of the many subgroups, or lineages, of the clan. Members of such subgroups can all trace their relationship to a remembered common female ancestor, after whom the group is named. Lineages have rights over certain areas of land for the purposes of cultivation, hunting and gathering wild foods, and collecting building materials and other natural resources. Some lineages also own the title to a chieftainship, with its attendant privileges, which the members bestow on one of their number when the incumbent chief dies.

More significantly, lineages traditionally also had rights over people—and in some parts of the region, they still do. A lineage, in a sense, "owns" its members. This is of little consequence until either a member is killed by someone from another lineage, creating a "blood debt" between the two lineages, or a woman of the lineage marries. Clearly, marriage creates a significant link between two lineages, and naturally enough, lineages seek to exert control over such matters. Until the middle of the twentieth century, it was still the case that a blood debt could only be settled by the slayer's lineage transferring to the victim's lineage control over the marriage of a woman, and of any daughters she may subsequently bear. As with a title, the members of the victim's lineage would then allocate these rights to one of their own. The man chosen could "cash them in", as it were, and marry the woman, but he would more likely keep the rights for use in settling other debts, or transfer them to a lineage member who had need of such rights. It is important to appreciate that such transfers were transfers of rights among men and very seldom involved the physical movement of the women involved.

◄O Cattle are rare among the matrilineal peoples of central Africa. The fish these women will catch will make an important contribution to their family's diet. Women in this region have combined to construct dams and individual fish ponds, and engage in a kind of fish farming. Salt plants, from which salt can be extracted, are grown around the ponds. The ponds are passed down from mother to daughter.

FRANS LANTING/MINDEN PICTURES

Men in a Matrilineal Society

Although membership of a lineage, and the property rights that go with it, descend through the mother's line, it is the males of the lineage who administer these rights and generally look after the group's interests. Despite the importance of lineages, however, the everyday tasks of farming life and raising children are carried out in family groups headed by a husband and wife. In walking though a settlement, one is much more likely to encounter family groups than lineage groups. Because lineage and family interests do not always coincide, people move about a good deal and villages are often only temporary.

Clearly, if the men of a lineage choose to live close together to better manage lineage affairs, their wives go with them. And just as their own wives had to leave their settlements to be with them, so, too, do their sisters move away, to be with their husbands. This means that their sisters' sons, who are their heirs, and their sisters' daughters, whose marriages they seek to control, are also scattered about the country. The only way of avoiding this situation would be to keep the sisters together in one place and to make their husbands come to live with them, instead of the reverse. But while this might suit the sisters' brothers, it would obviously not suit the sisters' husbands, as these men would then be dispersed around the countryside, while their own lands, and their heirs and sisters' daughters, would be coming under the influence or control of the strangers their sisters married.

Inevitably, then, people move about a good deal as men maneuver for advantage, with the ultimate goal of having their sisters and their sisters' children, as well as their own wives and children, living with them. A man who succeeds

in doing this is recognized as a powerful leader, and his followers are those men who, having married his sisters and daughters, decide to stay in his settlement. Young men of ambition will eventually seek to break away and become leaders of their own village, but others will resign themselves to being followers. To some extent, such maneuvering is assisted by the prevailing practice of shifting cultivation. After two or three years of continuous cropping, cultivated areas are allowed to revert to grassland and forest for several years, and people then move their place of residence to a site nearer the new areas under cultivation.

The Pressures for Change

Today, among urban workers and in those rural areas where farmers have commercialized their activities by investing in modern equipment, matrilineal values are being displaced by Western ideas of the family and responsibility for children. A commercial farmer or someone who has migrated to a town and has succeeded as a trader or gained professional qualifications finds himself in a dilemma. His sons are probably involved in his farm or business and contributing to its success. They are not likely to accept that on their father's death it should all become the property of some distant cousin, their father's sister's son, who may well be living far away in the countryside. Nor are they likely to accept that their inheritance from a poor farmer, their mother's brother, who has eked out a living by traditional methods, is adequate compensation. If, moreover, they have become Christians, this will have weakened their adherence to traditional matrilineal beliefs and values even further.

THE PASTORAL PEOPLES OF WESTERN AND NORTHERN AFRICA

M. RENAUDEAU/HOA QUI

🐂 Between the Guinea Coast cultures to the south and the Sahara Desert to the north are ancient centers of Islamic learning, such as the Great Mosque at Djenne, in Mali. These Fulani herdsmen are returning to their cattle camp after a day at Djenne market.

♀ The pastoralists of the great grasslands of the Upper Nile basin are a proud and independent people, who have resisted subordination by both colonial powers and their modern-day successors in Khartoum.

In the regions that extend west and south from the Ethiopian highlands, the distinguishing cultural trait is the prestige associated with cattle and, by implication, the pastoral life of the herder as opposed to the agricultural life of the farmer. This prestige is evident in many ways. Everywhere in this region, cattle are the most important components of the gifts given and received as part of the complex formalities of establishing a marriage. Although many small gifts are exchanged between the bride's and groom's families, they are overshadowed by the gift of cattle from the groom to the bride's family—who, of course, are giving him his wife. (Elsewhere in Africa, gifts exchanged in the course of a marriage can vary enormously from one society to another, ranging from bales of fine cloth, brass artifacts, iron implements, and ornamental spears to cowrie shells or free labor.) In communities that observe class distinctions—between nobles or aristocrats and commoners, the rulers and the ruled—cattle are invariably associated with the superior class. And in those areas where indigenous religious beliefs are still paramount, cattle are the supreme sacrificial offering to ancestors and the gods.

Nomadic Herders: The Bororro

Although the prestige of owning cattle is a unifying factor throughout this huge area, there are other, equally prominent, characteristics that distinguish the western region from the eastern and southern regions of Africa. In general, the western region south of the Sahara Desert and north of the forest zone is inhabited by nomadic pastoralists. Most notable among these are the pastoral Fulani, also known as the Bororro, who are found from Senegal, in the west, to the borders of Ethiopia, in the east. Other significant nomadic groups include the Arabic-speaking Baggara, in the Sudan, and those peoples of northern Kenya and Ethiopia who speak Nilotic and Oromo. To the north, in the Sahara, where the environment is too harsh for cattle, nomadic pastoralists such as the Tuareg, the Teda, and the Zaghawa herd camels and goats. In eastern and southern Africa, pastoral peoples live in permanent settlements, migrating seasonally from the valleys to the upland pastures.

The Bororro are true nomads, moving their camps every two or three days. Since they must travel light, their camps are largely constructed from natural materials that lie to hand. When the herd is out grazing, it is possible to pass within a few meters of a Bororro homestead without realizing that it is there. In general, the Bororro move north as the rainy season extends north from the forest zone to the desert fringe, and south as the rains retreat southwards.

ROBERT CAPUTO/AURORA

PETER CARMICHAEL/ASPECT PICTURE LIBRARY

Prestige and Interdependence

The Bororro feel themselves to be immensely superior to the sedentary peasants they pass by with their herds—peoples such as the Malinke, the Bambara, the Mossi, the Hausa, and the Fur—considering them to be little better than slaves. But while they move among these settled societies feeling aloof from them, they are in fact quite dependent on them. Bororro women, for example, often work as dairy maids, preparing milk and butter for sale in the markets, and with the proceeds buy cereals, tea, sugar, salt, tobacco, condiments, spices, gourds, cooking pots, dishes, and the like, as well as cloth from Hausa weavers, and weapons, such as swords and spears, from blacksmiths. As the herds move south after the rains, they travel though the peasants' newly harvested fields, eating well off the millet and sorghum stalks. In turn, the fields benefit from the cattle manure. A successful peasant cultivator will use his profits to buy cattle, which he may arrange for a Bororro to herd on his behalf. So, while the Bororro seem to be a separate society, their way of life is in many ways closely tied to that of other ethnic groups in the region.

The fact that different ethnic groups specialize in particular economic activities, to which varying degrees of prestige are attached—the Bororro herding; the Bambara farming; the Bozo fishing in the Niger River; the Tukolor and the Hausa weaving; the Dyula trading; while still others specialize in such crafts as leatherworking, pottery, and blacksmithing, or in singing, composing, and playing music—combined with the fact that some of these specialist groups do not allow intermarriage, has led some observers to conclude that a caste system operates in this part of Africa.

Although the Bororro enjoy considerable prestige as cattle herders, they do not hold positions of authority within the wider society. Nomadic pastoral societies are above all egalitarian and anarchic, and no individual recognizes another as superior. Other Fulani, however, do occupy positions of authority, as the rulers of traditional Islamic states such as Kano and Sokoto, whose capitals were once great centers of Islamic learning as well as of a long-distance trading network extending south to the forest and north to the Mediterranean coast. Although the authority of these traditional rulers is now overshadowed by that of the modern states of Nigeria and Niger, they still command respect for their knowledge of Islamic law relating to the family and inheritance.

⚱ During the rainy season, Bororro households are less dispersed than in the dry season. The grazing is good and milk yields are high, so it is a time for feasts and social events.

JAMES H. MORRIS

⚱ Hausa cloth has been an article of trade in West Africa for hundreds of years. Special patterns have properties that are supposed to protect the wearer from witchcraft.

133

Saharan Peoples of the North

To the north are found Saharan peoples such as the Teda and the Tuareg. The latter are usually described as Berber-speaking nomadic herders, but this is no longer accurate. The Tuareg are found extensively throughout southern Algeria, Niger, and Mali, and occasionally in Burkina Faso. The values of Tuareg culture are essentially aristocratic, society being divided into landowning nobles and various landless vassals (including the Iklan and the Harratin). Traditionally, the nobles pursued the aristocratic life of the mounted warrior while living off the surplus production of their vassals. This corresponded roughly with the division of labor in the oases between nomadic pastoralists and sedentary farmers, except that the Tuareg nobles' monopoly over camels—as opposed to the nomads' control over cattle—was more significant politically and militarily than economically.

The twentieth-century impact of the nation-state, with its particular economic and political demands, and of modern communications and transport, has tended to marginalize the camel-owning nomadic pastoralists and to favor sedentary agriculture instead. The new state bureaucracies are staffed by the sons and daughters of former slaves and vassals who have attended schools and colleges. At the same time, economic and environmental changes have helped to undermine the Tuareg pastoralists, and some have had to resort to subsistence agriculture. These upheavals have recently been expressed in outbreaks of violence by sections of the Tuareg against what they see as the agents of their cultural destruction.

In semi-arid zones of the Sahara and northern Kenya, camels are not only important as beasts of burden for pastoralists with herds of cattle, but are also herded by some peoples, such as the Muslim Kababish in northern Sudan and the pagan Rendille of Kenya, for their wool, milk, hides, and meat.

For the Bororro, cattle are also beasts of burden. Here, a Bororro family loads one of their animals with their household equipment as they prepare to move with their herds to fresh grazing lands.

FRANS LANTING/MINDEN PICTURES

♙ The cattle herd returns to a Masai homestead in the evening, after a day's grazing. There are several separate herds, belonging to several brothers, but they are herded together as one unit, as it was before the men's father died.

THE PASTORAL PEOPLES OF EASTERN AFRICA

In the cultures found in the eastern region of Africa, extending from the Ethiopian highlands to South Africa and Botswana, social stratification is strongly in evidence everywhere. People are divided into rulers and ruled, aristocrats and commoners—a division that reflects a sometimes real and sometimes mythical distinction between a conquering tribe and a conquered original population. Even kinsmen are ranked as senior and junior, elder brother and younger brother, and men have a higher status than women. Cattle are always associated with rulers and aristocrats, and with men. In general, a man and his sons herd the household's cattle, while his wife and unmarried daughters cultivate food crops. But there are also poor men limited to subsistence cultivation, and rich women living in towns who employ a man to herd their animals.

Aristocrats and Farmers

In Ruanda, the stratification of society into cattle-owning aristocrats and a commonality of farmers is particularly elaborate. About a fifth of the population is made up of Tutsi cattle owners, while the rest are mainly Hutu cultivators. In practice, however, the Hutu herd most of the cattle, even though the cattle are owned by Tutsi. This is the result of a more or less feudal system in which, typically, a Hutu farmer pledges his allegiance to a Tutsi in return for protection and support. As a mark of his subordinate status, the Hutu will be given a cow or several cows, which he will herd as if they were his own until the particular relationship is brought to an end. This institution, which is called *buhake* in Ruanda and in which almost everyone is involved, seems to be inherently ambiguous: does it ameliorate or amplify inequalities between the parties? Historically, the system can be traced to periods of instability, when there were violent outbreaks of repression by the Tutsi and resistance from the Hutu.

A Network of Relationships

Division of labor, with men herding and women farming, is observed more in principle than in practice. In fact, agriculture is the main means of subsistence, requiring the efforts of both men and women, while cattle are a means of storing wealth or forging political alliances through marriage. Throughout this area, a marriage contract always entails a gift of cattle from the groom to his bride's family, the number varying in different societies. The cattle are then distributed to members of the bride's family on the basis of strict conventions. In societies where a very large number of cattle are given, debts are incurred that will persist into the next generation. Such debts are highly valued, since they form the real basis of the relationship between different families, who can turn to each other for support in times of crisis. When he surveys his cattle, the owner can see before him the network of relationships and alliances that defines his involvement in his community. A man without cattle is not just materially poor but literally outside society.

The Threats to Tradition

Although these practices are still current in some areas, migration to the towns, money wages, and the extension of the cash economy have brought about considerable changes. Basically, cash has replaced cattle as the most common form of bride payment. Even more important, young men who would once have worked for their seniors, from whom they would have expected assistance in the form of loans of cattle (which, in turn, would have placed them under obligation to the older men), have repudiated this custom, preferring to work for money wages in the industrial sector or the mines of South Africa.

The consequences of the cattle raids that were a feature of low-intensity warfare in this region are also different in modern times, when raiders are more likely to be armed with automatic rifles than with spears, and intent on selling their booty rather than herding it. So, too, with drought. People who have prospered in the new industrial and commercial economies of the towns are buying up the cattle of destitute traditional pastoralists, and the men they employ as casual labor to herd their animals may once have owned their own herds. In southern Africa, grazing lands are being enclosed and turned into highly capitalized ranches. The pattern of animal husbandry is also changing. Herdsmen are now tending to keep their herds within the vicinity of the expanding townships, to supply them with milk and dairy products, rather than following the traditional routes of seasonal migration, and this has been detrimental to the environment.

Despite Africa's increasing integration into a commercial, global economy, and the dislocations of warfare, which have brought about irrevocable

TOM ANG/NHPA

social changes, some traditional religious beliefs and institutions have been revitalized in recent times. In southern Africa, for example, spirit mediums have once again risen to prominence: individuals through whom the ancestral spirits of the great chiefs, called "lions", speak to the people during times of crisis (such as the wars of independence in Zimbabwe). Some of the most powerful mediums, in terms of the area and the number of people under the influence of a particular spirit, are women, the spirit being linked to the fertility of the land. Traditionally, these mediums wielded such enormous influence that the colonial regimes felt compelled to arrest and imprison them.

🐂 Pastoralists of northern Kenya move their herds between the uplands, where they stay during the dry season, and the grazing areas on the plains—which they regard as their "homelands"— during the wet season.

PETER CARMICHAEL/ASPECT PICTURE LIBRARY

🐂 Among the pastoralists of eastern Africa, women own and cultivate most of the gardens and farms. The cattle a wife is allocated to support herself and her children is the nucleus of the herd her sons will inherit when their father dies.

CULTURES OF RESISTANCE

The hills and broken uplands that extend irregularly from south of the great bend in the Niger River to the hills between the Blue and White Niles, in the Sudan, are home to a number of diverse ethnic groups. These peoples have little in common, beyond that they have all sought refuge in these hills and uplands from the powerful nations and states of the forest region to the south, and from the Islamic states in the surrounding lowlands and to the north.

In the nineteenth century, these small-scale, independent societies, lacking the protection of a powerful overlord, were looked upon by their neighbors as reservoirs of potential slaves, to be raided with impunity. While slavery—at least in terms of selling slaves in open markets—has disappeared, they still suffer discrimination and harassment from outsiders. The Sudanese government in Khartoum, for instance, has applied the severest pressure to the people of the Nuba Hills to abandon their culture and adopt the impoverished way of life of Islamic Sudanese peasants, often on pain of death.

Not surprisingly, the hill peoples are often shy but truculent, and suspicious of strangers. Because of their cultural and social diversity, few generalizations can be made about them. The different ethnic groups tend to be small, numbering only a few thousand, and they each have their own language. Population densities, on the other hand, are often very high, perhaps twice that of populations in the surrounding plains and the southern forests. These high densities are supported by elaborate and skillful agricultural and pastoral techniques, encompassing a wide variety of crops and domesticated animals, including pigs. On the hillsides, terracing and other erosion and water control techniques sustain high yields. Today, however, many of these intensive upland agricultural practices are being abandoned, as people move down to the foothills at the edge of the plains to cultivate the grasslands.

Systems of Chieftainship

All these groups have a system of chieftainship, although the underlying ideology is often quite different. The Rakuba people of central Nigeria, for example, seem to consider their chiefs to be vehicles for maintaining the symbolic integrity and purity of their land by acting as a kind of scapegoat. The chief must observe restrictions on his personal conduct, what he eats, his conjugal relations. The chief's health is associated with the health of the land and the people, and epidemics and crop failures are linked to his health and conduct. In the Ingessana Hills, in the Sudan, chiefs are considered to be the descendants of strangers and therefore able to intervene impartially in disputes. What is common to all these societies, however, is that they have numerous chiefs, whose authority is limited to a particular small locality. In none of them is there a sovereign chief uniting the whole society as a political entity.

The Dogon of Mali

While a few of these hill peoples have been assimilated into the way of life of their more powerful Muslim neighbors, most have not only stubbornly preserved their own beliefs and practices but have also deliberately cultivated and elaborated unique social and religious institutions—and, sometimes, esoteric knowledge systems of startling complexity. The Dogon of Mali, in West Africa, have achieved international fame. Dogon systems of knowledge have been studied over decades by French anthropologists, and much has been made of the discovery that Dogon mythology includes the idea that the heavenly body we know as Sirius comprises two stars, when it was not until well into the twentieth century that Western astronomers, with the aid of powerful telescopes, discovered

🔥 The figure on the wall of this Dogon shrine represents the microcosm and the macrocosm, a theme that is symbollically repeated in Dogon architecture, agriculture, textiles, and artifacts.

♀ This view of a Dogon village shows dwelling houses, granaries with removable thatched roofs (or lids), and, on the left, the *toguna*, or men's meeting house, a sturdy structure with carved roof posts.

BRYAN AND CHERRY ALEXANDER

⚡ Potting and other crafts, including ironworking, weaving, leather tanning, wood carving, basketry, and beadwork, are all well developed among the hill peoples.

ROBERT CAPUTO/AURORA

⬅ The settlements of some hill peoples are tightly clustered together on outcrops of bare rock. These sites were chosen not only because they were defensible, but also to conserve areas of land that can be cultivated.

that Sirius is orbited periodically by a dwarf star. Dogon institutions also include ritual cycles that extend over a period of 60 years, suggesting a conscious commitment to the past and the future of Dogon culture.

Elaboration as Defense

Among the Rakuba, marriage rules prescribing who may and may not marry on the basis of kinship and marriage relationships have become extremely elaborate over the years and are now institutionalized. Among some other groups, marriages can take place only when two men agree to exchange sisters. In general, marriage agreements among the hill people involve a long period of service by the would-be groom,

working in the fields of his future wife's father and kinsmen and tending their herds.

In the past, customs like these were thought to be indicative of the backward or uncivilized state of such peoples. The current view is that these peoples have deliberately developed their elaborate institutions and beliefs in defiance of, and as a form of protection against, the cultures of the dominant groups around them. Sister-exchange marriage, for example, tends to promote marriage within the group: one of the most effective ways in which a powerful group can incorporate a weak neighbor is by accepting the neighboring women as wives while refusing to allow its own women to marry outside the group.

THE BUSHMEN: A TALE OF SURVIVAL

Wilhelm Östberg

THE MANY DIFFERENT PEOPLES outsiders refer to as "Bushmen" do not have a name for themselves. In Botswana, they are called Basarwa, but this is a Bantu word, and not accepted by Bushmen generally. Government authorities classify them, together with other underprivileged groups, as "RADs", meaning Remote Area Dwellers, a term the Bushmen similarly reject. In the scientific literature, they are commonly called the San, the Khoekhoe people's name for them. Since the Khoekhoe often use the term in a derogatory sense, the well-known name "Bushmen", coined by the early European settlers, is retained here.

The Bushmen are probably the best-documented contemporary group of hunter-gatherers in the world. They have been extensively studied by anthropologists, and have also attracted much popular comment. This has led to the paradox that, while many aspects of their economy, society, and culture are well known, the Bushmen are, at the same time, subject to widely conflicting stereotypes.

Through the years, the Bushmen's image has changed drastically among outsiders. They have been looked upon as a precious prototype for prehistoric humans, but also as vermin to be eradicated. They have been seen both as pitiful destitutes and as enviable adepts in the art of living, enjoying the original affluent society. More recently, they have been characterized as trackers of superhuman dimensions, when they were conscripted by the South African Forces to assist in their operations in Southwest Africa in the 1980s; while currently, they are seen first and foremost as a deprived indigenous people.

More than 80,000 people speak one of the Bushman languages. Of these, only a few thousand today manage to live as hunter-gatherers, surviving in bands of 20 to 30 members. The rest work as herders on commercial ranches or as laborers in work camps or the mines, or eke out an existence performing menial tasks in small administrative and trading centers. They are one of the most underprivileged and despised groups in the area.

Original Inhabitants

The Bushmen are the region's oldest inhabitants, their ancestors once extending over nearly all of southern Africa and parts of East Africa. Today, they survive as an independent culture only in the Kalahari, the vast plain of grass and sand that covers large parts of Botswana and Namibia. The extermination of Bushman society is a particularly horrifying aspect of the legacy of oppression and violence in South Africa.

The Bushmen fought the Bantu who began to spread into the region in the first centuries AD, but they also helped them to become established in the area. At different times and in different places over the years, they variously traded and intermarried with them, kept themselves aloof, or became dependants in a widespread patron–client system. But once Europeans brought firearms into the interior of the region, the Bushmen could not resist for long. Both black and white settlers took over large parts of their lands.

Women have a say in decisions as to where to move, and plan their own activities. But once settled in a village, they become more dependent on men.

Food gathered within an hour includes tsama melons, grewia berries, and a tortoise. Women use their mantle, the *kaross*, both to carry food in and as a cover.

Hunting in the Kalahari may involve great distances, and a bicycle comes in very handy. Hunting equipment is light, weighing just a few kilograms. But it has served the Bushmen well for thousands of years.

The Kalahari Today

Today, the Bushmen share the Kalahari with some 20 other ethnic groups. Seasonally, when the dry lands suddenly flourish, people from all communities will leave their settlement to collect mongongo nuts, roots, berries, green leaves, and tsama melons—an important source of fluid also in demand by ranchers as cattle feed.

Just as others help themselves to the resources the Bushmen have traditionally relied on, today's Bushmen take what they can from the modern society that has marginalized them. They queue for famine relief and odd jobs, and sell handicrafts to tourists. Some have become healers of renown in the new centers established in the Kalahari, while others have turned to farming and keeping livestock. In Eastern Namibia, some Bushmen have resettled their old lands after having spent long, miserable years in settlements run by the South African army. Bushmen today are trying out new ways of life in the Kalahari.

Major economic interests have invaded the Kalahari. Mining companies are closing whole areas off from other uses and pumping up huge quantities of precious ground water for use in industrial processes. Vast ranches similarly pump up ground water to support a profitable livestock industry. Tourism is making inroads into the few good hunting areas that remain.

ANTHONY BANNISTER/ABPL

Surviving in the Kalahari

In many parts of the Kalahari, there is no surface water for about 10 months of the year. Some years are even drier. It seems a miracle that people can survive here at all. During the dry season, one strategy is to stay close to permanent waterholes and to hunt the game that comes there to drink. But as more people arrive, food resources, such as tubers, run out, and people must go further afield.

All are faced with the problem of water shortage, but there are solutions.

For example, tubers are dug out, peeled, and grated, and the liquid squeezed out of the moist pulp. Water is sometimes found in hollow trees. Liquid can also be obtained from a kill, a large antelope containing some 100 liters (22 gallons). The Bushmen are even able to extract liquid from moist layers of sand—in the few areas where ground water lies close below the surface. They join hollow reeds together, sink them about 1.5 meters (5 feet) into the sand at selected spots, and, with tremendous effort, suck up the concentrated moisture.

◄● Most food is hidden under the sand. A digging stick is light to carry and ideal for loosening the ground, while the left hand is used to shovel sand aside. And up come tubers, larvae, eggs, rodents, termites …

Underground Food

Most of the food in the Kalahari is found beneath the sand. In the dry season, it requires an experienced eye to spot a dried-up creeper, signaling the presence of a tuber below. While meat is the favorite food, between 60 and 80 percent of what Bushmen foragers eat is collected: tubers, plants, nuts, larvae, eggs, rodents, berries, fruits, honey, termites. More than 100 plant species are gathered, of which some 30 are eaten regularly and about 12 are essential to the Bushmen's survival.

Hunting in the Kalahari

Bushmen hunt with light weapons, but they are able to kill big game, such as antelopes, and even giraffes and elephants, with the help of an arrow poison extracted from the larvae of a particular species of beetle (*Diamphidia simplex*). The poison acts slowly on the central nervous system, so an animal must be followed for many hours after it has been shot before it falls dead, or is incapacitated and can be dispatched at close quarters.

About 80 different animal species are considered edible by the Bushmen, of which some 30 are regularly hunted or trapped. On ranches, it has become common for Bushmen to hunt on horseback, using a spear or rifle. They also appropriate prey from lions and other animals by making a noise and scaring them away.

Life in the Kalahari is harsh. But when a good season comes around, you work two or three days a week at most, and the family has plenty to eat and drink. There is time to do odd jobs at the camp and to play with the children; time to visit, rest, and talk, and to play the music-bow or the thumb-piano. When you ask a Bushman to describe the Kalahari to you, he or she will lingeringly recall this short period of abundance. That is when the Kalahari is "the place where we have always lived, the place we know".

LIS STEINCKE

PETER JOHNSON/NHPA

◄● A cloak made from an old famine relief bag, worn in the same way as a traditional skin mantle, covers Western-style clothes.

🖐 Once an additional source of liquid, many sip-wells have now dried up, as mining companies and farms pump up the ground water.

HUNTING-GATHERING SOCIETIES

Africa's hunter-gatherers have attracted a good deal of attention, much of it controversial. The major groups are widely dispersed. Pygmy groups such as the Mbuti are found in the forests around the Ituri River in eastern Zaire, while the Baka Pygmies live in the forests of southeastern Cameroon. Around Lake Eyasi, in Tanzania, are the Hadza, and in the Kalahari region of Botswana are the Bushmen, sometimes called the San. (See the features *The Bushmen: A Tale of Survival* and *The Pygmies of Central Africa*.)

Some Surprising Facts

Systematic anthropological and archaeological research began in these areas in the 1960s. From this and subsequent research, three key facts have emerged, which many people have found surprising. The first is that hunter-gatherers typically enjoy a food supply that is at once reliable and highly nutritious, even in years of poor rainfall, when neighboring agricultural peoples are suffering food shortages.

Secondly, so-called hunter-gatherers in fact acquire more than 80 percent of their food by gathering, their diet consisting predominantly of fruits and vegetable matter, drawn from a wide variety of species. Over the years, hunting has appeared to outsiders to be more important than it is simply because it is a predominantly male activity and, therefore, something the men like to talk about. Early travelers and investigators tended to spend most of their time talking to men, and they therefore reported men's interests in their writings. In reality, the men are not very effective hunters. Among the Hadza, for example, half fail to kill one large animal in any year. Only a few men are sufficiently accomplished hunters to be regularly successful.

Thirdly, hunter-gatherers do not have to work hard to survive—and this, it seems, is at least partly why they pursue this way of life. It has been estimated that, on average, an adult works about 15 hours a week, which is the equivalent of two and half days. This simple but secure and relatively effortless way of life probably accounts for their confidence, prodigality, and apparent fecklessness—characteristics that settled peasants living less securely, and middle-class townspeople, tend to find very annoying.

A Baka hunter of the Cameroon forest takes aim at his prey, a chimpanzee, with a deadly accurate crossbow. The Baka eat some of the game they hunt, but much of it is exchanged in the villages for other goods.

GUY PHILIPPART DE FOY/EXPLORER/AUSCAPE

Meat is a scarce but prized commodity for hunting and gathering peoples. A successful hunter attracts people, but as his camp grows in numbers, so his share of his kills dwindles. Eventually, he and his family will move on.

ANTHONY BANNISTER/ABPL

An Open Society

The daily routine of hunter-gatherers is simple. Women and children set out from the camps in groups, gathering and eating nuts and fruit as they walk through the countryside. Two or three women may separate from the group to dig up roots and tubers, while others will collect wild seeds, which are brought back to the camp and cooked. Some of the men may go out alone to hunt for game, feeding themselves en route. Those who stay in the camp will cadge some food from the women when they return. Men also scavenge animal kills, and some, such as the Hadza and Bushmen, will even chase lions away from a kill.

⚥ A girl's first menstruation is greeted by Mbuti pygmies as a blessing. It is the occasion of one of the happiest of celebrations, the *elima*.

Hunter-gatherer societies tend to be open, individuals leaving and joining camps easily and frequently. Although they are generous in sharing all that they have, it does not follow that they are particularly humane: the old and senile are usually abandoned. And just as everyone has direct access to food without incurring any obligations, so, too, people are free to exact revenge for any wrong they may have suffered at another's hand, without fear that others will interfere.

Antiquity without History?

Focused as it was on groups that were living wholly by hunting and gathering at the time, the 1960s research added weight to a long-standing view that such people were "uncontaminated" remnants of a much earlier stage of human evolution, untouched by thousands of years of human history. Yet compelling contrary evidence, both contemporary and historical, was always at hand.

Perhaps most obviously, hunter-gatherers are not ignorant of agriculture and domestic animals. Some Hadza, for example, are themselves peasant farmers and intermarry with non-Hadza farmers. About a fifth of the Bushmen herd cattle for Herero and Tswana pastoralists. Some own their own cattle, and in years of good rainfall, they plant and cultivate cereals. Nineteenth-century travelers in southern Africa often reported seeing Bushmen with herds of cattle, sheep, and goats. But because the "Bushmen" had already been classified as primitive "savages", it was concluded that they must have stolen the animals.

Similarly, the Pygmies in the Ituri forest do not live their lives independently of the farmers who have established villages in forest clearings. Mbuti hunters, for example, use a netting technique they learned from the villagers, and the Efe Pygmies help the villagers to harvest their crops. There is a considerable amount of trade between Pygmies and villagers, wild meat and honey commonly being exchanged for cereals. Villagers respect the Pygmies for their knowledge of herbal medicine and regularly consult Pygmy healers. Pygmy boys are initiated along with village boys in village initiation rites. Clearly, the peoples of this region have been adapting to each other, as well as to their environment, over a very long period of time.

⚥ Bushman mothers and their children feed themselves while gathering nuts, fruit, and berries to take back to those who have remained in the camp.

⚥ As much as a half of forest Pygmies' food comes from cultivated crops grown by farmers in neighboring villages. Pygmies acquire the food in exchange for work, as well as for game, honey, and other forest products. Sometimes, they will steal crops from the villagers' fields.

THE PYGMIES OF CENTRAL AFRICA

SERGE BAHUCHET

SERGE BAHUCHET

THE PYGMIES have long been considered to be the original inhabitants of the African rainforest. Here, they live in an intimate relationship with their environment, knowing by name more than 1,000 plants and 300 animals. In the accounts of early travelers, these distinctive peoples were described in a variety of ways—from noble, egalitarian forest dwarfs to fierce, unruly savages who were seen as remnants of an earlier stage of human evolution.

In fact, the term Pygmy refers to a number of different ethnic groups. These groups share two main characteristics that distinguish them from surrounding peoples: they are of small stature, and they are (or were until recently) predominantly hunter-gatherers. But there are also some marked differences between different Pygmy ethnic groups. For example, different groups speak different languages, and often use distinctive hunting techniques.

Most Pygmies are dispersed throughout different parts of the

vast, dense, and humid forest that covers the Congo basin. The Aka inhabit the southern region of the Central African Republic and the northern part of the Congo; the Baka live in southeastern Cameroon, northwestern Congo, and northeastern Gabon; and the Mbuti (including the Asua and the Efe) live in the Ituri forest of northeastern Zaire. Some small groups, including the Tikar Pygmies of central Cameroon and the Cwa of Zaire, live at the edge of the savanna, while the Twa inhabit the mountainous regions of Ruanda.

Social Organization

The Aka and the Baka, like the Mbuti, live in small groups of related families, in camps of not more than 50 members. Individual families live in their own hut, made from branches and leaves. They move camp periodically within their vast territory, the composition of the group changing continually as families come and go to visit relatives.

🐛 During a caterpillar-gathering trip in the rainy season, Aka women of the Central African Republic stop to eat a fruit of *Anonidium mannii.*

Groups are formed around a male elder, who is the father, the uncle, or the father-in-law of other members of the group. He is an esteemed personage but not a chief. People respect his opinion, but he never gives orders, as it is up to each family to decide what they should do for their own and the group's welfare. Disputes are solved by lengthy discussion, by people moving away from the camp until tempers have cooled, or by special rituals designed to relieve tension. Rarely do they escalate to physical aggression. Subtle rules govern sharing in different situations, ensuring that food, goods, and valuables are distributed throughout the camp.

Marriage among Pygmies is mainly monogamous. The groom-to-be is required to put in a lengthy period of bride service with his future wife's family, but after marriage the couple can decide where they wish to live. Men and women have a more or less equal say in decisions, and children are lavished with affection and brought up permissively.

G. PHILIPPART DE FOY/EXPLORER/AUSCAPE

◀ Baka women and children in front of a typical hut, made with branches and leaves. Each family has its own hut within the camp.

Living off the Land

The Pygmies have a detailed knowledge of the forest, and carry out most of their subsistence activities collectively. Digging up wild yams, gathering edible leaves and mushrooms, and collecting nuts are largely the tasks of women. Sometimes, particularly at the height of the wet season, when the main activity is collecting caterpillars, their husbands accompany them. During the dry season, men search for honey in the hollows of large trees, climbing them with the help of a special belt wrapped around the tree trunk. A specially shaped axe is also made for this purpose, which can be balanced over the shoulder while climbing. Some groups, including the Aka, hold special rituals at the time of the honey harvest. For the Mbuti, it is a time when the camp breaks up into family units.

All Pygmy groups use a range of hunting techniques, depending on the kind of game, seasonal conditions, and the size of the hunting group. Large mammals, including red hogs, elephants, and gorillas, are most easily tracked in the rainy season, when groups of men set out armed with iron-tipped spears. The Mbuti and Aka also hold collective game drives, when the men, women, and children of several camps join forces to beat the bush and drive small antelopes (duikers) and porcupines into large nets stretched across areas of the forest. The Efe and the Baka have a similar practice, except that the Efe prefer to kill the fleeing animals with spears or arrows rather than net them, whereas the Baka always spear their prey. These communal hunts represent an important social occasion for peoples such as this who live in small, dispersed groups for most of the year. It is during such times that major religious ceremonies are held, and future marriages are planned.

Such hunting parties also provide a steady supply of meat for the camp. Porcupines and Gambian rats—the latter weighing up to 2 kilograms (more than 4 pounds)—are hunted by groups of two or three men. Arboreal monkeys are hunted by lone archers equipped with a small bow and poisoned

An Aka woman prepares caterpillars for eating. They are first grilled to remove their spines, and then boiled.

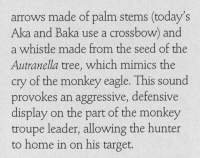
Aka pygmies extracting honeycomb. Like the Baka and the Mbuti, they make a special bark container for the honey.

This dance featuring a leaf mask is performed by the Aka to promote successful net hunting.

Several nets are necessary for an efficient hunting expedition. Only Aka (as here) and Mbuti use this technique.

Duikers are the Pygmies' major quarry, and are killed with spears or arrows.

arrows made of palm stems (today's Aka and Baka use a crossbow) and a whistle made from the seed of the *Autranella* tree, which mimics the cry of the monkey eagle. This sound provokes an aggressive, defensive display on the part of the monkey troupe leader, allowing the hunter to home in on his target.

Pygmies and Farmers

By their collective efforts, the Pygmies are able to gather a surplus of forest produce, which they can then exchange with neighboring farmers for such things as iron tools, pottery, salt, and agricultural products. Pygmy men also help farmers to clear fields during the dry season, using slash-and-burn techniques, and their wives help the farm women to harvest and process manioc and palm oil. In return, the farmers allow the Pygmies to harvest bananas, manioc, and, in the case of the Efe, wetland rice, for their own use. These carbohydrate-rich foods make a valuable contribution to the Pygmy diet, such foods being only seasonally available in the rainforest.

Throughout the Congo basin, Pygmies are also considered to have supernatural powers and are consulted as diviners and healers. They play a central role in a number of farmers' rituals, including initiation and circumcision ceremonies and funerals.

Music and Religion

Pygmies are well known for their polyphonic singing, which forms an integral part of their ceremonies. Everyone present at a gathering takes part in this. Some ceremonies are associated with hunting, especially the elephant hunt, but the most important ceremonies are linked to events affecting the group's survival, such as the end of a period of mourning or the establishment of a new camp site. Even though there are substantial differences between the religious beliefs of different groups, common strands run through most Pygmy religions. Of paramount importance is the belief in a Supreme Being, the Master of the Forest, who is invited to take part in large community gatherings under the guise of a mask or a sound, thereby bestowing good fortune on the humans present.

NORTHERN PEOPLES

Changing Times, Enduring Cultures

BRUCE GRANT AND SUSAN ROWLEY

SIBERIA HAS LONG BEEN CAST as a land of cold expanse and hardship. Stretching from the Urals to the Pacific, Siberia covers more than 8 percent of the world's land mass, much of it frozen tundra and dense forest. Few people realize, however, that for centuries Siberia has been home to more than a million and a half aboriginal peoples—a widely varied population of hunters, herders, fisherfolk, and farmers. Their history is traditionally told as a chronicle of physical survival in the face of tough natural odds. Yet their real struggle has been not with the environment, to which their cultures have long been well adapted, but with the changing aspirations of the Russian state that has ruled them for close to three centuries.

At this level, their story is part of the turbulent and often brutal history of colonization. But at another level, their fate speaks of the double-edged dilemma of Siberia itself, a land envisioned throughout Russian history as both a utopian frontier of new opportunity and a dark zone of suffering and oblivion. As a result, Siberian native peoples have been governed as savages both noble and crude. During the Soviet period, they were portrayed as children of nature, yet ironically, because of their perceived isolation and hence innocence from tsarist influence, they were also known as "the truest proletarians".

◀◎ An elderly Nenets woman of the Yamal Peninsula, in northwestern Siberia, feeds bread to draft reindeer during the migratory season.

◉ This wooden mask portraying a bird with outstretched wings was made for use in a sacred ceremony by the Inuit of southwestern Alaska. The distorted human face may represent the *inua* (spirit) of the bird or an evil being.
SHELDON JACKSON MUSEUM/WERNER FORMAN ARCHIVE

—— Tree line

NORTHERN PEOPLES

The cultures of circumpolar peoples make for a mosaic of political and economic formations across the north. Throughout Siberia, indigenous peoples were rigidly incorporated into the proletarian Soviet community from the 1920s onwards, while the northern peoples of Scandinavia, Greenland, Iceland, Canada, and Alaska have created different niches for themselves within capitalist market systems. In the post-Cold War setting, northern peoples across the globe are actively comparing strategies for protecting their rights in a new global environment.

CARTOGRAPHY: RAY SIM

The earliest records of contact between Russian and Siberian native peoples date back to the eleventh century, when explorers from the medieval Russian city of Novgorod first ventured across the Ural Mountains. It was there, "in the midnight lands", that they heard stories of "impure people of Japheths's tribe who ate all sorts of filth … and also ate their dead instead of burying them". It was not until the period of broader colonial expansion that took place in Europe in the seventeenth century, however, that Moscow began to turn its eye to the east. Hungry for

profits from the fur trade, Russia looked to the *inozemtsy*, or "people from a different land", as a new path to wealth.

By initial accounts, the newcomers often impressed their native hosts with unknown foods and wares. In a meeting between Russians and the reindeer-herding Evenki, one Evenk "chewed some bread for a while—and liked it. He said in Evenk: 'Good.' Then he took a cracker, ate it, and said: 'Delicious.' Then he ate some sugar. 'Don't even think about killing those good men,' he said [to the other]. So they threw away their bows and began to eat."

The newcomers' goals were nonetheless economic rather than altruistic. In order to extract a regular supply of pelts, they instituted a fur tax known as *yasak*. On paper, it became the obligation of every native male aged 15 and over to provide a fixed number of sable pelts, or the rubles equivalent, once a year to the Russian state. In practice, the institution of fur tribute began what was to be almost 300 years of organized plunder and degradation, with the Russians often taking hostages in order to ensure payment. *Yasak* debts were shared collectively and could be inherited. Entire peoples thus carried the burden of payment in perpetuity, under the threat of marauding gangs and a corrupt military. Numerous battles attest to native resistance, although rare groups, such as the Chukchi, from far northeastern Siberia, fought off the Russian invaders. Still, for Siberian peoples as a whole, the toll was staggering. In the 1640s alone, almost a third of the Russian state's entire revenue came from the fur trade.

During the reign of the Russian empress Catherine the Great (1762 to 1796), utopian plans for the Siberian colony envisioned the building of "our Peru", "our Mexico", "a Russian Brazil", and even "our East India". In 1763, in an only partly conciliatory gesture, Catherine sent an emissary to Siberia to "punish those responsible for the ruin of the 'timid and helpless yasak people'", but also to find a way to raise the fur revenues still higher.

The new Russian Peru, of course, never materialized. Few merchants and settlers were persuaded to take a chance in the vast new territories, where the climate was too cold and the distances too great. But the growing official interest in Russia's eastern colony resulted in a number of new measures to bring the natives under state control. Hundreds of Russian Orthodox missionaries spread out, primarily to convert the Siberian savages, whose cultures in many cases leaned toward Islamic, Tibetan, and shamanistic faiths. Despite the absurdity of mass baptisms being conducted in Russian, a language unknown to the converted, many natives agreed to be baptised, since conversion signaled the end of their "foreignness" and hence (at least on paper) the canceling of their *yasak* obligations. By the early nineteenth century, the Russian population in Siberia had grown enormously. But it could hardly be said that the example they set was a civilizing one. The Russian emperor Peter the Great introduced the idea of hard labor as a form of punishment in Russia in the early 1700s, but it

🔥 During the winter, many Udegei people, of far eastern Siberia, turn to trapping furs to augment their income from state farms and fisheries. These hunters are wearing the famous airtight Udegei jackets, which protect them from the taiga winds.

🔥 A Nenets reindeer herding camp at sunset. During the Soviet period, the government discouraged the seminomadic way of life of many Siberian reindeer herders, because it made them too hard to monitor.

⤷ Two Asian Inuit on the Chukotkan peninsula relax in their tent. Although the tents are small, the space inside is traditionally divided according to various ritual functions of food preparation and the entertaining of guests.

♦ A child's robe of the style worn by Nanaitsy in far eastern Siberia. Much of the ornamentation characteristic of the Amur River area, where the Nanaitsy live, was borrowed from ancient Chinese designs.
A. MILOVSKY

♦ In many cultures throughout Siberia, respected older women, such as this Khakass woman of central Siberia, negotiated marriages on behalf of younger members of their community.

was not until the 1800s that this was compounded by the scourge of exile. Disappointed with the failing economic performance of the enormous eastern colony, Count Nesslerode, foreign minister to Nicholas I (1825 to 1855), formally proposed that Siberia become a dustbin for Russia's sins, a dark colony of convict labor to which which criminals and political prisoners alike could be sent to be forgotten.

While the Russian colonial administration had made every effort to colonize the natives economically and politically, there were few efforts to colonize them culturally. Between the seventeenth and early twentieth centuries, they may have graduated from foreigner status, but it was clear that they were still very much burdened by the image of savagery. Missionary efforts had won over few converts to the Russian Orthodox faith, and few native children were permitted to attend missionary or state schools. On distant Sakhalin Island, in the Russian far east, one administrator acknowledged that schooling could have a potentially "favorable influence" on the native Nivkh children, were it not for the "certain odour" that precluded their being exposed to Russian playmates. As one early Soviet reformer put it, "Such was the dilemma: either shed the 'certain odour'

or remain in darkness. The latter alternative wins by default, since the [Nivkh] native—politically, economically and morally forgotten—has had no chance to attempt the former."

This spirited defense nonetheless belied the diversity of the Siberian native population on the eve of the Russian Revolution of October 1917. The larger Buryat, Yakut, and Tatar communities had extensive trading relations with their Mongol, Chinese, and central Asian neighbors, and hardly went unnoticed in the broader political and economic spectrum. Those smaller nationalities living on Russia's Pacific borders also had extensive networks of their own. Many Chukchi knew more English than they did Russian, as a result of their trade with the Americans. On Sakhalin Island and the banks of the Amur, it was common for Nivkh men to use both Chinese and Japanese in the course of their trade dealings. For most of the northern and far eastern peoples, however, their experience of imperial colonialism ranged from intimidation to the de facto enslavement of entire groups. Yet if Siberian peoples had been "forgotten" by European civilization at the turn of the century, the establishment of a Soviet Siberia meant that they were about to be recovered in a determined way.

THE NIVKHI OF SAKHALIN ISLAND

BRUCE GRANT

THROUGHOUT THEIR CENTURIES of tenure of Siberia's far eastern Sakhalin Island and the Amur River Basin, Nivkhi have thrived as fishermen and hunters. They worked in tandem with seasonal cycles of salmon, and relocated between separate winter and summer households to optimize access to bear, sable, and seal hunting grounds.

In the Nivkh world view, almost all natural phenomena were guided by spirits, and a complex system of rituals, such as feeding the sea with tobacco and sweets at the start of a new fishing season, was intended to supplicate spiritual forces. These animistic beliefs extended even to the construction of numerals in the Nivkh language, which to this day possesses 26 different ways of counting from 1 to 10, based on the material and spiritual qualities of the objects or persons in question.

With the incorporation of Sakhalin Island into the Soviet Union in 1925, many Nivkhi embraced the Soviet provision of free medical care and primary education, and the transition to "proletarian" collective fisheries, such as "New Life" or "Hammer and Sickle", proceeded relatively smoothly. As with all Soviet peoples, however, time soon left less room to maneuver. Nivkh shamans were hounded from their communities, the use of the Nivkh language was banned, and fewer and fewer Nivkhi were ready to risk their jobs or their family's security in the name of their spiritual beliefs.

In the 1990s, with new political freedoms, programs aimed at educating people in the Nivkh language and culture have begun in earnest, and a new Nivkh language newspaper offers refresher courses in Nivkh history and cuisine. Although fishing collectives of the Soviet period, such as "New Life" or "Red Dawn", now often have more Russian than Nivkh employees, their fishing brigades have begun new traditions of feeding the sea, as a nod to past ways.

♀ With the greater economic freedom in post-Soviet Russia, many Nivkh families are returning to once thriving village sites to rebuild homes and gardens.

ALL PHOTOGRAPHS BY DOUGLAS VOGT

♀ In the uncertainty of the post-Soviet economy, many younger Nivkhi are reviving the traditional art of drying salmon for the winter food supply.

♂ Zoya Ivanovna Agnyun is one of few Nivkhi still able to craft the intricately embroidered salmon-skin dresses traditionally worn by women.

♀ The often barren Sakhalin vistas can belie the vast fields of wild berries that were a mainstay of the Nivkh diet for centuries.

A. MILOVSKY

⚱ One of the early achievements of the Soviet administration in the Siberian north was to provide a medical service to even the remotest communities. Here, a Russian doctor examines Chukchi patients on the Kanchalan tundra.

Under Communist Rule

As their power consolidated, the new communist leaders were quick to criticize the prerevolutionary government for its abusive neglect of native peoples. However, for fear of alienating the support of the large local Russian population, on whom the new state depended, criticism of Russian influence over the Siberian aborigines became taboo. Moreover, in contrast to their more numerous republican counterparts, such as the Ukrainians or the Georgians, Siberian peoples were portrayed as being "without culture"—empty vessels, which the new state organizations would fill and define.

One of Lenin's first decrees was to recognize the equal rights of all peoples under the new Soviet system. The system of *yasak* payments was immediately repealed. Northern natives were exempted from all taxation (a measure that was to last only eight years). The sale of alchohol was prohibited on native lands, and trade with natives in general was extensively regulated in order to reduce exploitation. Nonetheless, despite these early positive measures, real native autonomy had little place in a society bent on world revolution and the eventual merging of all cultures. Maintaining that ethnic tension was class-based, the Bolsheviks held that the disappearance of the class struggle under communism would, in turn, cause ethnic differences to diminish in importance.

Free of oppression, Soviet peoples would flourish and come together as a new international community. Siberian peoples were to play an integral part in this new, modern society.

To meet the task, the administration of the Siberian indigenous population fell to the Committee for the Assistance to Peoples of the Northern Borderlands, or the Committee of the North, as it became known, founded in 1924. This Moscow-based working group set out three main priorities for northern native development: native self-government, economic reorganization, and social enlightenment. What the committee lacked in financial clout, it compensated for in energy and innovation. Immediately there were proposals for creating a network of northern correspondents, for starting a special fund to address northern problems, and for recruiting students to work in remote areas. Given its ambitious program, what is striking about the committee's early work is its high regard for existing native channels as an avenue of reform. Indeed, some of the most positive achievements of the Soviet period were set in motion during these early years. Hospitals and schools in which native languages were spoken were established. Agriculture was introduced, and credit was extended to native hunting, fishing, and herding collectives.

It is at this point that most Soviet accounts of native peoples stop short. Excepting brief notes on developments since the 1920s, the tendency in communist literature has often been to leap ahead to the present by pronouncing that socialism had been achieved for all. These omissions have given rise to the false notion that Siberian peoples were somehow set apart from the turbulent events that engulfed the Soviet Union after its formation.

⚱ A carved walrus tooth from the northeastern Siberian Inuit community of Uelen.

A. MILOVSKY

↪ With the new economic freedom of the post-Soviet Russian economy, many fishermen, such as this Chukchi man, have returned to traditional methods of walrus hunting as a way of supporting themselves.

A. MILOVSKY

BRYAN AND CHERRY ALEXANDER

Transforming the Economy

One of the most important measures to affect the native peoples was the process of mass collectivization on which the Soviet system was predicated. By eradicating private property and collectivizing the proceeds, the intent was to not only to create efficiently run, centralized economic structures, but also to provide a place for the hitherto excluded smaller nationalities. The technical aspects of renovating an entire cultural system were daunting. One Chukchi noted wryly of the new Soviet emissaries: " ... there comes an instructor who does not know a word of Chukchi and speaks through an interpreter who, not knowing scientific terms, says something completely different ... After that the instructor leaves a whole pile of directives and instructions, which the chairman of the [council] receives and puts in a sack, and there they lie until a year later when somebody else comes from the district executive committee."

On a deeper level, the special problem for the smaller nationalities was that their cultures thrived precisely on decentralized power bases. Among the nomadic Evenki of central Siberia, planning ahead was considered bad luck and therefore taboo. How were they to take part in a government Five Year Plan?

The transition to communes was least disruptive to fishing communities, many of which had been participating in fishing teams before the revolution. But for hunting and herding peoples, these factory-like organizations were completely foreign. Part of the ancient belief system of herders on the peninsulas of Chukotka and Kamchatka was that there was a spiritual bond between a reindeer and its owner. Even when reindeer were held by families, each animal was connected with a specific individual. To collectivize them was a sin. Across the entire north, herders began to slaughter their reindeer rather than collectivize them, with the result that the size of the Siberian herd was reduced by a third in only three years. In the mid-1930s, Anatolii Skachko, the acting head of the Committee of the North, assessed the debacle, noting that "we have paid for the transferral of [only] 20 percent of the herd into the socialist sector by destroying 35 percent of the reindeer".

The government struck back a local resistance by singling out the wealthiest as *kulaks*, from the Russian word for "tightfist". The term *kulak* quickly became a catchword for anyone in opposition to state policy. Among Siberian peoples, this spelled particular trouble for shamans, the spirit mediums and healers who acted as religious figures across the continent. Shamans were routinely harassed as reactionaries and exploiters by the new atheist government. Religious beliefs in general were pronounced to be "a waste of social energy".

Nenets reindeer herders travel routes so ancient that the reindeer often need little guidance. Oil development on the Yamal peninsula, where these herders live, has begun to curtail their access to these routes.

A. MILOVSKY

Reindeer herding has long been a central component of northern Siberian economies. Among Chukchi on the Kanchalan peninsula, a few herders are taking steps to establish private herds, as shown here.

✿ Zoya Agnyun, a Nivkh, takes pride in her Award for Heroism in Communist Labor, earned in state fisheries on Sakhalin Island.

✿ Konstantin Kekhan, a Nivkh, outside his home, No. 3 Soviet Street, in the town of Rybnovsk, on Sakhalin Island's northwestern shore.

It soon became clear that the objective was not simply rapid modernization but an express "war against the past". As the 1930s advanced, it became more difficult to determine which changes were voluntary and which were coerced. For northern social planners, a war against the past called not only for the eradication of shamans, *kulaks*, and class enemies, but also for the aggressive jettisoning of all forms of traditional life in favor of a new Siberia in step with history. In the darkest moments of the new order, the war on the past led to the mass arrest and killing of tens of thousands of northern peoples. The tolls were highest in those areas where the natives had previously had trading contacts with foreigners. On the Chukotkan peninsula, 37 percent of the native population were branded as *kulaks*. To the south, on Sakhalin Island, early KGB (NKVD) documents indicate that more than a third of native Nivkh men were imprisoned or killed in 1937 and 1938 alone.

The Second World War proved to be a turning point for Siberian native peoples in the Soviet world. For the men, it was an opportunity to confirm their citizenship by taking part in Soviet missions. While they were off at war, it was also a chance for the government to finally coax women into the workforce. Native women across Siberia had been among the most reluctant to take part in the new collective economy. With many of their men absent, women took up much of the work left behind. Indeed, after the war, the Siberian economy as a whole began to prosper. Siberian industry thrived when hundreds of thousands of people were evacuated eastwards during the fighting, and the construction of large hydroelectric plants further transformed local landscapes.

✿ Galina Pshenichnaya, a Russian, works as a baker in the Nivkh community of Rybnoe. Yeast is often in short supply, as it is diverted for the brewing of home spirits.

A Disastrous Policy

The relative calm and prosperity of the postwar period was shaken in the 1960s by a controversial decision made by Prime Minister Nikita Khrushchev to further concentrate the entire Soviet population into special agrocenters. In the larger republics, this dubious, politically motivated proposal was for the most part ignored. But in Siberia, still the Russian province most vulnerable to the caprice of changes from on high, it was widely implemented. For the native population, already dramatically transformed by the first wave of collectivization, this was a further blow. Many groups had managed to maintain their cultural identity by keeping as much distance as possible between themselves and the central government. Others lived in remote areas because of the natural resources they depended on. Across the board, when provincial officials were pressed to relocate sometimes as much as two-thirds of the local native population, they often resorted to force. One Nivkh fisherman recalled:

"None of us could believe the news when we first heard it. The town had grown to about 700 people, about 300 of us Nivkhi. The government had spent so many years building us up! There was a school, a laboratory, two clubs, a fishery … they had only just finished a whole new set of houses and a two-story hospital on the edge of the village. A new rail line, too. I had been a communist party organizer there before, and I didn't know a thing. They called a meeting of

the whole village. The district council explained that small settlements were no longer profitable for the country, that they were too broadly spread out and maybe even dangerous. Then they tried to tell us that the town was badly situated, that there was a danger of flooding. There's never been a flood there, ever!"

The moves were absurd in their lack of foresight. Across the native north, the most prosperous villages were emptied, and the populations moved to show-villages of up to 5,000 people. Many natives lost their jobs altogether in these new settlements, which were distinguished by their proximity to government centers rather than to a resource base. In this disastrous campaign, the government not only failed to strengthen the economy, they also failed to cut native ties to traditional lands, as had been hoped. Rather than moving natives forward into a brave new world, the resettlement campaign generated a retrospective force that caused many natives to start criticizing the state of their affairs.

The downward slide of the Siberian peoples since the 1960s is a sobering one. As a government report of 1988 observed in retrospect, "The results of sixty years' worth of development are not very comforting: from highly qualified reindeer herders, hunters and fishermen, native northerners have been transformed into auxiliary workers, loaders, watchmen and janitors." Public health statistics from the early 1990s indicate the extent to which decades of official self-congratulation omitted any mention of the considerable problems.

A. MILOVSKY

After the Soviet Union

The dramatic events of perestroika and the tumultuous collapse of the Soviet Union breathed new life into this expansive community of peoples. In the mid-1980s, complaints about the state of native education, language rights, and access to traditional resources grew louder and louder. In March 1990, the first Congress of Native Peoples was held in the Kremlin in Moscow, marking an historic and cathartic turning point. Speaker after speaker mounted the podium to rail against decades of discrimination, shameless historians, government fictions, and ecological disasters. But as in previous times, the prospect for real improvement hinges on the direction taken by the Russian state.

What seems certain under any circumstances is that the aboriginal voice in Siberia will now be heard to a much greater extent. After a roller coaster of social change in the twentieth century, when their languages and ways of life were discouraged and then encouraged, repressed and then rehabilitated, ignored and now revived again, Siberia's northern peoples are rightly calling for social policies set on their own terms. Across Siberia, native-language newspapers are flourishing, and the first steps are being taken towards re-introducing native languages in schools. While the future of these peoples may be up in the air, this new surge of native activism turns the tide in their favor for the first time.

Bruce Grant

OMEGA/CAMERA PRESS/AUSTRAL INTERNATIONAL

◄◐ Roughly half of Siberian indigenous peoples, such as the Inuit woman photographed here with her children in the northeastern town of Novoe Chaplino, live in urban or semi-urban environments.

DOUGLAS VOGT

◉ Vera Kekhan at home with her grandson. She is among the few Nivkhi who regularly speak their native language.

◄◐ A Ket couple living along the Yenisei River, in central Siberia.

THE SAAMI: A PEOPLE OF FOUR COUNTRIES

Louise Bäckman

THE SAAMI, commonly known as the Lapps, occupy the arctic and subarctic regions of Fennoscandia, which extend over the northern parts of Norway, Sweden, and Finland (the Laplands), and the Kola peninsula, in Russia. About 2,000 years ago, their homeland was much more extensive. Saami inhabited the entire region of what is now Finland and also a part of Karelia, and extended further into the southern parts of Scandinavia. The Saami language belongs to the Finno-Ugric branch of the Uralic language family, and there are somewhere between 60,000 and 70,000 Saami speakers, of whom nearly 6,000 are reindeer herders, leading a nomadic way of life.

A seventeenth-century drawing of a Saami shaman (*noaidi*), with his drum (*goabda*), during a séance.

In spring and autumn, a Saami family traditionally lived in a permanent house known as a *gamme* or, in Saami, a *darvhe-goatie*, consisting of a framework of poles covered with turf. This group of Saami was photographed in northern Norway in the 1930s.

Fishers, Hunters, and Herders

While the Saami are most widely known as reindeer herders, this has not always been their way of life. Like many other peoples, they once subsisted by fishing and hunting, their major prey being wild reindeer. Over the years, however, some Saami began to concentrate on herding reindeer, while others continued to hunt and fish, supplementing these activities with small-scale farming. Herding wild deer, like hunting them, requires a cooperative approach, and the structure of Saami herding communities reflects this. Each household belongs to a *siida*, which can be understood as a team of reindeer owners who migrate with

Outside his portable tent (*loavht-goatie*), a man packs dried and softened sedge, which will be used to line boots.

their herds within a certain area. A Saami village or district is a union of *siidas* within a larger region, with the function of promoting the deer herders' common interests.

The Saami in History

The earliest written descriptions of northern Europe, from the first centuries AD, mention a people skilled in deer hunting called Fenni or Skrithifinoi, who are believed to be the Saami. The Icelandic sagas, which were written during the early thirteenth century, describe the Saami—here called Finns—as being

knowledgeable about witchcraft and occasionally dangerous. This was in part a reference to the figure of the shaman (or *noaidi*) in Saami society, a person who had special knowledge of the supernatural world. During séances, the shaman would fall into a trance, and on awakening, would relate the will of the gods or deliver messages from the dead. The *noaidi* used his drum, the *goabda*, as an instrument of exaltation, but as far as we know, he never used drugs.

Gods, Goddesses, and Ancestors

Traditional Saami religion followed a pattern common to the northern Siberian region, and was based on living in harmony with nature. The Master or Mistress of Places and Animals was an important deity, because he or she protected the animals people relied on for food

and influenced the rate of reproduction of all living things. The Sky God, Tiermes, was more distant, but revealed himself through such phenomena as the sun, the wind, and thunder. These natural phenomena were worshiped with animal sacrifices, as was the Sky God himself, on occasion. In Saami myths, deities assumed human characteristics, but the idols made to represent them were roughly fashioned, consisting of little more than wooden blocks. Female divinities played an important role in traditional Saami religion. The Mother Goddess, *Madter-Akka*, and her three daughters promoted fertility in both humans and animals, and protected families. Ancestors were venerated, and the shaman was the guardian of religious and social order. By the end of the eighteenth century, however, the Saami had officially abandoned their old religion and become Christians.

An Enduring Culture

Until the twentieth century, cultural differences between the Saami and other European peoples were clearly evident. The Saami were set apart by their egalitarian social structure, the way they utilized natural resources, and by their language. During the last three centuries, the Saami's central area has attracted many immigrants. Rich ores are being mined, hydroelectric power stations have been built, and the forests are being cleared for timber. The high mountain area attracts tourists and holiday-makers, and this has had a big impact on the Saami way of life. Pollution from factories and from the nuclear power station at Chernobyl has reduced the pastures available for reindeer, and many reindeer herders have had to switch to other occupations. For hundreds of years, both the Nordic countries and Russia (and its successor, the Soviet Union) have tried to assimilate the Saami, and Saami culture has inevitably been weakened by the gradual infiltration of Nordic and Slavic cultural elements.

Reindeer herding followed the traditional pattern until the mid-twentieth century. During the summer months, the entire family lived with the herd in high mountain areas or on the islands along the Atlantic coast. As winter approached, the family followed the herd to winter grazing in the woodlands. When following the herds, the Saami lived in portable tents, but during the spring and autumn, they stayed in low mountain regions, living in wooden huts known as *kåta* or *gamme*. Where once people had a special relationship with their herds, today herding is highly motorized. The use of cars, snowscooters, snowmobiles, airplanes, and helicopters has made the work easier, but it has also turned herding into a business more than a way of life, and deer into a commercial product.

There have been political upheavals among the Saami since the Second World War. National Saami organizations as well as local associations have gradually emerged to promote Saami interests. The inaugural body was the Nordic Saami Council, founded in 1956, and the first Saami parliament, or *Saamidiggi*, was established in Finland in 1973. Saami parliaments followed in Norway, in 1989, and in Sweden, in 1993. The members of the parliaments are elected by Saami from among their own communities. The parliaments are financed by the respective national governments, and have, in the main, consultative authority concerning Saami issues.

Under the rule of the Soviet Union, the Saami on the Kola peninsula became workers in reindeer communes, in which the deer were owned by the state. Today, they strive to promote their independent status through such organizations as economic unions for herders and cultural associations. Their contact with the Saami in the West is very important in this regard, and since 1992, they have been members of the Nordic Saami Council.

☉ Weaving a band for a traditional Saami dress. The loom is made of deer antler.

◂ A mother carries her baby in the *gietka*, the traditional Saami cradle.

☞ The traditional dress of each Saami village is distinguished by particular colors. The girl at right comes from Kautokeino, in northern Norway.

☞ Herders recognize their own deer among the herd by cut marks in the ears.

☞ The weather on the Aleutian Islands is very severe: on days when there is no fog, there are strong winds. As there are no trees on the islands, semi-subterranean houses are built to provide protection from the winds. Here, Billy Dushkin is chopping driftwood, collected from the seashore, to light and heat his home.

STEVEN C. WILSON/ENTHEOS

STEVEN C. WILSON/ENTHEOS

🐚 Aleut unloading cod for processing at the local fish plant at Dutch Harbor, on Unalaska Island. Commercial fishing provides a cash income for some Aleut.

ALEUT AND INUIT

The northern coasts of North America and Greenland are the homelands of two distinct peoples: the Aleut and the Inuit. Collectively, these people occupy the Arctic and Subarctic coasts from 53°N to 83°N and from 172°E in the west to 18°W in the east. Glottochronologists, who study the history of languages, suggest that the Aleut and Inuit spoke a common language more than 6,000 years ago.

The Aleut occupy the southern tip of the Alaska Peninsula and the Aleutian Islands, a chain of more than 70 volcanic islands. In the mid-1700s, when they first came into contact with the Russians, the Aleut population was estimated at approximately 15,000. Today, about 3,000 people regard themselves as Aleut. Although their indigenous language is spoken by less than a third of the population, the Aleut are working to revive their language.

The Inuit speak two languages, Yup'ik and Inupiaq. Yup'ik speakers occupy the eastern-most tip of Siberia, St Lawrence Island, and southwestern Alaska. The Inupiaq language is the most widespread in the world, spanning a region of 6,000 kilometers (3,800 miles), from Siberia, across northern Alaska and Canada,

to eastern Greenland. The Inuit population is estimated at approximately 135,000. Yup'ik and Inupiaq are both vital languages, spoken by about 25,000 people and 100,000 people respectively.

The Inuit and Aleut occupy two ecological zones: the Arctic and the Subarctic. In these zones, the food chains are short and the eco-systems fragile. The climate is both harsh and unpredictable. Despite the challenges of this environment, these peoples have thrived for thousands of years. Contact with the outside world over the past 400 years has posed a greater threat to their survival.

While contact with outsiders occurred at very different times across this region, it in-variably followed a similar pattern: exploration, exploitation, and then colonization. From that of independent peoples, the Inuit and Aleut found their status altered to that of colonial subjects. Today, these people are part of four nations: Russia, the United States of America, Canada, and Greenland (Denmark).

Contact led to massive disruptions in all spheres of aboriginal life: economic, social, and spiritual. Before describing contemporary life, it is necessary to provide a background against which to understand the magnitude of the changes these people have had to undergo and their tenacity in maintaining their separate identities.

Traditional Society

Before European contact, people subsisted by hunting and gathering. They had an intimate knowledge of their environment: land, sea, ice, animals, and plants. Animals and their gifts of food, clothing, shelter, and light were treated with respect. Traditions related the dire consequences awaiting those who abused animals. To ensure survival, skills and knowledge were coupled with a philosophy of sharing.

The Aleut and Inuit lived in very different settings. Rich maritime resources and the warming effect of the Japanese Current enabled the Aleut to maintain permanent settlements. Among the Inuit, most groups followed a seasonal cycle, moving from camp to camp within a particular territory to take advantage of the availability of different game species, but resources in southwestern Alaska, St Lawrence Island, and along the north slope of Alaska were conducive to permanent settlements.

All Aleut and Inuit social organization was based on kinship relations, but there were also special partnerships, or alliances, formed on the basis of friendship and respect. Some were primarily economic, such as trade and seal sharing. Seal-sharing partners exchanged parts of every seal they caught when seals were few. In this way, most members of the group had some food. Other alliances were mostly social, and included joking, dancing, and singing partnerships. Joking partners were especially close. They were always making fun of each other, pointing out the other's weaknesses through jest. Singing and dancing partners exchanged their private songs and danced to these melodies, thus creating a strong bond. However, all these alliances carried obligations in times of stress. If starvation threatened in one region, the people could count on assistance from their partners in neighboring regions. These alliances provided security, given the unpredictable nature of the weather and food resources.

Northern societies were egalitarian within limits. Certain families were accorded a higher status than others. Elders were the repositories of cultural heritage and were respected because of their life experiences and knowledge. Among the Aleut, there was a well-defined social hierarchy with hereditary chiefs. In contrast, leadership among the Inuit was not inherited. The community leader, or *isumataq* ("one who thinks"), would be recognized because of his hunting prowess and his knowledge of the land. With the help of the elders, he also administered justice.

Across the circumpolar regions, the universe was seen as consisting of many delicately balanced layers. Through injudicious actions, people could upset this balance and create discord. Harmony

BRYAN AND CHERRY ALEXANDER

♂ A hunter from northwestern Greenland raises his rifle to shoot a seal at the floe edge. Although the Inuit now make use of modern technology for hunting, no species has been endangered as a result.

♀ Inuit are hunters. Their knowledge of and respect for animals enables them to survive in the Arctic. Here, a hunter from Igloolik waits patiently for a seal to surface at one of its many breathing holes.

BRYAN AND CHERRY ALEXANDER

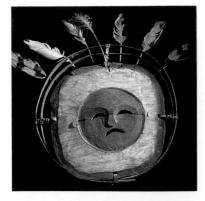

⬧ This wooden mask is an expression of Inuit cosmology. The face in the center represents one of the important spirits, that of the moon. The surrounding hoops are the different layers of the universe, while the feathers are the stars in the heaven.
SMITHSONIAN INSTITUTION/WERNER FORMAN ARCHIVE

♀ Inuit often have to travel long distances on foot when hunting caribou. This hunter is using an Inuit-style backpack with chest and forehead tumplines to carry a dressed caribou.

could be restored by the shaman. Shamans could communicate across usually impassable boundaries, such as the boundary between the world of the living and that of the dead. Through this ability, they could determine the sources of problems in the world of the living, and prescribe solutions. Often, there were many shamans in a community. Some had only healing powers, while others were able to undertake fantastic spirit flights into other realms. Usually, these individuals worked as holistic healers for the group's good. Sometimes, however, they operated solely for their own benefit, manipulating members of the group through fear to provide for them and their families.

In the unpredictable environment of the north, societies had to be extremely flexible. Slow response was often deadly. Any change in caribou migration routes, for example, necessitated an immediate change in people's seasonal cycle. This ability to adapt rapidly to new and unexpected events has helped to ensure the survival of these people throughout the period of European contact.

Early European Contact

In the eastern Canadian Arctic and Greenland, the earliest contact with Europeans was during the westward expansion of the Norse (about AD 1000). Despite Norse colonization of southern Greenland, this contact appears to have been limited—probably some trade and several disagreements. Troubles with Inuit groups moving into southern Greenland

may partly explain the disappearance of the Norse colony there in the fifteenth century.

The main period of European expansion into the north began with British voyages in search of the fabled Straits of Anian—a mythical Northwest Passage connecting Europe to the riches of the Orient. This passage would obviate the need for excruciating overland expeditions or long and dangerous marine expeditions around either the Cape of Good Hope or Cape Horn and into waters controlled by the Spanish and Portuguese. Martin Frobisher's voyage to southern Baffin Island in 1576 marks the beginning of this period.

The indigenous populations living on either side of the Bering Strait have been in constant contact with each other, except during the Cold War period (1945 to 1990). Chukchi and Inuit traded and raided across the waterway. In 1741, the Danish explorer Vitus Bering, employed by the Russian Crown, crossed the strait that now bears his name. Bering died on this voyage, but the bundles of rare and valuable sea otter pelts brought home by the survivors ensured continued Russian interest. The Russians added this region to their empire, and the Aleut and some Yup'ik speakers were forced into the *yasak* taxation system. In 1799, the Russian American Company was granted monopoly trading rights by the Russian Crown and ruled Alaska as a virtual fiefdom. In 1867, the Russian Tsar sold Alaska to the United States of America for $7.2 million in gold. What followed, for all Alaskan peoples, was a period of laissez-faire capitalism. There were few government officials to patrol this vast region, and traders, miners, and others came and went as they pleased, sometimes employing native people but otherwise paying little attention to them.

In what was to become the Canadian Arctic and Greenland, an initial period of exploration was rapidly followed by one of exploitation, as a capitalist economy armed with the technology to extract resources at rates previously unimaginable competed with a subsistence economy based on the sustainable use of resources. The north was the fringe of this economy, and was generally regarded as uninhabited by civilized peoples. As such, it experienced a boom and bust economy —as it still does today.

Tragically, the boom periods have been just as destructive to northern societies as have the bust periods. Russian exploitation of sea otters led to subjugation of the Aleuts, along with the virtual extinction of the sea otters, by the early 1800s. In the 1800s, Europeans and Americans began hunting bowhead whales for their baleen and oil in both the eastern (beginning in 1821) and western (beginning in 1860) Arctic. The whalers employed Inuit crews to assist in the hunt, finding them both cheaper and more experienced than imported crews. The Inuit traded their services for the goods they desired. By the beginning of the twentieth century, bowhead whales were close to extinction. When these

JOHN EASTCOTT/YVA MOMATIUK/PLANET EARTH PICTURES

industries collapsed, the Inuit and Aleut were left with little access to the goods on which they had grown dependent. Their societies had also been severely affected by the exploitation of and reduction in their resource base and the introduction of new goods (such as guns, iron, cloth, flour, and tobacco). In addition, they were ravaged by such introduced diseases as measles, tuberculosis, smallpox, and syphilis.

Few outsiders remained in the north during the bust periods. Those who did were traders, missionaries, and a few government agents, including police. The missionaries came from many different faiths. While both the Inuit and the Aleut adopted Christianity, this did not alter their basic philosophy. The missionaries simply replaced the shamans, usurping their role as intermediaries with the spirit world, and Christian beliefs were incorporated into Inuit and Aleut cosmology.

The missionaries, eager to translate the Bible, were the first to develop written scripts for the Aleut, Yup'ik, and Inupiaq languages, most of them based on Roman orthography. The earliest script was created for Inupiaq by Hans Egede, who established the first mission in Greenland in 1721. Greenland has a long secular publishing history, beginning with the journal *Atuagagdliutit*, established in 1861. In the late 1800s, the Reverend J. Peck, working in the Canadian Arctic, altered the syllabic script, a phonetic script developed for the North American Cree language, for Inupiaq.

HULTON-DEUTSCH/THE PHOTO LIBRARY, SYDNEY

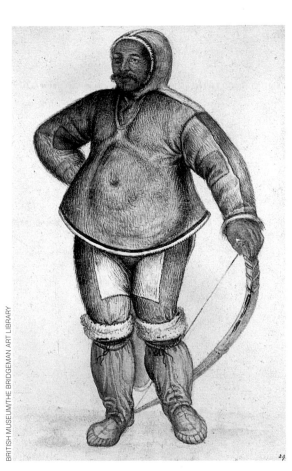

BRITISH MUSEUM/THE BRIDGEMAN ART LIBRARY

⊕ An Inuit woman and child drawn by C.F. Lyon in 1821. The woman is wearing an *amautiq*, a jacket with a pouch in the back for carrying an infant. The large shoulders enabled the mother to bring the baby to her breast without removing it from the *amautiq*.
NATIONAL MARITIME MUSEUM, LONDON/THE BRIDGEMAN ART LIBRARY

⊕ This mother and child, photographed about 1914, are both dressed in caribou skins. In cold weather, Inuit wore two layers of skin clothing. On the inner layer, the animal hair lay against the wearer's body, while the outer layer had the hair on the outside.

Meeting the Challenge

Following the Second World War, Canada, Denmark, and the United States began to take a greater interest in their northern frontiers. New government policies were initiated. In Canada, the government favored rapid assimilation of the Inuit into mainstream Canadian society. To this end, residential schools were established for Inuit, where students were removed from their communities and speaking Inupiaq was actively discouraged. Health care became more proactive. Anyone suffering from tuberculosis, by then an epidemic, was removed from the north and sent to a sanatorium in the south. In the early 1950s, almost 10 percent of the Canadian Inuit population was in southern health facilities.

⊕ In 1577, Martin Frobisher abducted three Inuit from southern Baffin Island —a man and (from a different location) a woman with a baby—forcing them to return to Britain with him. All three contracted diseases and died. This illustration by John White shows the man, Kalicho, with his bow.

BEN GIBSON/IMPACT PHOTOS

☞ Snowmobiles enable Inuit living in permanent communities to go hunting on the weekends and to travel long distances rapidly during most of the year. Some people still prefer to use dog teams, however, because dogs don't break down.

🏺 This ivory float plug is decorated with the image of a woman's face, complete with tattoos below the lower lip. It was used to plug holes in the sealskin floats Inuit used to hunt marine mammals.

ALASKA MUSEUM OF ESKIMO ART/ WERNER FORMAN ARCHIVE

MICHIO HOSHINO/MINDEN PICTURES

🏺 In the past, Inuit supported themselves entirely from the products of the land and sea. Here, a woman is using an *ulu*, a semilunar-shaped knife, to cut up fish.

To speed up the assimilation process, permanent settlements were constructed for these nomadic peoples beginning in the 1960s. Access to schools, health care, and social security was one of the benefits of living in the settlements rather than on the land. Even for a flexible society, the rapidity of this change was overwhelming. It brought about tremendous social upheaval, which continues today. Alcoholism and substance abuse are rampant. The suicide rate for Canadian Inuit is twelve times that of southern Canadians. This problem is particularly acute among young men, who feel that they are no longer "real Inuit". They find themselves torn between two worlds. They no longer have the skills to survive on the land, and they are unable to find jobs in northern communities, where the unemployment rate is usually over 70 percent. The Aleut and Inuit living in the United States and Greenland face these same economic and social problems.

The Alaskan peoples began to organize politically in 1912, with the establishment of the Alaska Native Brotherhood. The aboriginal population of Alaska had never entered into treaties with the United States government, and in 1967, the Alaska Federation of Natives presented the United States government with a land claim proposal. The importance of this claim was driven home to the United States government by the discovery of a major oil field at Prudhoe Bay, on Alaska's North Slope. The Alaska Native Claims Settlement Act was passed into law in 1971. In exchange for just under a billion US dollars and

18 million hectares (44 million acres) of land, the indigenous people agreed to extinguish their aboriginal rights to the land. This claim, with all its subsequent problems, became the reference point for other Inuit groups formulating claims.

Greenland was a colony of Denmark from 1721 until 1953. During this period, the Danish government acted in an isolationist and protectionist fashion, making trade with Inuit a state monopoly and closing Greenland to foreigners in 1776. Colonial status was abolished with the passage of the Danish constitution in 1953. Greenland became a province of Denmark, with two elected seats in the Danish parliament. Active and astute Inuit politicians continued to seek greater independence, self-government, and self-determination for their constituents. In 1975, a Danish Parliamentary Committee recommended the development of home rule, which was achieved, after much negotiation, in 1979. This status gives the people of Greenland the right to control their own affairs except for three important areas: finance, defense, and foreign relations.

In Canada, the Inuit founded the Inuit Tapirisat of Canada (ITC) in 1971. In 1977, they submitted a land claim titled *Nunavut* (*Our Land*) to the Canadian government on behalf of the Inuit of the Northwest Territories. Complicated negotiations then began. Following the discovery of oil at the mouth of the Mackenzie River, the people of the western Northwest Territories, recognizing the parallels with Alaska, negotiated their own agreement. At the same time,

Inuit living in Quebec and in the Canadian provinces of Newfoundland and Labrador, who were not part of the ITC land claim, began to develop their own claims. In a situation again analogous to Alaska, the people of northern Quebec settled their claim in 1975 when the Quebec government announced plans for the massive, and still highly controversial, James Bay hydroelectric power project. The Inuit of Newfoundland and Labrador submitted their claim in 1978. As the provincial government saw no benefit in expediting land claims, it stalled the negotiations process for many years, and this land claim has still to be resolved.

The *Nunavut* land claim was finally settled on 9 July 1993. At the same time, a plebiscite was held on whether to divide the Northwest Territories into two: Denedeh in the west and Nunavut in the east. The people voted for division. In Nunavut, the Inuit form a large majority. The *Nunavut* land claim and the new territory of Nunavut have effectively achieved, for the first time in Canada, self-government for an aboriginal people.

The land claims process has continued the rapid pace of change in the north. But this is a different kind of change, as these people take active control of their own affairs and begin to shape their own destiny.

Developing a Stable Economy

The economy of the north continues to be problematic. Following the collapse of whaling at the beginning of the twentieth century, the fur industry was developed in the Arctic, most notably by the

HANS BLOHM/MASTERFILE/STOCK PHOTOS

Hudson's Bay Company, a privately owned British firm that had been involved in the Canadian fur industry since 1670. This industry was based mainly on the sale of white fox and seal pelts. It appeared to follow the already well-established boom and bust pattern of resource exploitation, but while prices fluctuated according to the fashions in the outside world, demand remained constant enough to provide many northern hunters with the income required to sustain their way of life. In addition, the animal

🐾 In 1993, the *Nunavut* land claim agreement, which redefined the relationship between the Inuit of Nunavut and the Canadian government, was signed. Left to right: representing the government, then Prime Minister Brian Mulroney; representing the Inuit, Paul Quassa, Mary Simon, Rosemary Kuptana, and Martha Flaherty.

BRYAN AND CHERRY ALEXANDER

BRYAN AND CHERRY ALEXANDER

🐾 Until the early 1980s, sealskins provided many Inuit with their livelihood. This sealskin warehouse is in Savissavik, Greenland.

🐾 The Polar Inuit of northern Greenland are the world's northernmost inhabitants. To preserve their environment, the people have enacted strict local hunting ordinances. Here, a man is disentangling a seal caught in a seal net.

☛ *Ulus* were most often used by women. Their semilunar cutting blade is ideal for cutting up meat and for working on skins.
SMITHSONIAN INSTITUTION, WASHINGTON/ WERNER FORMAN ARCHIVE

♀ Each spring, the whalers of northern Alaska gather at the floe edge in anticipation of the arrival of the bowhead whales. This period of waiting is a time of physical and spiritual preparation for the whale hunt.

populations were not overexploited, as had happened in the case of sea otters and bowhead whales.

In the late 1960s, environmental groups such as Save Our Seals (SOS) and Greenpeace began massive campaigns against seal hunting. These organizations were targeting the harp seal pup industry of Newfoundland. However, the Inuit, who were not involved in this, became the unintended victims of animal rights activists more concerned with the welfare of animals than with human lives. The concerted efforts of environmental groups led the European Union (then the European Economic Community) to ban the import of the pelts of juvenile harp and hooded seals in 1983. As a direct result of this action, the market for all seal pelts, both juvenile and adult, crashed. This had a dramatic impact on the Inuit of northern Canada and Greenland. In one year, these communities lost up to 80 percent of their cash income. In 1985, Greenpeace formally apologized to the Inuit for the unintentional harm caused by the campaign against the Newfoundland harp seal industry, but no apology, however well meant, could make up for the devastation caused to a people whose livelihood had been stripped away.

Today, well aware of the pitfalls of the global economy, Inuit are working towards a goal of sustainable economic development. Training of

Inuit for northern jobs (such as in government, in construction, and in education) as well as the development of light industry (such as small-scale commercial fisheries and the manufacture of leather goods from sealskins) are important steps towards this goal. In addition, the people of the north want to ensure that the quality of their environment is maintained. Pollution has become a major concern, and future development will have to be environmentally sound.

A Heritage of Whaling

While developing a new economic base, the Aleut and Inuit are also striving to maintain their culture and heritage. One of the most striking examples is provided by the Inuit of northern Aslaska and St Lawrence Island. The bowhead whale hunt was extremely important to these cultures. Their social structure was based on the structure of whaleboat crews, the *umialit* (owners of whaleboats) being the leaders of the community. Whales were also central to their cosmology and spiritual life. In economic terms, the meat, skin, oil, and bones they obtained from whales allowed these Inuit to sustain a way of life based on large, permanent villages.

In 1946, the International Whaling Commission (IWC) recognized the fundamental importance of whaling to aboriginal groups and exempted it from the ban on hunting gray and bowhead whales. In

MICHIO HOSHINO/MINDEN PICTURES

1977, the IWC, concerned about the decline in the bowhead population, revoked this exception, making it illegal to hunt bowhead whales. In response, the Alaskan Inuit formed the Alaska Eskimo Whaling Commission (AEWC) and hired scientists, historians, and anthropologists to demonstrate that limited harvesting of the bowhead population was not only sustainable but also necessary for the people's cultural survival. As a result of this research, the Alaskan Inuit were successful in obtaining permission from the IWC to harvest a small quota. Then in 1981, in an unprecedented move, the United States government, through a cooperative agreement, handed over responsibility for the administration and management of the Alaskan bowhead whale population to the AEWC. Recently, the quota has increased from the 1977 quota of 20 whales harpooned or 14 harpooned and landed to 44 whales struck or 41 landed per year, owing to new estimates of the bowhead population. While the quota is still set by the IWC, it is now based on more accurate estimates

of sustainable use of the resource as well as on the Inuit's requirements. In 1992, when the Alaskan communities did not take their full quota, they gave the right to hunt one whale to the Inuit of the Mackenzie Delta. The capture of this whale was the first by these people in the twentieth century. It was the occasion not only of a great celebration but also of an important cultural revival.

A United Voice

In the 1970s, the late Eben Hopson, then mayor of Barrow, in Alaska, perceived the need for an organization that would promote Inuit unity and identity. His vision led to the founding of the Inuit Circumpolar Conference (ICC) in 1977. The aims of this organization are to foster Inuit unity, to maintain Inuit culture, to protect the Arctic environment, and to facilitate the transborder exchange of information among Inuit. The ICC acts as the Inuit's international voice and is recognized by the United Nations as a nongovernment organization with consultative status. One of its major objectives is to ensure that the Inuit are directly involved in decision-making that affects the north.

For many years, the ICC was unable to have representatives from all four nations at its meetings. As a constant reminder of their absent relatives living in Siberia, a chair was left vacant at the conference table. Since 1989, this seat has been filled, and the Inuit are once again able to communicate throughout the entire north.

The Inuit and Aleut today are following in their ancestors' footprints. They are adapting their culture to contemporary circumstances, while still maintaining their separate identity.

Susan Rowley

⚓ Entitled *Fisherman*, this soapstone sculpture is by Inuit artist Davidee Inqumiak, of Quebec, Canada. Soapstone carving as a commercial art form began in the 1950s. Inuit artists use this, and other media, to create powerful images evoking their intimate relationship to the land and its animals. Art and tourism are also seen as important components of the development of a sustainable economy.
BECKETT/AMERICAN MUSEUM OF NATURAL HISTORY, NO. 60.2–5538

⚓ In the past, history was passed on orally from the elders to the younger people. Today, this chain of transmission is being broken, but some people are working to preserve indigenous knowledge. Here, Mike Immaruituq listens to Rosie Iqalliuq tell of the past, as he records her words for the benefit of future generations.

SHAMANISM: AN ANCIENT TRADITION OF SPIRIT MEDIUMS

Åke Hultkrantz

DURING THE LAST CENTURIES, shamanism has been a characteristic feature of, in particular, the Arctic or circumpolar peoples and their neighbors in Siberia. The word shaman itself, as *sama* or *saman*, originates from one of the Siberian peoples, the Tungus (now also called the Evenki, their own name for themselves), and refers to a person who has secret knowledge. Shamanism is thus the complex of beliefs, rites, and traditions clustered around shamans and their activities. What kind of secret knowledge do shamans possess?

A. MILOVSKY

ROBERT BRAUNMÜLLER

In many so-called scholarly works, shamans have been presented as little more than jugglers, who, thanks to their magic tricks and dexterity, persuade their tribesmen that they can change the ordinary course of events. Others have portrayed them as medicine men able to cure sick people with their magic. Some psychotherapists have even maintained that shamans are typically of low intelligence and exhibit a pathological, hysterical state of mind. (Women can also be shamans, but the masculine pronoun is used here for convenience.)

⚜ A Nganasan (Samoyed) shaman from the Taimyr district, in northern Siberia. To keep him on Earth during his trance, when his soul is transported elsewhere, he is attached to a pole with a chain.

Mediators with the Spirit World

Recent anthropological research has shown that shamans are people with a perfectly normal personality and, often, above-average intelligence. Their special role is to mediate between human beings—usually the members of their own tribe or social group—and supernatural powers. With the aid of an instrument, often

⚜ This Tungusian shaman's costume represents a bird, indicating the shaman's ability to fly while in a trance. The pendants on the costume depict guardian spirits in bird form.

a drum or a rattle, and/or intoxicants in the form of psychotropic herbs, mushrooms, or drinks, the shaman enters into a trance, thereby passing over into another, spiritual dimension. In the trance, he dispatches his soul to other realms, such as the sky, the

ocean, or the underworld, or to remote places on Earth. Here, it meets with gods and spirits and receives information from them, or snatches back the soul of a person that has been stolen by the dead: a cause of illness. Sometimes, the shaman calls on the powerful spirits and, in his trance, consults them about matters of importance to the community. He thus acts as an intermediary in many situations: as a diviner who foretells the future or the whereabouts of

The membrane of a Saami shaman's drum, from Swedish Lapland. The figures represent the sun and other gods and spirits.

A. MILOVSKY

A Nganasan shaman's drum, made of reindeer hide and decorated with symbolic animal figures.

game, as a finder of lost persons and articles, as an oracle who reveals what offerings or sacrifices the supernatural powers demand, and, occasionally, as a sacrificial leader. Most shamans are also medicine men, who can restore a lost or stolen soul to its ailing owner, or exorcise disease agents in the form of evil spirits or dangerous objects from the victim's body.

Guardian Spirits

The shaman's expertise derives from a combination of factors, including inheritance, ascetic training, and help from guardian spirits. In northern Siberian families, the position of shaman is sometimes inherited from a parent or other relative. In such families, the necessary quality of heightened nervous sensitivity is usually an hereditary trait. Or a young person aspiring to shamanhood

may submit to a lengthy period of fasting, thirst, sexual abstention, and isolation, until he becomes so weak that he loses consciousness and experiences a meeting with the spirits. Sometimes, particularly in South America, drugs are used. The spirits that appear in his dreams and visions become his helpers or guardian spirits.

When a shaman sinks into a trance, these spirits lend the assistance he needs. We hear, for example, of guardian spirits in the form of animals or birds that fly with the shaman's soul to the other world in order to retrieve a sick person's soul. Sometimes, the shaman transforms himself into one of his guardian spirits on this flight; at other times, he sends his guardian spirits on his behalf. In Siberia, Mongolia, and on the American Northwest Coast, shamans are occasionally possessed by their main guardian spirit, which then takes over the shamanic act: the shaman may speak with a foreign voice, or behave like an animal. Often, the shaman dons a mask, thereby assuming the spirit's personality.

The Shamanic Ritual

The shamanic experience usually takes place in the course of a ritual. The entrancement follows intensive drumming and singing by the shaman and other participants in the séance, or the taking of psychotropic substances. Sometimes, the shaman falls into a cataleptic trance, from which he must be awakened to tell of his experiences. In other cases, he sinks into a light trance, during which he describes his journey, lifts the figures of small animals when talking about his spirits, climbs a tree representing the world tree, in order to reach the supreme powers, and so on. When a shaman is possessed by his spirit, a very dramatic scene usually ensues.

There are also séances where several shamans together make an imaginary journey to the other world in a boat represented by wooden frames on the floor of the lodge. The pantomime is accompanied by mock fights with the dead and other theatrical events. The degree of trance on such occasions is, of course, open to interpretation.

COLLECTION VIOLLET

An Altaian shaman drumming, by means of which he will pass over into a trance. Most ethnic groups in the Altai mountains are Tatars, and their shamans often wear bird costumes.

An eighteenth-century engraving showing a Tungus shaman in action. The antlers on his head signify that he is a reindeer shaman, who may appear in a trance as a reindeer.

COLLECTION VIOLLET

The focus here has been on shamanism in the circumpolar area, but traces of shamanism are found in other areas as well—in South America, Southeast Asia, Oceania, China, and Korea. In the light of present-day knowledge of the history of ancient cultures, it would seem that the circumpolar area is the last refuge of Paleolithic cultural elements, as

modified by later developments. The practice of shamanism derives from a world of hunters, and the Paleolithic was the time when all humans were hunters, gatherers, and fisherfolk. There can be little doubt that the roots of shamanism go back to Paleolithic times, and that shamanism is one of humankind's oldest belief complexes.

TRADITIONAL PEOPLES OF NORTH AMERICA

A D   1 4 9 2   –   T H E   P R E S E N T

Survival and Persistence in the Wake of Invasion

FREDERICK E. HOXIE

BEFORE THE ARRIVAL of Europeans, the indigenous communities of North America faced numerous challenges in their day-to-day life as they sought to feed their families and defend their homelands from rival groups, all the while adjusting to environmental and technological changes. To survive, people throughout the continent had constantly to adjust their habits and ideas to new conditions, and to find practical solutions to unexpected problems. The products of their struggle, representing the sum total of thousands of adaptive strategies and inventions, were the hundreds of cultural traditions that had evolved by AD 1500. These ranged from the innovative farming strategies of southwestern desert dwellers, through the immense temple cities of Mississippian chiefdoms, to the elaborate rituals celebrated at midwinter in the cosy longhouses of northeastern farmers.

With the coming of Spanish adventurers in the sixteenth century, the challenges facing these "Indian" communities, as they were called, escalated dramatically. Waves of disease swept the continent, disrupting countless lives. Some groups fled; others were to die out completely. In the wake of this invasion of pestilence, armies of soldiers and settlers swept through the continent, breaking down complex trading and alliance systems that had been built up over hundreds of years, transforming the physical environment, and leaving many ancient homelands uninhabitable.

◄● Preparing for a celebration in Sheridan, Wyoming, these girls proudly put on the traditional dress that identifies them as descendants of North America's original people.

◉ A Salako kachina, carved by Arizona Hopis about 1900.
DENNIS LYON COLLECTION/JERRY JACKA

NORTH AMERICA AT THE TIME OF EUROPEAN CONTACT

Hundreds of tribes and communities, many of which had disappeared by the time of large-scale European colonization, do not appear on this map. Shown here, in the locations where Europeans first encountered them, are most of the Native American groups that played a significant role in Indian history after 1492. These groups include confederacies, such as the Iroquois, Blackfoot, and Creek, that encompassed smaller units; communities, such as the Chumash and Erie, that had nearly disappeared by 1900; and others, such as the Navajos and Ojibwa, that grew in size and influence during the same period. The map also identifies "new" tribes (Mashpee, Seminole, Lumbee, and Catawba) that consolidated their identity in the postcontact world of dislocation and change.

CARTOGRAPHY: RAY SIM

The newcomers declared themselves to be the "conquerors" and "tamers" of North America. In the eighteenth and nineteenth centuries, their descendants announced their intention to bring forth new nations on the land they had come to call Canada and the United States. These expansive plans did not include the indigenous peoples and their ancient traditions. There was a grudging promise to offer membership in the new societies to all Indians who would abandon their previous habits and beliefs in favor of Christianity, the English language, and adherence to European standards of governance and property ownership. But there was no willingness to accept Native American ways of life as an integral part of the national life.

Surviving the Onslaught

Remarkably, many communities survived this horrific onslaught. We cannot know the names of all the groups that disappeared, whether as a result of destruction, disease, or a private decision to disperse and start a new life among neighbors and allies, but they were many. From a precontact population of between three and five million in 1492, North American Indians had shrunk in number to fewer than one million by 1800. By 1900, the United States Census Bureau counted no more than 250,000 people living in Indian communities in that country, while its counterpart in Canada reported another 100,000. From this low point, the Native American population began to rise. (Disputes continue in both countries as to each government's enumeration techniques and skill in counting isolated groups of indigenous people, but the trend during the twentieth century has been unmistakably upward.) In 1990, more than two million Indians were living in the United States and Canada.

We know that some infectious diseases had affected Native Americans before 1492. Tuberculosis, for example, has been detected in some ancient human remains. But the principal killers in the centuries of conquest following Columbus's first voyage were the diseases brought across the Atlantic from Europe. Smallpox arrived soon after the Spanish had established a beachhead in Mexico in 1519; the plague came to New England with the Basque and Norman fishermen who camped and traded along this stretch of coastline during the sixteenth century; and influenza, diphtheria, and measles accompanied explorers to every corner of the "New World". The endemic diseases associated with the stressful conditions Indians faced as European settlement spread were also very destructive. Diabetes and alcoholism, for example, shortened life expectancy and reduced birth rates in native communities across the continent.

The survival of Indian people into the modern age has required them to confront a grim biological reality. Members of shrinking and harassed communities felt compelled to seek marriage partners outside their village or locality. Families that were prey to intruders, diseases, and persistent ill health were often forced to migrate or to seek help from churches and government agencies. Children left without parents or homes found their only refuge in adoptive families (both Indian and white) or in government-run orphanages, boarding schools, and charitable institutions. In order to survive, native groups have had to merge both with other native groups and with the non-Indian majority.

Despite these disruptions and changes, the communities that have survived to the present day remain intimately linked to the world of 1500. Some of these links are tangible. Native languages, despite the addition of new words, have retained their distinctive grammars and perspectives. Expressive of unique concepts of tense and person, they encompass the distinctive philosophical outlook of whole communities of Native Americans as well as a universe of place names, family designations, and terms to describe the natural world.

Similarly, certain locations have continued to represent a particular community's origins or its links with the spiritual world. Arizona's San Francisco Peaks, for example, are still the home of the Hopi deities called kachinas, despite the fact that this area has been incorporated into a national forest and desecrated by the building of a modern ski resort. Other physical links to the past include art forms such as basketry and carving, community festivals, and traditional forms of dress.

Far more compelling in forging a link with the past, however, are community activities that celebrate distinctively Indian ways of life and thereby sustain the traditions of individual groups. It is the people who have kept their traditions alive who have been the principal architects of Native American survival into the modern era. They include individuals who still speak their native language, elders who worship at sacred

sites, and artists who practice ancient weaving or carving techniques —but also religious leaders who have created and sustained new native rituals in the recent past, political leaders who have helped shape fresh approaches to community governance, and economic innovators who have devised new ways of surviving in an age of railroads and fax machines. Distinctive Indian communities have also grown out of the remnants of earlier groups, including disparate Indian refugees living in North America's mammoth cities and tribal bands occupying the same government reserve, or neighboring reserves.

Meeting the challenges of the past 500 years has required North America's native people to use all the ingenuity and creativity at their disposal. The strength of their spirit has enabled many groups to retain their language, their arts, and other concrete ties to the ancient past, and has also brought new community traditions into being.

Traditional peoples have survived into the present in many guises. Perhaps most easily recognizable are those who have preserved and safeguarded both the language and the splendid ceremonial dress of their ancestors, but there are also dedicated fishermen and ranchers who look upon their enterprises as community resources, and individual workers and professional people who have managed to uphold ancient values and community loyalties in an impersonal, urban environment.

NORTH AMERICAN INDIAN LANGUAGE GROUPS, c. 1492

While it is not always possible to trace postcontact communities back to their "prehistoric" roots, language families have had an enduring presence in many parts of North America. Shown here are the approximate locations of major language families at the time of Columbus's voyages. Language "families" include numerous local languages that appear to be related to one another and that probably evolved from a common parent tongue.
CARTOGRAPHY: RAY SIM

♀ Hopi women from Third Mesa make wicker baskets like this to supplement their family income and also to keep an ancient craft alive.

THE GRANGER COLLECTION

🔥 Amos Bad Heart Bull (1869 to 1913) captured the drama of mounted warfare in this portrait of the fighting near Montana's Little Big Horn River in 1876. Here, Sioux and Cheyenne warriors pursue the Seventh Cavalry, led by Colonel George Armstrong Custer. Bad Heart Bull drew in the pictographic style of his tribe and captured details supplied to him by men who had fought in the battle.

THE GREAT PLAINS: THE COMING OF THE HORSE

On the Great Plains, the arrival of Europeans signaled a dramatic cultural shift. The vast grasslands of the American interior had beckoned hunters for centuries, but large groups could not survive in this treeless environment for any length of time, and few communities ventured very far from the region's major river systems, the Missouri, the Platte, and the Arkansas. Following the successful Pueblo uprising against the Spanish in 1680, however, horses were suddenly loosed on the prairies. Some ran free, but most were rounded up to form a new currency for trade. Within 50 years of the expulsion of the Spanish from the Rio Grande, horses were a prominent feature of North American tribal life as far north as Montana and as far east as Kansas. Mounted on their ponies, the ancestors of the modern Sioux, Cheyennes, Comanches, Arapahoes, Osages, and Kiowas swept out onto the plains, taking what game they needed and moving their tipi camps across vast distances.

For these plains groups, as well as for their more sedentary neighbors, the Gros Ventre, the Mandans, the Pawnees, and the Arikaras, horses were a visible sign of God's blessing, bringing freedom and prosperity. In the eighteenth century, when the Europeans once again drew near, the Indians of the American West looked down on them from the backs of their ponies and battled fiercely to retain their new way of life. Led by such famous warriors as Crazy Horse, Roman Nose, and Satank, they fought the American soldiers in defense of their families, their horse herds, and their hunting grounds. Even when the bluecoat armies finally gained the upper hand at the end of the nineteenth century, the plains communities persisted in their struggle to keep their horses and the way of life they represented.

Cattle Ranching and Rodeo Riding

On a spring evening in 1806, the American explorer William Clark was camped along the Yellowstone River when a vast, migrating herd of buffalo passed nearby. The sound of their hooves was so deafening that he could only sit in wonder as they thundered past. Eighty years later, wild game had disappeared from the plains, and the Indian communities for whom horses had become a way of life had turned to other pursuits. Of these, ranching was by far the most attractive, and for the next half-century, Native Americans on the plains strove to establish themselves as cowboys and cattlemen.

As Indians retreated to reservations and the rail lines snaked across the west, entrepreneurs from the east saw this region as ripe for ranching. Running herds on public lands or leasing large tracts from defeated tribal leaders seemed a quick way to get rich. As early as the 1880s, non-Indian cattlemen were active from southern Arizona, on Pima and Papago lands, to the Dakotas and Montana, where they leased the Sioux, Crow, and Blackfeet reserves.

Even as white businessmen were flocking to join the cattle industry, Indians began to see the enterprise as a means of retaining some of their community integrity. Life on horseback had great appeal, and by working as cowboys and ranch hands, Apaches, Sioux, Blackfeet, and Cheyennes could work with their kinsmen in rhythm with the seasons. They could avoid the stifling atmosphere of the factory or cornfield, and hold on to a landscape filled with ancient associations. In 1900, Blackfeet ranchers had replaced buffalo with a herd of 10,000 Hereford cattle. Other groups followed a similar pattern, as tribal herds were established at the San Carlos Apache reserve in Arizona, among the Northern Cheyennes in eastern Montana, and among the Comanches in modern-day Oklahoma. In some cases, success stories occurred on a smaller scale. When the Rosebud, Standing Rock, and Cheyenne River Sioux reservations were opened to outsiders, for example, a number of tribal members were able to continue as cattlemen.

❦ In the age of the horse, even a bag for holding a pipe could be emblazoned with heroic images of the Plains Indians' new, mobile way of life.

❦ *Left*: This "horse dance stick" illustrates the way Plains Indians brought the powerful spirits of their horses into religious rituals as well as their daily lives.

❦ *Above left*: Even as they lost ground to white settlers, Plains Indian groups such as the Blackfeet celebrated their association with horses in decorated riding gloves and other paraphernalia.

❦ By the end of the twentieth century, Plains Indian people had lived with horses for more than two centuries. While no longer essential for hunting or travel, horses continue to be a part of everyday life: on ranches, as objects for decoration and display, or as prized possessions to be raced and traded.

THE NORTHWEST COAST: THE "RIGHT OF TAKING FISH"

In 1500, the Northwest Coast encompassed some of the most densely populated areas of North America. Villages stretched from the Oregon coast to southeastern Alaska, their inhabitants ranging from groups living north of modern-day Vancouver to communities on Vancouver Island and the many smaller islands that fill the bays and waterways for 1,600 kilometers (nearly a thousand miles). Living in elaborate, multifamily dwellings in settlements that hugged the coast, these Indian communities felt the bounty of nature all around them. Before the arrival of Europeans, streams and rivers teemed with fish, and whales and seals swam within reach of the shore. The dense coastal forests offered such a wealth of wild plants that there was no need for intensive agriculture.

➥ Separated only by time from his canoe-bound ancestors, this fisherman brings home the salmon he has just gathered from his nets near Puget Sound.

SEATTLE POST-INTELLIGENCER COLLECTION/MUSEUM OF HISTORY AND INDUSTRY

ROYAL BRITISH COLUMBIA MUSEUM, VICTORIA, B.C. NO. PN 242

🔥 Along the bays and inlets of the Northwest Coast, native communities built their cedar-plank houses to face the sea and decorated them with painted images of deities and family heroes. Other family symbols stood nearby, atop tall cedar poles, and the beach provided space for work, gossip, play, and commerce.

But the wealth of the Northwest Coast was more than material. The people of this region have long been oriented towards the sea as the source of their livelihood, but they also felt a deep sense of kinship with its creatures. The Haida of the Queen Charlotte Islands, for example, still say that the first human emerged from an open clam shell. Whaling captains from the Nootka tribe of Vancouver Island, who commanded dug-out canoes that ventured far out into the Pacific, believed that their success in stalking and killing their mammoth prey was conditional on their

showing the proper respect for these fellow creatures. This took the form of elaborate rituals requiring the harpooner to live apart from his family, fasting and praying for a successful hunt.

People who lived by fishing, hunting, and gathering similarly felt a deep affinity with the natural world, and expressed their respect for individual animals and plants in an intricate series of rituals and taboos. Even today, the first salmon to appear in the annual migrations each spring is welcomed into many coastal communities as a visitor. The fish is caught, roasted, and shared among the entire group. Only after this ritual is complete can the salmon harvest begin.

With the resolution of the Oregon boundary dispute between the United States and Great Britain in 1846, the Northwest Coast was opened up to rapid settlement by non-Indians. Territorial laws offered 130 hectares (320 acres) of land free to Americans who would settle in Oregon and Washington, and the government north of the 49th parallel in British Columbia offered similar incentives. Soon, settlers moved into a number of areas near Vancouver Island, around Puget Sound, and in the Willamette Valley.

Sawmills and Fisheries

There were few formal controls to constrain these newcomers, and within a decade, dozens of sawmills were operating along the riverways that had been the lifeblood of Indian subsistence. Loggers pushed back the dense forests that had covered hillsides for hundreds of kilometers along the coast, while immigrant fishermen moved into native fishing grounds. Much the same happened in Canada, but here there were fewer immigrants, and they did not have such ready access to eastern markets.

For the fishing communities of Puget Sound and the coast, anxiety over the pace of change was greatly reduced in 1854, when the American government sent Issac I. Stevens to the newly demarcated Washington Territory to negotiate a series of peace treaties with them. In the space of a few months, between the end of 1854 and the beginning of 1855, Stevens concluded four separate treaties with the Indians of western Washington. In exchange for pledges of loyalty and grants of land, the government agreed to assist tribal groups, to protect their lands, and to ensure that "[their] right of taking fish at usual and accustomed grounds and stations" would

tended by crews in steam-driven boats, could capture a huge proportion of the salmon that coursed annually along the Pacific coast. Inevitably, these new techniques overshadowed Indian netting and fishing practices and intruded on the tribes' "usual and customary" fishing grounds.

Led by the Lummi and other Puget Sound tribes, Indian spokesmen protested against the seemingly uncontrolled growth of the new fishing industry. Prodded by the tribes, the Indian Office brought a suit against one of the worst offenders. But the case failed, and the fishing industry continued to expand. By 1915, there were 41 canneries in the Puget Sound area, and state officials went unchallenged when they asserted that the regulation of Indian fishing was a local, not a federal, concern.

The culmination of this long struggle came in 1974, when Federal District Judge George Boldt stunned the entire region by ruling that the Stevens treaties were indeed binding on Washington State authorities. He further stated that the Puget Sound tribes were entitled to half the harvestable fish passing through their "usual and customary" fishing sites.

⚓ Made of wood and iron, this hook was designed to both lure and capture Pacific halibut. It was lowered to the bottom with a cotton cord.
EDUARDO CALDERON/THOMAS BURKE MEMORIAL WASHINGTON STATE MUSEUM, CATALOG NO. 4259

be secured "in common with [that of] all citizens of the Territory". This statement, which Stevens and his colleagues saw as a simple recognition of the tribes' dependence on the sea, was destined to become the instrument of a remarkable case of Indian survival.

In 1866, the first commercial salmon cannery opened alongside the Columbia River. Eleven years later, a cannery was established on Puget Sound. It was not until the 1890s, however, that commercial fishing, centered on sockeye salmon, emerged as a dominant industry along the Pacific coast. By 1899, 19 canneries were producing nearly a million cases of salmon a year, providing employment for hundreds of workers and fishermen.

While the early canneries were happy to process fish caught in the traditional way by members of the Puget Sound and other Northwest tribes, the rapid rise in the level of production encouraged experimentation in new technologies. In the course of the 1890s, it became clear that fish traps and purse seines (vertical nets drawn by two boats, which can be closed like a bag), laid out and

By the time the Supreme Court affirmed Boldt's decision, in the summer of 1979, Indians along the Northwest Coast had weathered five years of antagonism and local resistance. State officials refused to enforce court orders, non-Indian fishermen openly violated the new regulations, and other local agencies tried to lure the tribes into signing away their victory. Despite this opposition—and the attendant claim that the courts were creating "chaos" along the coast— the 1979 decision endorsed a broad federal effort to protect tribal fishing rights.

⚓ Carved for display at the 1893 World's Columbian Exhibition, in Chicago, this model shows a Makah whaling captain and his crewmen about to harpoon a Minke whale. In fact, Makah whaling crews typically contained eight men, and their prey were at least as long as their boats.
EDUARDO CALDERON/THOMAS BURKE MEMORIAL WASHINGTON STATE MUSEUM, CATALOG NOS. 96, 97

CHIEFLY FEASTS: ARTIFACTS AND MASKS OF THE POTLATCH

ALDONA JONAITIS

THE KWAKIUTL OF Vancouver Island hosted some of the most splendid potlatch ceremonies of all those held on the Northwest Coast, and created some of the most dramatic art ever made by Native Americans. Potlatches were hosted by high-ranking families for several reasons: to commemorate someone who had died; to acknowledge a family member's chiefly status; to celebrate the raising of a totem pole.

The potlatch was also the means by which a family validated its chiefly position. Among the Kwakiutl, status was embodied in material objects such as masks, feast bowls, and ceremonial regalia, as well as in speeches, songs, and dances. At a potlatch, the host family would display its unique objects and perform its special dances before an audience of invited guests. At the end of the event, the family would distribute vast quantities of goods, such as blankets, as well as cash, to the guests. This was a form of payment to the audience, whose role was to acknowledge the host family's claim to chiefly status. By accepting the goods, the guests validated their hosts' high position.

In 1885, in an attempt to assimilate the Kwakiutl into white society, the Canadian government outlawed the potlatch, believing it to be wasteful and pagan. Despite that law, and the fact that some people were imprisoned for potlatching, the Kwakiutl tenaciously held on to their traditions. The ceremony was decriminalized in 1950, and today, the Kwakiutl proudly continue to host potlatches.

⚲ One of the most dramatic types of art displayed at a potlatch was the transformation mask, which represents a legend from its owner's family history. This mask, when shut, depicts an eagle. The dancer pulls some strings, and the mask snaps open to reveal a human-like face.

ROYAL BRITISH COLUMBIA MUSEUM, VICTORIA, B.C., NO. CPN 13685

☝One of the most significant articles displayed at a potlatch is the copper, a shield-shaped plate of beaten copper that embodies a family's history and status. Today, families still proudly display their copper at potlatches.
HILLEL BURGER/PEABODY MUSEUM, HARVARD UNIVERSITY

◀This trade blanket featuring appliquéd images of a tree and coppers was bought by the Kwakiutl from merchants of the Hudson's Bay Company.

📍 This mask represents a hero known as Born-to-be-Head-of-the-World, who was mocked by his family for laziness. One day, he was magically transported to the Undersea Kingdom, where he encountered a number of supernatural beings. After he had traveled through the Undersea Kingdom, he returned home to his family, to whom he showed masks and other items of regalia he had obtained from the creatures of the Undersea Kingdom. He then became a great and respected chief.
LYNTON GARDINER/
AMERICAN MUSEUM
OF NATURAL HISTORY
NO. 4507(2)

FRANS LANTING/MINDEN PICTURES

◀The Kwakiutl potlatch tradition continues to be strong today. Here, Chief Fred Smith of Hee Gums hands out money at the end of the potlatch he held in 1984.

📍 This transformation mask is also associated with the legend of Born-to-be-Head-of-the-World.

LYNTON GARDINER/AMERICAN MUSEUM OF NATURAL HISTORY, NO. 4577(2)

177

OKLAHOMA: THE PEYOTE ROAD

◑ Peyote buttons like these were gathered along the Texas–Mexico border near Laredo and shipped north by railroad to fuel the expansion of the Native American Church. Dry and easily packed in boxes and barrels, peyote buttons could be distributed to Native American communities across the United States and Canada.

The survival of traditional values in yet another region of North America can be linked to the coming of the railroad, one of whose unexpected effects was to spread a previously obscure religious ritual among a large number of Indian communities in Oklahoma.

At the end of 1881, two rail lines entered the dusty, Rio Grande river town of Laredo, in Texas. As the new line cut across southern Texas, it passed through part of the tiny area of North America where the species of cactus known as peyote (*Lophophora williamsii*) grows. Long known to local peoples for their effect as a stimulant, peyote buttons had been used in religious rituals in the Rio Grande valley for centuries, giving participants the sensation of seeing and communicating with spiritual beings. Suddenly, they could be transported in bulk to tribes living outside the areas where the cactus grew—along with this powerful religious ritual.

Several elements of the new ritual had particular appeal for the reservation communities in Oklahoma at this time. The ritual was portable, focusing on the peyote button itself as a source of inspiration rather than on a particular place or tribal tradition. It promised to restore participants' health through prayer as well as through such practical measures as group sanctions against alcohol abuse. Singing in tribal languages and drumming were important traditional elements. And finally, like many tribal celebrations, the ritual usually lasted the entire night, ending with a communal meal.

At the turn of the twentieth century, the appeal of the peyote ritual was unmatched. Between 1900 and 1920, the religious use of peyote spread across the new state of Oklahoma, and then moved north to the Winnebagos of Nebraska; west to Taos Pueblo, in the Rio Grande valley; and far to the northwest to Plains Indians in Wyoming and Montana. Peyotists posed no threat to the government. They accepted most of the Indian Office's regulations enforcing Anglo-American norms of monogamy and sobriety, held their meetings on Saturday night and Sunday morning, and preached the virtue of hard work.

During the early years of the new century, the peyote ritual produced a new generation of Native American religious leaders. These people (most of whom were men) created a network independent of the federal government or any pre-existing tribal structure. They were comfortable with the English language and the workings of American law. Their main concern was to defend their ritual and to spread it to a wider audience.

Oklahoma peyotists formed the Native American Church in 1918 "to foster and promote the religious belief ... in the Christian religion with the practice of the Peyote Sacrament ... and to teach ... morality, sobriety, industry, kindly charity and right living ..." Celebrating a traditional ritual whose origins lay in North America rather than in Christian Europe, the peyotists understood the unique way it bound them to each other and to the ancient cultures of their land.

🔥 Painted in 1913 by Shawnee artist Ernest Spybuck, *Delaware Peyote Ceremony* shows male and female participants praying, singing, and drumming around the central fire. They wave eagle-feather fans and shake gourd rattles. The inset shows the morning farewell that ends the service.

Many stories surround the origins of the peyote ritual in Oklahoma, but most sources agree that during the 1880s, men of the Lipan branch of the Apaches, from southern Texas, began to conduct all-night ceremonies centered on the use of the drug among the Comanches and Kiowas living near modern-day Lawton and Anadarko. In a blending of old and new religious elements that became known as the "Peyote Road", the practitioners of this new rite sought to establish contact with Jesus Christ and with dead ancestors, and to promote both the spiritual and physical well-being of their communities.

THE INVISIBLE TRIBES OF THE EAST

East of the Mississippi, Native Americans were often forced to reinvent their communities in order to win recognition of their heritage from the whites who surrounded and vastly outnumbered them. Following the establishment of the United States and Canada, native people living close to European settlements were gradually forced westwards. Few tribal communities could survive amidst the nationalist fervor of the nineteenth century.

Influenced by popular stereotypes, white easterners had come to believe that the only "real" Indians lived west of the Mississippi. They could not accept the native people who lived among them as the kinsmen of western warriors or the inheritors of a tribal past. Forcing non-Indians along the Atlantic coast to recognize the region's native communities was one of the greatest victories won by Indian people in the modern era.

The process began in North Carolina in 1885. In that year, the local Indian people, who had always held themselves apart from both whites and blacks, rejected their designation as "free people of color" and petitioned the state legislature to recognize them formally as the Croatan Indians. The Croatans were descended from coastal communities that had been decimated and dispersed by Anglo-American settlers in the eighteenth century. When the legislature acted, eventually designating them as the "Lumbee Tribe" (after the river of the same name), the group was free to develop its identity as an Indian community. Exempted from attending nonwhite schools, the Lumbees formed their own educational system. They were offered support, albeit meager, to build their own classrooms, and in 1887, they founded a teacher training institution, Pembroke State College.

Another example of community redefinition occurred in Massachusetts. In 1869, the state legislature lifted a series of protective statutes, known as the Mashpee laws, that for centuries had prevented individual Indians (principally those living on Cape Cod) from selling their land to outsiders. Wealthy Bostonians immediately moved into the region, buying up cranberry bogs and ocean-front

lots and gradually replacing the local fishing economy with tourism and commercial agriculture. By the 1920s, much of the land in Mashpee, the largest Indian settlement, was owned by whites, even though Indians continued to harvest fish, game, berries, shellfish, and firewood.

Remarkably, even as they saw their land base evaporating, the Mashpees and other groups in the region continued to regard themselves as members of independent communities. They managed to retain most of their local leaders, along with a set of social customs that reinforced their sense of distinctiveness. In Mashpee, two young men, Nelson Drew Simons and Eben Queppish (the latter a veteran of Buffalo Bill's Wild West Show), were at the forefront of a movement to revitalize the community's sense of its Indian heritage. Simons, the town clerk, declared himself "chief" of Mashpee in 1921, while Queppish was designated the town's "medicine man". In 1928, in conjunction with leaders of surrounding communities, they formed a new organization known as the Wampanoag Nation. The following year, the group held its first powwow.

With its revival of traditional dances and ceremonies, the Wampanoag Nation helped to galvanize the loyalty of Mashpees and other Massachusetts Indians to their tribal past. These communities appointed their own leaders, continued to produce traditional handicrafts and to use folk medicines, and supported their local churches. As recently as the 1970s, the strength of their commitment became apparent when the white majority in Mashpee elected a local government dominated by non-Indians that was intent on implementing an ambitious program of real estate development. In response, the local Indians formed a tribal council and took the land developers to court in an attempt to win back some of their ancestral land. During the same period, the Indians of Martha's Vineyard successfully petitioned the federal government to formally recognize them as an Indian tribal government.

Although the Mashpees lost their lawsuit in 1978, they have retained a fierce sense of social solidarity along with their community traditions and ties. Similar struggles took place in communities across the region—in Maine, Connecticut, South Carolina, and New York—reminding the white majority that native people are a vital part of modern life along the Atlantic coast.

Early in the nineteenth century, government policies forced most tribes to remove themselves west of the Mississippi River. Nevertheless, groups of hardy tribespeople eluded the troops and agents and survived in isolated pockets. These "eastern" Cherokee women belong to a North Carolina community founded by men and women who escaped the government's grasp.

While contemptuous of people whose technologies did not include iron, Europeans quickly learned to appreciate the light and sturdy bark-covered canoes Passamoquoddy and other Algonquin groups used to navigate the rivers and bays of eastern North America.

THE GREAT LAKES: WINNING BACK THE "HARVEST OF THE WOODS"

The law has also figured prominently in the cultural survivals of the Great Lakes region. Here, in the centuries following 1492, the rich variety of hunting and semihorticultural societies that had occupied the lakes and rivers surrounding North America's vast inland seas had been gradually replaced first by Ojibwa bands, who pushed their rivals west and south, and then by European settlers. Mesquakies, Potawatomis, Kickapoos, Sioux, and many other groups gradually moved, or were forced to move, across the Mississippi. By 1900, enclaves of Ojibwa people lived as far west as North Dakota and as far east as Ontario. Scattered between them were remnant enclaves of Winnebagos, Oneidas, Potawatomis, and other peoples, as well as the Menominees, a group that had maintained a fairly permanent claim to the forests of northeastern Wisconsin throughout the period of white expansion.

Occupying the northern margins of the continent's arable lands, the Great Lakes Ojibwa and their neighbors were closely attuned to their forest environment. With little opportunity for agriculture, they had learned to harvest the resources of their wet, seasonal homeland. By moving in accordance with the migratory patterns of birds, the spawning habits of fish, and the seasonal habits of the larger animals, they "farmed" the creatures of the Great Lakes as efficiently as they tapped the region's maple trees and harvested its berries in summertime. Their reliance on the earth and its bounty was a mark of faith in Kitchie Manido, the creator. But this faith also required that the Ojibwas recognize another deity, Nanabush, the trickster, who could disrupt well-planned projects and irreverently thumb his nose at even the most sacred figures. Nanabush, too, was a part of Kitchie Manido's creation.

For many Indian people in the Great Lakes region, the survival of their traditions was tied to the survival of their forest environment. Even after the railroads reached the southern shore of Lake Superior, in the late nineteenth century, and lumbermen began clear-cutting the immense pine forests of northern Wisconsin, the Ojibwas and other groups rejected the idea that "progress" required a transformation of the landscape. Not surprisingly, the defense of these forests, along with that of traditional subsistence activities such as fishing, hunting, and gathering wild rice, came to represent the defense of Native American life in the Great Lakes region.

☙ Traders supplied Ojibwa artists with the colorful beads that adorn the sash holding this bag. The bag itself is decorated in an older style, with porcupine quills dyed with indigo and blood root.
HILLEL BURGER/PEABODY MUSEUM, HARVARD UNIVERSITY

♀ In warm weather, Ojibwa bands gathered in birch-bark wigwams to fish, trade, and renew their friendships. Villages such as this one, recorded by artist Paul Kane in 1845, often reappeared at favored fishing sites each season.

THE GRANGER COLLECTION

Enforcing Old Promises

Twentieth-century Indians in this region were fully aware that when their grandfathers and great-grandfathers had agreed to sell their lands to the United States and Canada in the first half of the nineteenth century, they had been careful to reserve their right to hunt and fish on the property they were ceding. Since the white population centers were so far away at the time, and the white negotiators were so certain that Native Americans would either disappear or be assimilated into "civilized society", it seemed a small matter to add guarantees of this kind to most land-sale agreements. As the non-Indian population began to multiply in the first decades of the twentieth century, however, white settlers and state officials found it convenient to overlook the old promises. Like their counterparts in the Pacific Northwest, provincial state and federal officials pointed out that it was no longer practical or efficient for the Ojibwas and their neighbors to continue to harvest the woods and lakes.

But the Indians who were still living in the Great Lakes region had little reason to abandon their old ways. American and Canadian expansion was apparent in the long reach of the railroad and the rise of the tourist industry, but the woods remained uncrowded, the streams continued to produce fish, and stands of wild rice could still be found along the lakeshore. Conditions were undoubtedly changing, making the boundaries between reservation land and surrounding white areas more important, but the Ojibwas and the other communities of Ontario, Wisconsin, Michigan, and Minnesota still lived within reach of their ancestral territories.

Challenges to native ways of life accelerated during the twentieth century. In an effort to remove Ojibwa, Menominee, and Winnebago children from the influence of traditional beliefs, the government and various missionary societies established a number of boarding and day schools. Timber merchants and settlers lobbied the government to divide tribal lands into individual plots for homesteads to be sold to non-Indians. Although much of the forest remained, the Great Lakes peoples grew increasingly uneasy.

Many communities in the north woods turned to religion for solace and support. The Dream Dance or Drum Dance, an eclectic ritual that emerged at the turn of the century and passed from the Winnebagos and Ojibwas to the Menominees, became popular on several reservations. With its emphasis on cooperation, generosity, and celebrations marked by singing and dancing, the new sect reinforced traditional beliefs and offered a form of group support. Among the Ojibwas, the Dream Dance was often promoted by followers of the Midewiwin, or Grand Medicine Lodge, a much older society, whose priests continued to induct members and to exert an influence on community affairs.

HIROJI KUBOTA/MAGNUM

The tendency of non-Indians to overlook the Great Lakes Indians' commitment to their traditions was exemplified in recent years by two political confrontations. In the 1950s, the federal government legislated that the Menominees should manage their vast timber resources without the protection of federal reservation status. The group was therefore "terminated" and transferred to the jurisdiction of the state of Wisconsin. Their reservation became a county.

Within a decade, it was clear that this had been a mistake. Unable to compete economically with better-equipped logging operations, harassed by state officials, and preyed upon by local land developers, the Menominees launched a sophisticated campaign to reverse the government's decision and return Menominee county to tribal status. Their victory in 1973 was unprecedented.

Even more dramatic were the efforts of a number of Ojibwa bands to exercise the fishing and hunting rights guaranteed them under nineteenth-century land cession treaties. After a federal judge ruled in 1983 that these rights extended to off-reservation lakes and public forests, 13 reservations joined together to form the Great Lakes Indian Fish and Wildlife Commission, with the aim of regulating native hunting and fishing—a move that met with violent opposition from sport fishermen and the tourist industry, but did not deter the native people from asserting their legal rights and celebrating their cultural heritage.

⚬ Each autumn, Ojibwas, Menominees, and others travel to the shallow waters of inland lakes to harvest wild rice (*Zizania aquatica*). Continuing an ancient technique, one person usually poles a canoe through the grass, while a second uses sticks to bend the stalks and "beat" the kernels into the boat.

CATHLYN MELLOANTS/THE PHOTO LIBRARY, SYDNEY

⚬ Even though the Great Lakes region has become heavily industrialized, Indian people, like these Menominee girls, still find occasions where they can wear traditional dress and enjoy each other's company.

NATIONAL MUSEUM OF THE AMERICAN INDIAN

FREDERICK E. HOXIE

FEW INSTITUTIONS better symbolize recent shifts in relations between American Indians and the general public than the National Museum of the American Indian. Founded in New York in 1916 as the "Museum of the American Indian", the original institution was rooted in the belief that native cultures were destined to disappear. Its original goals were to "collect and preserve for future study the aesthetic, utilitarian, and ceremonial objects of the tribes".

For 70 years, the museum sponsored expeditions, mounted exhibits, and welcomed scholars to its research facilities. Over time, however, the cost of sustaining its programs far exceeded its resources, and the institution's leaders grew uncomfortable with its narrow mission. As Indian communities persisted into the twentieth century, and growing numbers of native people entered the fields of history and anthropology, it seemed that the nearly one million objects in the museum's collections should be more closely linked to living Indian communities.

A Living Link

A resolution of the conflict between the museum's falling resources and rising ambitions emerged in the 1980s, when Senator Daniel Inouye, a champion of resurgent tribal communities, became convinced that an affiliation with the Smithsonian Institution could both revive the museum and provide an innovative link between Native Americans and the nation's premier cultural institution.

By 1989, both institutions had agreed on a formula under which the museum would become the National Museum of the American Indian, a part of the Smithsonian Institution's complex of museums, but would be governed by a 25-member Board of Trustees, 12 of whom would be Native Americans. The agreement also stipulated that the museum would have a new home in Washington, DC. Legislation introduced by Senator Inouye to implement this agreement was approved by Congress and signed into law by President George Bush in November 1989.

A New Era

W. Richard West, Jr, a member of the southern Cheyenne tribe, became the National Museum's first director in 1990. He announced an innovative series of programs that involve tribal representatives in museum policy making, re-evaluate the ways in which museum personnel handle and exhibit Indian artifacts, and move the institution into the fields of contemporary art, educational outreach, and the training of native museum professionals.

The new museum will come to life during the last decade of the century. In 1994, a revitalized New York exhibition facility opens in Manhattan's financial district; in 1997, a new cultural resources center will allow the museum's collection to be transferred to the outskirts of Washington, DC; and in the year 2000, the main facility, designed by Native American architect Douglas Cardinal, will open its doors at a site at the foot of Capitol Hill, placing native people and their heritage squarely in the center of the nation's most important cultural displays.

The confidence and pride of Plains Indian men are reflected in this magnificent headdress of eagle feathers, secured at the base with flannel, beadwork, and strips of fur. Such items have become greatly sought after by collectors. This headdress was made by the Prairie Crees of Saskatchewan, in Canada.

NATIONAL MUSEUM OF THE AMERICAN INDIAN, SMITHSONIAN INSTITUTION, NO. 14/7957

In Plains societies, social and ceremonial occasions called for special costumes, such as this beaded and fringed shirt made for a Crow child.
DAVID HEALD/NATIONAL MUSEUM OF THE AMERICAN INDIAN, SMITHSONIAN INSTITUTION, NO. 15/2395

Tribesmen of the Great Plains often carried shields like this into battle. Adorned with divinely inspired objects and designs, they symbolized the spiritual power warriors carried with them when they faced their enemies.
NATIONAL MUSEUM OF THE AMERICAN INDIAN, SMITHSONIAN INSTITUTION, NO. 22/8539

These dragonfly hair ornaments were made of rawhide and feathers by the Cheyenne of Montana.
DAVID HEALD/NATIONAL MUSEUM OF THE AMERICAN INDIAN, SMITHSONIAN INSTITUTION, NOS. 24.2440, 24.2441

Many museum collections contain objects, like this Seminole doll, that were made in the early twentieth century for daily use or for sale to visitors. While they seemed ordinary to their makers, such pieces have preserved an aspect of tribal life that might otherwise have been lost to future generations.
DAVID HEALD/NATIONAL MUSEUM OF THE AMERICAN INDIAN, SMITHSONIAN INSTITUTION

183

SPAIN'S FRONTIER "EMPIRE" IN THE SOUTHWEST

On the surface, the survival of Indian communities in the American Southwest has been a straightforward affair. Travelers in modern-day New Mexico and Arizona cannot help but see evidence of Native American life in the region's architecture and social life. Adobe buildings, Indian handicrafts, and colorful celebrations all communicate the continuing presence of indigenous peoples. Most striking is the huge Navajo reservation, home to more than 200,000 citizens of the Navajo nation, and a place where the Navajo language and Navajo religious practices thrive. Also impressive are the Pueblo communities of Arizona and New Mexico—from the Hopi towns perched on the mesas of central Arizona to the Rio Grande villages stretching south from Taos—which appear to have retained most of their ancient ways of life.

Unlike the indigenous traditions of the Pacific Northwest or Oklahoma, where traditional practices have been transformed and revised, the cultures of the Southwest appear to have remained largely unchanged during 500 years of contact with Europeans. Navajos herd their sheep across scenic landscapes; Pueblo communities celebrate their harvests each year. But as appealing as these tableaux might be, they are misleading. The Southwest did not escape the cultural pressures brought to bear on other parts of North America by foreign invaders. They simply experienced them at a different time and from a different source.

Unlike most other areas of North America, where initial contact was rapidly followed by large-scale European settlement, the Southwest remained on the periphery of the Spanish and American empires until well into the nineteenth century. Moreover, in contrast to Indians in other areas, who experienced the onslaught of Anglo-American settlement in the eighteenth and nineteenth centuries, the Navajos and Pueblos first encountered Europeans in the form of the Spanish. While there was a substantial time-gap between initial exploration and the onset of large-scale settlement in some other areas, such as the plains, nowhere was the interval between those two events so great as in the Southwest. And while other areas, such as Florida and California, started out under Spanish rule, they were later overtaken by the English and the Americans, who replaced Iberian and Mexican rulers with legions of Anglo-American settlers.

The first European incursion into the Southwest came in 1540, when Francisco Vasquez de Coronado and a troop of several hundred mounted soldiers, following tales of the golden city of Cibola northwards from Mexico, entered the Rio Grande valley. After subduing the Pueblos there, Coronado and his men continued eastwards as far as modern-day Kansas before becoming convinced that Cibola did not exist.

More than 50 years passed after the conquistador's brutal first foray before any significant attempt was made at Spanish settlement. In 1598, Juan de Onate entered the Rio Grande from the south, accompanied by several hundred colonists and more than 1,000 head of cattle. The Spanish established a series of permanent settlements, founded a capital at Santa Fe, and dispatched Franciscan friars to dozens of Indian villages. But just as suddenly as this frontier empire was created, it was swept away.

In 1680, a San Juan Pueblo religious leader, named Pope, led a general revolt of Indian villagers against Spanish rule. They killed two-thirds of the region's priests and nearly 400 settlers before the colony was abandoned and the remaining authorities retreated to El Paso.

🔥 The beauty of Pueblo pottery has been a constant thread in Southwestern culture, despite dramatic historical change.
JERRY JACKA

🌿 Perched at the north end of the Rio Grande valley for a thousand years, Taos Pueblo has withstood assaults from military enemies, missionaries, and legions of modern tourists.

JERRY JACKA

↪ *Opposite:* While most modern Navajos no longer rely on herding for their sustenance, the care of sheep, goats, and horses remains a valued feature of tribal life. These women tend their animals in Arizona's Monument Valley.

INDIAN CENTERS: CULTURAL OASES IN THE URBAN WILDERNESS

C.B. CLARK

MOST AMERICAN INDIANS today live in urban areas far removed from reservations. The 1990 Census of the United States population found 1,009,234 American Indians living in or very near cities and towns, and 950,000 living on or near reservations, out of a total of 1,959,234. For many Indians, the community centers that have become known as Indian Centers are a lifeline, providing the only warmth and friendly Indian faces they ever experience in the cold city environment.

An Urban Lifeline

Modern Indian Centers have their genesis in the dance or social clubs American Indians formed as a response to the profound cultural shock and alienation they experienced when they moved to cities. The first such clubs were established in big cities, including one in Los Angeles in the 1930s, and in the 1950s, the idea spread to smaller, provincial towns—Sioux City, in Iowa, being a notable example.

During the Second World War, many Indians left their reservations in search of work or to enter military service. A federal policy of relocation introduced in 1952 then induced a further 30,000 Indians to move into cities. This influx of relocatees, and the relatives who followed them, taxed the limited resources of both the clubs and those churches that were willing to assist the new arrivals. Of necessity, the clubs expanded their social services, developing into fully fledged urban Indian Centers in the 1960s. Since that time, these Centers, largely staffed by volunteers, have become the focal point of a complex network of intertribal organizations, providing a range of religious, health, economic, social, cultural, and athletic services for urban Indians.

Community Service

The Sioux City Indian Center, for example, offers a staggering range of social and cultural services. Located near two Indian reservations, this Center serves both reservation Indians and those living in the metropolitan region. Although Sioux City's estimated urban Indian population is only about 3,000, an astounding 46 different tribes are represented. Led by a Winnebago–Omaha Indian named Ernie Ricehill, the Center runs a meals program and a program called Project Care, which serves the needs of the elderly. Ricehill also sponsors cultural classes, oversees training for workers involved in rehabilitation programs for alcoholics, and organizes an annual Native American week filled with activities for the whole community, including community parties, hand games, and dances, as well as an AIDS awareness powwow. The Sioux City Indian Center is also a focus for action on Indian-related issues of community concern. In 1991, for example, the Center's leadership helped to keep the nearby Winnebago Hospital open, a move that benefited all residents in the nearby surrounding states.

Other Indian Centers provide services ranging from food banks to temporary shelter for transients. St Augustine's Indian Center in Chicago, founded in 1962, offers counseling, emergency cash assistance, legal and medical aid, job training, various forms of cultural enrichment for young Indians, summer educational and recreational activities, foster home placement help, and advocacy services in the local courts for both Indian children and adults. Like many community centers, however, Indian Centers suffer from a chronic lack of money, and are vulnerable to the whims of Congressional funding.

Keeping Tradition Alive

One of the most important functions of Indian Centers is to preserve the heritage of American Indians. The pow-wows they organize, featuring intertribal ceremonies, foster the exchange of Plains Indian symbols, songs, and tribal ways, which has reawakened feelings of tribal pride throughout Indian Country.

The Centers also preserve Indian traditions in less spec-tacular ways. An elder might give instruction one evening a week in beadwork techniques or basket-weaving styles. Another night, Indian men instruct young people in traditional singing and drum-ming. All the while, in the course of conversation, people are recalling their memories of the reservation they have left behind, and the relationships they knew there. A young girl sitting in a corner half-listens as two of her aunts doing beadwork swap stories with other Indian women of how Coyote continues to play tricks back home on the reserve. The pull of Indian tradition contin-ues even in the city.

CARRIE GOERINGER/RED EARTH, INC.

Two young children confer before they return to performing the circles upon circles of dancing at the Red Earth Festival in Oklahoma City, Oklahoma, June 1993. They, too, will experience the tribal affirmation, pride, and renewal that lie at the heart of the ceremonies.

Blending Ways of Life

Between 1680 and 1698, when the native peoples of the Southwest had regained control of the region, the horses and sheep left behind by the Spanish became valuable items of exchange within Indian trade networks, which ran north to the Great Basin and the Great Plateau and east to the plains. By the time the Spanish returned to New Mexico, these animals and other new commodities had permanently altered the Indian way of life across the entire western half of the continent. Within 50 years, horses were a common sight as far north as the Yellowstone Valley, and sheep were being grazed in central Arizona. In the Rio Grande, Indian farmers added melons and wheat to their repertoire of crops, while chickens and donkeys were part of village life.

Because the new rulers remained few in number—ruling from such towns as Santa Fe, El Paso, and Albuquerque—they did not displace their "subjects" from their ancestral homelands. The Pueblo people added the required Catholic church to their towns, but they did not forget

♀ With access to Spanish silver and freedom from direct domination, Hopi jewelers began to produce and market objects of extraordinary beauty.
WADDELL TRADING CO., TEMPE/JERRY JACKA

Pueblos of the Southwest has led anthropologists to coin a term to describe this remarkable ability to accommodate distinctive, even contradictory, practices and values within a single community: "compartmentalization".

The Navajos owe their cultural survival to two things: the Spanish practice of ruling from a distance and their remote location. Living on the periphery of the Spanish and American spheres of influence, they adopted a variety of European practices, including sheep-raising and silversmithing, but the dispersed nature of their settlements and the vast distances separating them from the Spanish and American garrisons protected them from direct control. At the same time, with their experience of the Rio Grande valley behind them, the Spanish had little interest in conquering the Navajos. The Navajos were eventually conquered, but not until 1868, and then by the Americans, more than 20 years after the latter took control of New Mexico. Even then, the Navajo people's resistance and resilience was merely blunted, not destroyed.

![St Jerome chapel image]

⚱ St Jerome chapel was built across the plaza from Taos Pueblo following the reimposition of Spanish authority in the Rio Grande valley.

their sacred mountains, springs, and shrines. They learned the Spanish language, but still retained their own languages, along with many of their older ceremonies and customs. As anthropologist Edward P. Dozier (himself a Santa Clara Pueblo) has written, "the Pueblos reserved the inner core of their culture to themselves and effectively warded off influences which might have disorganized and disrupted [their] tightly integrated … way of life".

The pattern established in the late seventeenth century has continued into the present. As the Mexicans succeeded the Spanish, and the Americans the Mexicans, Pueblo leaders accepted their new rulers without significant resistance. They agreed to accept priests and to obey the laws of the new regime. In return, they expected the newcomers to allow them a good measure of autonomy within their villages. Their cultural freedom was bought with political obedience. The unique history of the

♀ Like other Pueblo people, these dancers at San Ildefonso incorporate traditional forms of dress and instruments into community rituals that honor both their native and their Christian pasts.

FLIP NICKLIN/MINDEN PICTURES

Just as these Inuit hunters have made snowmobiles part of their daily life, so native people across the continent have adopted what is useful from the culture of the newcomers.

Modern Hopi carvers fashion replicas of their spiritual guardians as works of art and a source of income. This Mountain Sheep figure is the work of Myron Gaseona.

MᶜGEES BEYOND NATIVE TRADITION GALLERY, HOLBROOK/JERRY JACKA

EXPLODING THE MYTH OF A "DISAPPEARING RACE"

One theme unites these and other examples of native survival in North America over the past 500 years. No Indian community has remained unchanged by the onslaught of Europeans. For this reason, no group's survival can be attributed to its resistance to change. On the contrary, the tradition of adaptation that allowed indigenous peoples to adjust to new conditions and to take advantage of new resources for thousands of years before the coming of Europeans has been vital to their survival as distinctive communities during the last 500 years and into the present.

Examples of this ongoing tradition are to be found throughout the continent. In the Arctic, ancient subsistence practices have been overtaken by the arrival of the rifle and the snowmobile, but Inuit communities have incorporated this new technology into a long-standing village way of life, in which family ties provide a social "safety net" of mutual support in a harsh environment. Similarly, in the 1980s, groups of Florida Seminoles sponsored high-stakes bingo games in order to support village communities whose history can be traced back more than a century, thereby making use of tourism and entertainment to reinforce traditional Seminole relationships and customs.

A Tradition of Innovation

Two other features of modern Indian life have affected cultural survival across the continent. First, the population decline that began with the first European contacts in the fifteenth century has been reversed. American Indian populations began to rise in the first decades of the twentieth century. In 1890, there were fewer than 400,000 native people living in the United States and Canada—probably only 10 percent of the population existing in 1492. This figure had doubled by 1960, and had doubled again by 1980. By the 1990s, there were more than two million Indian and Inuit people in the United States and Canada. This rising trajectory of growth has fueled community optimism, increased the political influence of native communities, and, most important, exploded the myth of the "disappearing race" that had become so widely accepted at the end of the nineteenth century.

Second, there has been a revolution in the attitudes of the ruling authorities. For centuries following the arrival of Europeans in the Americas, native peoples were perceived as the antithesis of "civilization". "Savages" could be driven from their homes, separated from their families, robbed and tortured, all in the name of progress and the "development" of the "New World". This belief probably reached its apotheosis in Canada and the United States in the late nineteenth century, when military action against Indian noncombatants, vicious programs of forced acculturation, and government-subsidized missionary efforts were all carried out by men and women who claimed to be acting on behalf of some greater good. Then, almost as suddenly as this wave of ethnocentrism peaked, it crested and began to decline.

Clearly, racial animosity did not disappear in the twentieth century. But pity for the suffering of Indians, and curiosity about a culture that could continue to hold the allegiance of people through such long periods of intense suffering, gradually grew into a genuine interest in native ways of life. Since the time of the Spanish empire, isolated individuals have expressed sympathy for Indians, but in the early twentieth century, with the growth of professional anthropology and the rise of a campaign for racial and ethnic understanding in the United States, there emerged a critical mass of intellectuals, reformers, and government officials who could lead the public in a dramatically new direction. Playing a vital role in this process was the first generation of educated Native Americans— men and women such as Charles Alexander Eastman (Ohiyesa), Arthur C. Parker, Gertrude Bonnin (Zitkala-Sa), and, in Canada, Levi General (Deskeheh).

The administration of United States Commissioner of Indian Affairs John Collier ended official opposition to Indian dancing and religious ceremonies in 1933, while Canada's 1951

THE GRANGER COLLECTION

MICHAEL CRUMMETT

Indian Act repealed that government's ban on potlatch ceremonies and the sun dance, both of which are traditional to the Northwest Coast. Potlatch ceremonies had involved the distribution of massive gifts, and the sun dance often required self-mutilation. Both offended Euro-Americans. Nevertheless, in both Canada and the United States, modern tribal leaders emerged who spoke powerfully in defense of their communities' rights.

As the five-hundredth anniversary of Columbus's voyages passes, and the twentieth century draws to a close, it is clear to all North Americans that the Indian people have survived and will continue to survive as a vital element within the continent's social mosaic. Native communities exist in every region, and native people can be found in nearly every profession and trade. Uniting them across the vast landscape of their homeland is a common allegiance to each other, a common loyalty to their ancestry, and a remarkable ability to adapt and reformulate their traditions. But altered, diminished, or transformed, these traditions continue to shape the rhythms of community life and to define what it means to be an Indian.

♦ This modern depiction of the Cherokee tribe's forced exodus from Georgia suggests how Native American persistence has often overcome great odds. The sad but heroic figures elicit sympathy, turning the tables on the nineteenth-century politicians who thought the United States should be rid of its "savage" inhabitants.

♦ Gathering at dawn to absorb the strength of the sun, these Crow sun dancers symbolize the determination of contemporary Indians to hold fast to powerful traditions. The sun dance is a widely practiced religious festival of the Plains tribes, held annually in the late spring or early summer. Lasting for several days, it follows a closely pre-scribed format, from the choosing of the central lodge pole to the solemn placing of sacrificial gifts at an altar. Both men and women paint themselves and perform ritualized dances.

189

POWWOW: A POWERFUL CULTURAL REVIVAL

GEORGE P. HORSE CAPTURE

S AID TO BE a Narragansett Indian word meaning "medicine man" or "shaman", the word "powwow" has been given various meanings over the years, including that of a discussion, a meeting, or almost any kind of gathering. It is still commonly used to describe such events, but in Indian Country, it has kept its original sense of "power"—for powwow is the fastest-growing cultural activity within Indian communities today.

Powwow is the contemporary Indian's celebration of life and cultural survival, and is acclaimed across Indian Country. It is a festive ceremony of the past and the future, incorporating dance and song. Groups of singers and drummers, together with dancers from different age groups and different tribal traditions, join together to engage in friendly competition. Everyone is involved: young and old, men and women, all celebrating their Indianness.

A People, a Drum, and Joy

Every viable Indian community has a powwow, and its components are simple: a people, a drum, and a cultural joy. Sponsoring such a complex event is the responsibility of a rotating dance committee, which hosts various fund-raising events to finance the food, gifts, and prizes that will ensure its annual powwow is well attended and a great success. Since the sponsors of the event must also feed their guests, the dance committee has a responsibility to the entire camp.

The best powwows are held out-of-doors in the summer months, when the weather is good and hot. Somewhere in Indian Country, a host community will provide a large, centrally located arena (which can be roofed or open to the sky), outhouses, and a supply of fresh water.

People begin gathering on a Thursday, their "camps" ranging from recreational vehicles to nylon pup tents or stately tipis, all arranged in a large circle around the arena. When they are not themselves performing, they will watch the events from their own lawn chairs or from the permanent benches at the sides of the arena, which is always open to the east.

Dances Old and New

The celebration begins on the Friday evening with the children's dance events. These are junior equivalents of the adult categories, which start the next day. On Saturday, the contests and excitement continue, with events for teenage boys and girls. The finals of all categories are held on the Sunday evening, when the winners are announced. Throughout the weekend, dancing contests alternate with intertribal dances, where everyone dances for pure pleasure.

Contestants in all categories must follow the rules relating to age and form of dress. The word "costume" is considered to be demeaning: the accoutrements of the different dances have been handed down for hundreds of years, and represent the authentic traditions of the Indian people.

ALEX WEBB/MAGNUM

⬅ Grass dancers wear flashy, multi-colored bustles fashioned out of long, brightly colored yarn fringe, which sway and twist as they dance.

➡ Young girls in traditional dress stepping high in the dance category known as fancy dancing.

Each day there are two identical dance segments, one starting at midday and the second taking place in the evening. The Grand Entry opens both segments. Each event follows a prescribed format, or ritual. The singing groups sit around their drum, near the perimeter of the dance area, ready to perform in turn. The host drum then begins the first song, leading the dancers into the arena.

Walking side by side, the honor guard, who are always military veterans, carry the flags: the stars and stripes, and the crooked feather lance—the Indian flag. Following closely behind are the dignitaries: a veteran's group, a tribal politician, the sponsoring dance committee, and the Indian princesses. Then come the traditional men—the warriors, the spiritual leaders, and the chiefs. Some wear the time-honored eagle-feather warbonnets, but most are dressed in the old way, adorned with the black and white feathers of the golden eagle. Their style of dancing is slow, stately, and respectful.

Next come the male grass dancers (formerly known as fancy dancers), wearing flashy, multi-colored bustles fashioned out of long, brightly colored yarn fringes, which sway and twist as they dance their flowing style. Young boys then perform in exactly the same events.

The women have similar dance categories. Traditional dancers dressed in their elk-tooth or beaded buckskin apparel lead, and the fancy, or shawl, dancers follow, along with the new "jingle" dress style. Young girls, wearing similar outfits, then perform in the same events.

All the participants, dancing in the same rhythm, enter with a sense of tradition, pride, and glory, making the dust fly and the earth tremble. Their hearts soar.

The dancers all wear eagle feathers in some form as a mark of respect for this honored bird. The eagle is not only beautiful and strong, but also has the ability to fly the highest in the sky, perhaps delivering prayers

JIM BRANDENBURG/MINDEN PICTURES

to The One Above. These qualities make it special.

Armbands, headbands, belts, harnesses, purses, leggings, moccasins, and most everything else are brightly decorated with quillwork and glass beadwork. This form of Indian art adds color everywhere, and draws the generations closer together. Animal furs are plentiful, too, adding their ancient beauty to the proceedings. The painted faces and vivid symbols add another deep meaning, and express the close bond between different tribal beliefs.

Powwow is a happy, joyous time of celebration. As people dance, they greet and shake hands, enjoying one another. They look around, taking a mental inventory, seeing who has made it through the harsh winter. They notice the many new dancers on the floor—a sure sign of cultural continuity. They note the new dance outfits and wonder what new styles may appear, for change is essential to growth. One can survey the dance arena enveloped in a milieu of sound, color, and Indians. This world is totally ours. Perhaps this world is the closest we can ever get to the days of old, when things were better. However, this celebration provides us with strength for the future. We are close to The One Above here.

A Sioux dancer from the Rosebud Reservation in South Dakota. Outfitted from head to foot like the old ones, people come to powwows to dance. As the tempo quickens, they dance harder, until the music and the unifying rhythm are overwhelming.

A Celebration of Life

These dances and ceremonies are vital to us, and more and more of them are performed at powwows. It is here that ceremonies and presentations take place: children receive their Indian names; a deceased mother is remembered; a young child dances for the first time; a graduating college student or returning war veteran is honored.

After the Grand Entry and the intertribal dances, some participants rest. Removing their fragile feathers, they stroll around the arena, enjoying the celebration of life, eating Indian fried bread, buying beadwork. Kids and dogs scurry around, while the girls giggle and the young men strut. The laughter, noise, songs, color, scents, and everything else add to the excitement. It is a grand time. It is good to be an Indian, for this is our world.

American Indians have suffered in many ways since 1492, and suffer even to this day. In His infinite wisdom, The One Above provided a positive balance to the bad things: He gave us Spirituality, Earth, and Powwow.

JIM BRANDENBURG/MINDEN PICTURES

191

192

TRADITIONAL PEOPLES OF SOUTH AMERICA

A D 1 6 0 0 — T H E P R E S E N T

From Tierra del Fuego to the Amazon

ROBERT L. CARNEIRO

ONSIDERABLE CONTROVERSY still surrounds the date when human beings first entered South America. But we know from radiocarbon analysis that by 8000 BC, Paleoindians, as the earliest known inhabitants of the New World are called, had reached the southern tip of the continent, and earlier radiocarbon dates indicate that they were living in more northerly regions of South America a few thousand years before that. By the time Europeans arrived on the scene, no major part of the continent remained uninhabited.

The Indians the Europeans encountered varied greatly in their degree of cultural development, ranging from the tiny, simple, nomadic bands of the Yahgan to the vast, powerful, and complex empire of the Inka. The larger, wealthier societies were those that most aroused the cupidity of the Spaniards, and were therefore the first to fall to their crossbows and arquebuses. The societies that proved best able to survive, with most of their culture intact, were the small, unobtrusive groups scattered over lowland South America. It is the representatives of these societies that will be sketched here, as they existed at the time Europeans first encountered them.

Beginning our survey at the southern tip of South America and proceeding up the continent is not only geographically convenient but also successively brings into view more complex cultures.

◄ᴑ Among the Yanomami, who live in the border area of Venezuela and Brazil, young women decorate themselves with thin sticks inserted into small holes around the mouth and through the septum of the nose.

◉ Ornaments like this one, made of macaw, tanager, and honey creeper feathers, are worn by men of Brazil's Urubú-Kaapor tribe in an opening in the lower lip.

PEOPLES OF TIERRA DEL FUEGO

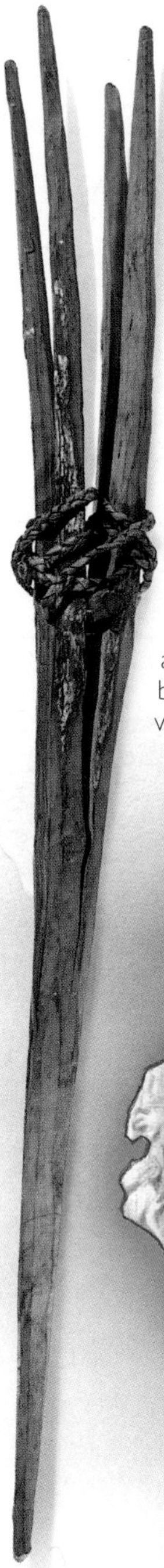

◀◎ Living along the southern coast of Tierra del Fuego, in present-day Chile, the Yahgan used four-pronged wooden spears like this to catch sea urchins.
J. OSTER/MUSÉE DE L'HOMME

◉▶ A Yahgan man shows how to throw a spear or harpoon. The spear, in the foreground, has a wooden shaft and a barbed bone point lashed with a rawhide thong.

Tierra del Fuego, the most southerly inhabited island on Earth, was the home of two quite different tribes, the Yahgan and the Ona, often contrasted as "Canoe Indians" and "Foot Indians".

The Yahgan: The Most Southerly People on Earth

Along the numerous isles and inlets of the extreme southern coast of present-day Chile lived the Yahgan. At a latitude of about 56 degrees south, they were the most southerly people on Earth. Existence on those rocky shores was hard, and the Yahgan enjoyed few amenities. Charles Darwin encountered the Yahgan in 1833 during the voyage of the *Beagle*, calling them "the most abject and miserable creatures I anywhere beheld".

In their simple bark canoes, the Yahgan ranged along their rugged coastline, subsisting mainly on fish and shellfish. Using special wooden forks, women dislodged mussels from the rocks and dived into the icy waters to strip shellfish from their underwater beds. Women also caught fish with a baited line, without a hook, or with a two-pronged spear, and men hunted sea mammals with spears and harpoons. Every once in a while, a beached whale provided a surfeit of food, and on such occasions, several normally independent bands would gather together to feast on the carcass.

A common type of Yahgan shelter was a beehive-shaped hut, consisting of a circular framework of boughs bent over at the top and then covered with grass, brush, or beech bark. Flimsy and drafty, they afforded little protection from the biting cold and piercing winds, and Yahgan clothing was similarly scant. Besides a leather pubic covering, the Yahgan wore only a small square of animal skin draped over their back, moving it from one shoulder to

SOUTH AMERICA
Although many tribes have become extinct, hundreds of them still survive in South America, especially in Amazonia, where the dense rainforest environment has protected them from outside encroachment until recently. The tribes located on the map are those mentioned in the text.
CARTOGRAPHY: RAY SIM

[Map of South America with labels:]
Orinoco River
Magdalena River
YEKUANA
GUIANAS
WAYANA
YANOMAMI
Rio Branco
Rio Negro
WAIWAI
TUKANO
Putumayo River
Amazon River
JÍVARO
YAGUA
OMAGUA
TAPAJÓ
TUPINAMBÁ
Ucayali River
Purús River
Tapajós River
Juruá River
MUNDURUCÚ
Xingú River
Araguaia River
INKA
SHIPIBO
Madeira River
KAYAPÓ
Tocantins River
SURUÍ
TAPIRAPÉ
AMAHUACA
Guaporé River
TXICÃO
KARAJÁ
CAMPA
YAWALAPITÍ
KAMAYURÁ
GRAN PAJONAL
MOJOS PLAIN
KUIKURU
São Francisco River
MANASÍ
SHAVANTE
Paraguay River
MBAYÁ
GRAN CHACO
LENGUA
PILAGA
MATACO
TOBA
TUPINAMBÁ
ABIPONES
Paraná River
PUELCHE
PAMPAS
TEHUELCHE
PATAGONIA
ONA
Tierra del Fuego
YAHGAN

⚓ A Yahgan family. The woman is wearing a typical small mantle of animal skin with the fur inside.

MUSÉE DE L'HOMME

MUSÉE DE L'HOMME

the other according to the direction of the wind. For protection from more intense cold, they smeared their bodies with grease.

The Yahgan lived in bands of five or six to a few dozen people, which camped in the same spot for no more than two or three days, unless a lucky catch allowed a longer stay. Although there was no chief, a man known for his intelligence, experience, and good judgment was more influential than others when group decisions had to be made.

The Yahgan had two important ceremonies, usually held when a stranded whale brought several bands together. One was a puberty initiation ritual, the *čiexaus* ceremony, which both boys and girls had to go through twice before they could marry, and involved a great deal of moral instruction. The other, the *kina*, served to reinforce the subordinate status of women through the recounting of a myth of a time when women dominated men, until the men, discovering that the women were merely impersonating the spirits by donning masks, overthrew them and established their own dominance.

⚓ The Ona were "Foot Indians", who occupied the interior of Tierra del Fuego, in present-day Chile and Argentina. They dressed for warmth in cloaks of guanaco skins, worn with the fur side out. The guanaco was the favored prey of these hunters, but they also hunted smaller game, using bows and arrows made with great skill.

◀ Ona men wore body paint, down, and bark or hide masks to impersonate spirits in the *klóketen*, the male initiation rite. Women and uninitiated boys were not supposed to witness this ceremony, which took place over several months.

The Ona: "Foot Indians"

North of the Yahgan, in the interior plains and hills of Tierra del Fuego, in present-day Chile and Argentina, lived the Ona. These people were "Foot Indians", who exploited the food resources of the prairies and forests.

Ona shelters were not unlike those of the Yahgan, consisting of semicircular windbreaks made of a framework of poles draped with guanaco hides. (Guanacos are thought to be closely related to the wild ancestor of llamas.) But the Ona dressed more warmly than the Yahgan, in cloaks made of guanaco skins, worn with the fur side out. The guanaco was

the Ona's principal quarry, but they also hunted smaller game, such as foxes, wild fowl, and a small burrowing mammal called a *tuco tuco*. Their weapon of choice was the bow, which they made with consummate skill, and their tiny arrowheads were the most delicately chipped of all in South America.

Although their languages were not related, the Ona and the Yahgan had some contact with, and influence on, each other. An example is the Ona's *klóketen* ceremony, which was a male initiation rite and a symbolic means of keeping women in subjection—similar, in that respect, to the Yahgan *kina* ceremony.

GUNTER ZIESLER/BRUCE COLEMAN LTD

⚇ Guanacos graze at sunrise near the foothills of the Andes. The favorite prey of the Tehuelche, who inhabited present-day Argentina, as of their neighbors the Ona, guanacos are wary animals and difficult to catch. They were hunted on horseback, and also stalked on foot with the help of camouflage and, sometimes, a tame young guanaco used as a decoy.

⚇ In this engraving made in 1602, a tall Patagonian Indian swallows an arrow to cure his stomachache, as a small European looks on. In early Spanish accounts, the Patagonians were described as giants.
THE GRAINGER COLLECTION

⌖ A Tehuelche woman moving to a new camp site, her horse loaded with the family's possessions.

THE TEHUELCHE OF PATAGONIA

Across the Straits of Magellan, stretching 1,600 kilometers (1,000 miles) northwards along the length of Patagonia, in present-day Argentina, were the lands inhabited by the Tehuelche. Linguistically, the Tehuelche were related to the Ona, both speaking a language of the Chon family. When first encountered by Magellan, they were probably much like the Ona as just described, but by the end of the eighteenth century, their way of life had been totally transformed by the acquisition of the horse. Horses that had escaped from Spanish ranches near Buenos Aires provided their first mounts, and the Tehuelche soon became expert horsemen. The present-day gauchos, the cowboys of Argentina, learned their style of riding from the Tehuelche, the Puelche, and other equestrian tribes of Patagonia and the Pampas.

The name "Patagonia" itself derives, in a peculiar way, from the Tehuelche. When Magellan landed on the southern coast of this region, the first traces he found of its inhabitants were huge footprints in the sand. These were the imprints of the Tehuelche's bulky footwear, fashioned from guanaco hide, with the fur side out, and stuffed with straw. Magellan called these unseen people "Patagones", which is Spanish for "big feet".

The Tehuelche were imposing physical specimens—tall, broad-shouldered, and muscular. Indeed, for more than two centuries, they were reported to be giants. Pigafetta, the chronicler of Magellan's voyage, wrote that a Spaniard standing at full height came only to the waist of the average Tehuelche. Later navigators, following suit, described these Indians as being 3 to 3.5 meters (10 to 12 feet) tall. But later observers gradually whittled them down to their true size, an average of about 180 centimeters (5 feet, 11 inches), which still makes them the tallest Indians in South America. They wore large mantles sewn from guanaco skins, worn fur side in, and belted at the waist with a leather thong.

The Horse and the Bolas

Horses transformed Tehuelche culture in much the same way they transformed the culture of the Plains Indians of North America. Tehuelche bands were always fluid in composition, but before the introduction of the horse, they probably did not exceed 50 or 60 people. Horses not only gave them greater mobility, but also made it possible for them to congregate in larger groups. Foreigners traveling with the Tehuelche in the 1830s and 1840s reported bands ranging from several hundred up to a thousand or more. Large bands camped together during the winter, but in spring, people broke up into smaller groups. Mounted on horses, they were able to range 1,600 kilometers (1,000 miles) or more over a year.

The Tehuelche were hunters par excellence, their favored prey being the guanaco and the rhea. (The rhea is one of two species of South American ostriches.) Plant foods played a very minor role in their diet. Once they began to hunt on horseback, they abandoned the bow and arrow in favor of the *bolas* (meaning "balls" in Spanish). The *bolas* are a weapon consisting of two, or sometimes three, leather cords about 2.5 meters (8 or 9 feet) long, each with a stone ball attached to one end. The *bolas* are whirled around the head until centrifugal force drives the balls apart. At that moment, they are released, and go spiraling towards their target, usually the legs or neck of a guanaco or rhea. Entangled in the *bolas*, the animal was immobilized and could be dispatched with a knife or a club. Tehuelche men became extremely adept with the *bolas*, and could hurl them accurately even at full gallop.

NORTH WIND PICTURE ARCHIVES

Patagonia is a harsh environment, described by one observer as "wild, bleak, blasted, and weird". Winters are cold and snowy, with winds of astonishing violence, capable of blowing a man clear out of his saddle. But between the lava beds and boulder fields, the Patagonian plains support vast numbers of guanacos. The animals live in groups of some 20 to 30 during much of the year, but during the mating season, herds of 500 or more may form. Throwing off their mantles to free their arms, the Tehuelche would gallop into the midst of such a herd, swinging their *bolas*, letting them fly, and entangling one guanaco after another.

In small herds or singly, guanacos are wary animals and hard to catch. In such cases, they were stalked on foot, perhaps using a tame young guanaco as a decoy. When the hunter had worked his way to within striking distance of his quarry, he would dispatch it with a lance.

Rheas, whose meat the Tehuelche preferred to guanaco, were sometimes run down with the aid of dogs, which were apparently present in prehispanic times. When a nest was found, the eggs were eagerly seized. The contents were removed through a small hole drilled in one end and cooked, omelet-style, while the shell was kept for use as a water bottle.

Skilled and mobile hunters, with access to abundant game, the Tehuelche enjoyed a secure subsistence. When there was a surplus of meat, it was cut into thin strips, lightly salted, and dried in the sun. The result, known by the Quechua term *charquí*, is the source of the English word "jerky".

A Mobile Society

When encamped, each Tehuelche family lived in a curved, skin-covered windbreak called (from the Spanish) a *toldo*, sleeping on horse hides laid on the ground. When the band broke camp, the *toldos* were dismantled, and the poles and skins loaded on horseback and carried to the next camp site.

A Tehuelche band was organized around the person of a *cacique*, or chief. In peaceful times, the chief chose the camp site, decided the route of the day's march, and, when necessary, directed communal hunts. Beyond this, he had little authority, and a family dissatisfied with his leadership was free to leave the band and join another.

When hostilities broke out, the *cacique* took on the role of war leader. In combat, the Tehuelche used a long lance and the *bola perdida* (literally, "lost ball")—a single *bola* hurled at the target to strike rather than entangle it. Prisoners taken in war were kept as slaves of a sort, being forced to do such menial tasks as fetching wood and drawing water, but otherwise lived much as everyone else.

Considerable differences in wealth developed among the Tehuelche, manifested primarily in the number of horses a man owned. Bride payment took the form of horses, ranging from 7 mares for a girl of no particular status to up to 100 for the daughter of a wealthy *cacique*.

The Tehuelche believed in the existence of a variety of evil spirits called *gualichus*, and had various strategies for ridding themselves of their baleful influence. For example, a group of men might ride at dawn across the plains, howling and gesticulating wildly, in an attempt to scare away the spirits.

Gualichus were said to cause illness by invading a person's body. A shaman called in to effect a cure took the victim's head between his knees and shouted into his ear to drive out the offending being. When a person died, the body was placed on a hilltop and a cairn of stones built over it. The more important the person, the bigger the cairn. When passing the cairn of a great chief, people were expected to add a stone to it. At a man's death, his favorite horse was killed, stuffed with straw, and mounted on four posts by his grave.

The Tehuelche were inveterate gamblers. On a few rolls of the dice (carved from the thigh bone of a guanaco), a man might bet, and lose, his *bolas*, his lasso, his saddlery, and even his horses. They also enjoyed vigorous sports, including horseracing and a form of field hockey, in which opposing teams slapped at a puck made from a round knot cut from a tree "apparently without clear order or system", according to a nineteenth-century observer.

♂ A Tehuelche horseman about to kill a puma by hurling a one-ball *bolas* at its head. The Tehuelche hunted guanacos, rheas, and deer using two-ball and three-ball *bolas* to entangle their legs.

♂ The rhea, a large South American flightless bird, was hunted for food and feathers by the Tehuelche.

◄ A Tehuelche family in front of their *toldo*, a lean-to dwelling covered with skins. At the birth of a male child, a mare was slaughtered and the newborn placed briefly in the mare's open chest cavity to help the child to grow up to be a good horseman.

THE LENGUA OF THE CHACO

❦ Among the Lengua, of present-day Paraguay, a ceremony known as the *yanmana* was held in honor of a girl's coming of age. Holding cane staffs with deer-hoof rattles at the top, the women danced in a circle, chanting and marking time by striking the staff on the ground.

Further north, beyond Patagonia and the Pampas, lies the Gran Chaco, a region now divided among Argentina, Paraguay, and Bolivia. The several dozen tribes who once lived here were originally all Foot Indians. With the arrival of the Spaniards early in the seventeenth century, some Chaco tribes, such as the Abipones and Mbayá, took to using horses, thus creating the distinction between "Horse Indians" and "Foot Indians". The Lengua, of what is now the Paraguayan Chaco, were a typical Foot Indian society.

The Chaco is a transitional zone between the grassy pampas to the south and the tropical rainforest to the north. It is one of the flattest regions on Earth, the land sloping to the southeast at an average grade of only 6 or 7 centimeters per kilometer (a few inches per mile). It is also an area of great climatic extremes, with summer temperatures often reaching a high of 41 degrees Celsius (106 degrees Fahrenheit) in the shade, making it the hottest region in South America. The ground becomes so hot that the Lengua, despite their hardened, calloused feet, wore sandals when traveling across open country in summer.

Along the margins of the rivers, gallery forests provide strips of arable land, which some Chaco tribes, including the Lengua, farm on a small scale. Away from the rivers, the grasslands were interspersed with patches of arid-zone vegetation, such as cactus and *caraguatá*, or wild pineapple. Fibers extracted from *caraguatá* leaves were widely used in this region to make cordage.

The Chaco supported a great variety of animals and plants, offering the local tribes a broad-based subsistence. Tribes such as the Lengua, Toba, and Pilagá were predominantly hunters, fishers, and gatherers, but practiced a little agriculture.

The Lengua relied principally on hunting for their food supply, and this activity occupied most of Lengua men's time. It required great skill, fortitude, and endurance, since hunters had to spend many hours searching for game under an intense sun, all the while subjected to relentless attacks by clouds of insects and lacerations from razor grass in the savanna and thorns in the forest.

During the wet season, the areas of swamp expanded, becoming home to millions of wild fowl, which were a major source of food. Game birds were hunted in various ways: by sneaking up on them and clubbing them with sticks, or diving underwater, grabbing them by the feet, and pulling them under.

The most important game bird, however, was the rhea, called the *ñandú* in the Chaco. Somewhat larger than the Patagonian rhea, it is known for its curiosity, and was often taken by subterfuge. A hunter, hiding behind palm fronds and imitating the cry of a young rhea, would sneak up on a bird until close enough to loose an arrow.

To hunt deer, tapirs, peccaries, and capybaras, the Lengua generally used bows and arrows. Jaguars were caught in pit traps. Hunting the white-lipped peccary was a particularly dangerous enterprise. The Lengua would sneak up on a herd, run suddenly into their midst with a great shout, and club the slower animals to death as the rest fled in all directions.

Late in the rainy season, fish became abundant, and for two or three months provided the Lengua's main food. They were variously shot with a bow and harpoon arrows, or caught with fishhooks, nets, and traps.

Palm hearts and honey were considered to be delicacies. If tender, palm hearts were eaten raw; otherwise, they were boiled or roasted. A few plants were cultivated, but living a nomadic life, the Lengua could not closely tend their gardens. The principal crops were sweet potatoes, maize, and manioc, tilled with a simple wooden spade.

A Fluid Social Structure

Being so dependent on wild food, for most of the year the Lengua moved in response to the seasonal cycle. At the height of the dry season, they

🔥 Camouflaged with foliage, a Lengua hunter stalks rheas, his bow and arrow held in readiness.

congregated around any remaining lagoons or waterholes, or camped along rivers. During the rainy season, they frequented the swamps, where fish might be found in abundance.

Lengua bands averaged well under 100 people, and because their sources of food were sparsely distributed, the people, too, were scattered. In the course of a day's march, they might easily cover 15 to 30 kilometers (10 to 20 miles).

The Lengua built two types of huts. One was made of boughs set into the ground in a circle and then bent over and interlaced at the top, with grass, rushes, or palm leaves heaped on the framework to help keep out the rain. The second consisted of a simple, rectangular frame with a roof made from a couple of reed mats. Inside, animal skins served as sleeping mats, but unless it was raining, the Lengua preferred to sleep under the stars.

For clothing, men wore a heavy woolen blanket, which was woven by the women on a vertical loom. The garment covered the whole body and was held around the waist by a leather belt. Women wore only a woven, wraparound skirt. Formerly, men wore a tongue-like wooden plug hanging from the lower lip —hence the tribal name Lengua, meaning "tongue" in Spanish.

The nuclear family was the basic unit of Lengua society, and families enjoyed a great deal of autonomy. Like the Tehuelche, those dissatisfied with a particular band could join another. A man of experience and ability was informally recognized as headman of the band. His primary role was to determine when the group was to break camp, in which direction it was to travel, and where it would set up a new camp. A headman's authority was limited, however, and important decisions were usually made by consensus. Generosity was prized in a headman, and he was expected to bestow gifts freely on his followers. This usually resulted in his becoming the poorest member of the community.

Feasts, Ceremonies, and Warfare

Lengua bands lived independently for the most part, coming together only for feasts and ceremonies, often connected with life cycle rituals, and warfare. Conflict was not uncommon, the Lengua's traditional enemy being the Mataco to the southwest. When it came to war, several bands joined forces and chose one man as war chief. Attacks were not wild, disorganized charges but were carefully planned. Unlike some other Chaco tribes, the Lengua did not scalp their war victims. Women and children were taken prisoner more often than men and were readily incorporated into the band of their captors.

Before marriage, a mock abduction of the bride was staged, but the married couple settled down with the bride's band rather than the groom's. A man was allowed to have more than one wife, but monogamy was the rule.

Like the Tehuelche, the Lengua attributed most diseases to possession by spirits. Malevolent spirits called *kilyíkhama* were thought to enter people during sleep. While someone's soul was off on a dream adventure, a *kilyíkhama* was able to take possession of the body, making it impossible for the returning soul to re-enter it. A person thus afflicted quickly sickened, and unless a shaman could expel the evil spirit, death was sure to follow.

A dead body had to be buried by sunset; otherwise, the soul was thought to hover around the camp, threatening the well-being of others. After death, a person's property was burned, so that it could accompany him or her to the afterworld. For fear of ghosts, the band abandoned the camp site as soon as the corpse had been disposed of.

The Lengua greatly enjoyed feasting, and made a fermented beverage from the beans of the carob-like *algarroba* tree. Most members of the group joined in the revelry, but a few would abstain to keep watch and ensure that none of the participants, their usual restraint dissolved by alcohol, tried to settle old scores or begin new quarrels. Like the Tehuelche, the Lengua were also addicted to gambling with dice and played a rather undisciplined version of field hockey.

🔥 This Lengua man wears a woolen blanket woven by his wife and his best feather finery, with shell necklaces and a flat wooden whistle around his neck. The feather anklets protected against snakebite.

⚲ In the *wainkya* ceremony, held to mark the coming of age of Lengua boys, relays of men beat pots or drums incessantly, day and night.

TROPICAL FOREST TRIBES

☞ Two men of Brazil's Yawalapití tribe, wearing their traditional shell necklaces and feather armbands, stand next to the entrance of a communal house. Like the Kuikuru, the Yawalapití thatch their houses with grass rather than palm leaves. In the whole of Amazonia, this custom is found in only nine villages in the Upper Xingú region, each occupied by a distinct group, or tribe.

F urther north, across the Guaporé and Upper Paraguay rivers, lies the vast region covered by the Amazonian rainforest. The cultures that have developed here have a number of major features in common, and are classified by anthropologists as of the "Tropical Forest" type. Two characteristic groups, the Kuikuru of central Brazil and the Amahuaca of eastern Peru, will be described here.

Unlike the groups previously outlined, many of the Amazonian Indians still survive, their cultures little altered by outside contact. The Indians of this region live in autonomous villages that range in size from 15 to 300 people. (See the feature *The Yanomami:*

☞ Kamayurá village, on Lake Ipavu, in Brazil. The houses are arranged in a circle, with the men's "club" house in the center. Paths lead to the lake and the manioc gardens.

☿ Txicão children in front of the framework for a *maloca*, a large house that will be home to several related families. The frame will be thatched with grass. Txicão village is located in the Xingú National Park, in Brazil.

Amazon Survivors in Peril.) Most villages are moved every few years, but some remain in the same location for decades. Houses, usually round or oval in ground plan, consist of a pole framework thatched over with palm leaves. The Kuikuru are all but unique in Amazonia in thatching their houses with grass. Generally, Amazonian houses are thatched to ground level, but among some tribes, such as the Amahuaca, only the roof is thatched and the sides of the house are left open.

Dwellings may be small, housing only a nuclear family, but more commonly, they are large communal structures called *malocas*. Among the Tukanoan tribes of northwest Amazonia, the entire village may consist of a single *maloca*. Amazonian houses have

VICTOR ENGLEBERT

LOREN MCINTYRE

☗ A Yanomami woman crosses a stream in the border area of Venezuela and Brazil. A bunch of peach palm fruit hangs from a tumpline worn around her forehead.

relatively little furniture, but an almost universal feature is the hammock, an Amazonian invention that has spread to the ends of the Earth.

Amazonian villages vary in layout. Some, like those of the Amahuaca, consist of a scattering of small huts, often out of sight of one another. More commonly, huts are tightly clustered in a circle around a central plaza. In some villages, such as those of the Kayapó and Mundurucú of central Brazil, there is also a men's house, located in the center of the plaza. Such structures are often associated with warlike tribes, and young boys are brought there to live away from the womenfolk and begin their training as warriors. But some peaceful societies, such as the Kuikuru, also have a men's house, which serves as a place for men to gather socially or engage in handicrafts, receive visitors, and store their ceremonial trappings.

Making a Living

Virtually all Amazonian Indians practice the simple type of cultivation known as swidden, or slash-and-burn, agriculture. To make a new garden plot, a man waits for the rains to end and then clears a tract of forest of between half a hectare and a hectare (1 to 2 acres) in size. Formerly, this was done with a stone axe, but today, steel tools are almost universally available. The fallen vegetation is allowed to dry on the ground until just before the next rains, and then

burned. The resulting wood ash acts as a fertilizer. Crops are planted for two or three years, after which the soil is depleted and weeds become a problem. The garden is then abandoned, and a new one cleared.

By far the most important crop plant of Amazonia is manioc, *Manihot esculenta*, a tuberous root best known to the Western world as the source of tapioca. (See the feature *Manioc: The Reigning Crop*.) Other crops include maize, sweet potatoes, and yams, as well as a variety of fruit trees, including papaya and the peach palm.

To satisfy their need for protein, Tropical Forest Indians also hunt and fish. The Kuikuru and other tribes living near lakes or large rivers well stocked with fish rely more on fishing than on hunting.

☗ Xinguano men inside a men's house in Kamayurá village, in Brazil. Here, the men come to chat, to make artifacts, and to ornament themselves for ceremonial occasions. It is here, too, that the sacred flutes, played in threes and used in exclusively male ceremonies, are hidden from the sight of women, who are subject to gang rape if they should lay eyes on them.

♀ Wearing traditional wooden lip-plugs but using steel axes, two men of Brazil's Kayapó tribe clear a garden plot for cultivation.

LOREN MCINTYRE

MANIOC: THE REIGNING CROP

Robert L. Carneiro

THE MANIOC PLANT, whose tuberous roots yield large amounts of starch, is the staple crop of most Amazonian Indians. Although there is only one species of manioc (*Manihot esculenta*), it occurs in two distinct forms, known as bitter and sweet. Bitter varieties (of which there are hundreds) contain prussic acid, a deadly poison, which must be removed before the tuber can be eaten. Sweet manioc, on the other hand, contains little or no prussic acid, and is rendered edible by roasting the tubers in ashes or cutting them into chunks and boiling them.

An Amazonian Finger Trap

Over the centuries, Amazonian Indians have devised various ways of ridding bitter manioc of its poison. The tuber is first grated and reduced to a pulp, and one of several methods is then used to remove the prussic acid. The most common is a cylindrical press called a *tipití*, consisting of a tube 1.5 to 2 meters (5 or 6 feet) long plaited from strips of stiff palm stems, with one end left open and loops woven into both ends.

The *tipití* works on the same principle as the well known "Chinese finger trap". When pushed in from both ends, the cylinder widens as it shortens, and in this position, it is stuffed with the pulp. The *tipití* is then hung outside from the end of a rafter. A stout pole is inserted through its lower loop, one end of which is tied to the bottom of a house post, while a woman sits on the other end. Her weight stretches the *tipití*, and as it narrows, the pulp inside is compressed, causing the juice to be extruded through the mesh and to trickle down the outside of the tube. The process usually takes 20 or 30 minutes.

The Detoxification Process

A pot underneath catches the juice, which also contains in suspension the fine starch flour we know as tapioca. The prussic acid is boiled off, leaving a thick, potable liquid. Sometimes, the pot is first set aside to allow the tapioca to settle to the bottom, and the juice is then carefully decanted and boiled. This produces a thinner liquid.

The coarse flour remaining inside the *tipití* is removed and dried in the sun to help get rid of the last traces of poison, and then boiled

🔥 After harvesting, manioc tubers are first peeled, and then grated and strained to remove the poisonous prussic acid they contain.

in water to produce a thick gruel. Sometimes, this coarse flour is mixed with the fine manioc flour that has settled to the bottom of the pot, spread over a large clay griddle, and then baked into flat cassava cakes. The greater the proportion of fine flour in the mixture, the higher the quality of the cakes. In the Guianas, cassava cakes are baked crisp, but in the Upper Xingú, they are only lightly toasted, leaving them soft and pliable. Pieces are then torn off, boiled fish paste is placed on top, and they are served as open sandwiches.

A Valuable Energy Food

Manioc, which is always planted from cuttings, never from seeds, takes about 8 months to produce tubers of edible size. Indians prefer, however, to leave the roots in the ground for 18 months, by which time their starch content is at its

◄ In Brazil and French Guiana, Wayana women remove the poisonous juice from grated manioc pulp with the aid of a *tipití*, a manioc squeezer made of basketry. The dried flour is then made into cassava cakes.

► A Brazilian man carries a basketful of manioc cuttings to be planted in a garden cleared by slash-and-burn.

LOREN MCINTYRE

LOREN MCINTYRE

♨ A woman of Brazil's Upper Xingu region bakes thin cassava cakes, made from a mixture of the coarse and fine (tapioca) flour derived from manioc, on a clay griddle.

◄◙ Using a mat strainer, a simpler device than a *tipití*, a woman of Brazil's Kuikuru tribe molds coarse manioc pulp into loaves, which are then dried in the sun and stored inside the house.

⚘ These Campa women of the Gran Pajonal, in Peru, are chewing manioc and spitting it into a log trough, where, aided by the ptyalin in their saliva, it will ferment into a beer called *masato*.

Manioc is not a particularly nutritious food, containing only 1 percent or less of protein and having only slight amounts of vitamins and minerals. Its virtues are that it grows well in poor tropical soils, resists drought and insect pests, and yields large amounts of carbohydrates. For peoples for whom getting enough kilojoules (calories) is a serious concern, its high yield is a great asset. After the European discovery of America, manioc was carried throughout the Old World tropics, and today it forms the staple food of millions of people, from West Africa to Polynesia.

maximum. Once pulled from the ground, the tubers quickly spoil if they are left unprocessed. Reduced to flour and stored in baskets, manioc will last for six months or more.

Athough manioc has been grown in Amazonia for perhaps 5,000 years, how it first came to be domesticated is still a mystery. One theory is that the root was originally used as a fish poison, and that people gradually found ways of removing the poison so that the rest could be eaten. Another is that wild manioc may have produced little starch and contained virtually no prussic acid, but as it came under cultivation and plants were selected for their starch yield, the prussic acid content increased accordingly. Rather than give up what had been a valuable food plant, Indians then experimented until they hit upon ways of removing the toxic element.

VICTOR ENGLEBERT

⊕ Standing in an unstable dugout canoe, this fisherman of Brazil's Kamayurá tribe has to aim his arrow slightly below where the fish appears to be, to allow for the refraction of light in the water.

♀ A man of an Upper Xingu tribe of Brazil inspects fish traps set into a weir. The check throat of the traps prevents the fish from escaping.

🔥 A Kayapó man returns home with a small jaguar he has shot. Killing a jaguar is a rare event, and the heart of the animal is eaten by the men of this Brazilian tribe to instill courage.

⊕ A rainforest tree with large plank buttress roots, which are used for various purposes. With their expert knowledge of their habitat, Amazonian Indians find virtually everything they need for a secure livelihood in the rainforest.

Most commonly, they shoot the fish with bows and arrows, but they also use a variety of traps, often set into weirs. The most productive fishing method of all is to poison the water with vines known collectively as barbasco or timbó. These plants contain a powerful alkaloid that stupefies the fish, making it easy to catch them by hand. If the lagoon of a large river is poisoned, it may yield as much as half a tonne (about half a ton) of fish.

Dugout or, as among the Kuikuru, bark canoes are used for fishing by some tribes. Water-craft, which probably go back thousands of years in Amazonia, have played an important part in the development of Amazonian culture, allowing Indians to penetrate to the far reaches of the Amazon basin. This helps to account for the very wide distribution of such major language families as the Carib, Arawak, and Tupí–Guaraní.

In headwater regions of Amazonia, well away from large rivers, live tribes such as the Yanomami and the Amahuaca, who rely more on hunting than on fishing for their protein.

The main weapons used by Amazonian hunters are the bow and arrow and the blowgun. (See the feature *The Blowgun: The Silent, Deadly Tube*.) The bows used here are the longest in the world, often exceeding 180 centimeters (6 feet) in length, while arrows may be even longer. A variety of arrowheads is used, depending on the game. Tipped with a sharpened piece of monkey bone or the spine of a stingray, they are well suited to killing small game. For bigger prey, such as tapirs, peccaries, jaguars, and (in war) human beings, a large, lanceolate bamboo point is preferred.

Throughout much of western Amazonia, the blowgun has displaced the bow as the hunting weapon of choice, especially for arboreal game, such as monkeys and birds.

THE BLOWGUN: THE SILENT, DEADLY TUBE

ROBERT L. CARNEIRO

RIVALING THE BOW AND ARROW as the weapon of choice among Amazonian Indians is the blowgun. This consists of a tube about 2.5 to 3.5 meters (8 to 12 feet) long and 3 to 4 centimeters (one to one and a half inches) in diameter, through which the hunter blows a poisoned dart. Among those tribes that have adopted it, the blowgun has generally displaced the bow and arrow. It is used mostly to hunt monkeys and birds in the trees, while the lance is used against terrestrial game. Some tribes, though, use the blowgun for both types of prey.

An Ecuadorian boy carries a blowgun and a quiver filled with curare-tipped darts. A monkey struck by curare will fall out of the treetops within minutes.

LOREN MCINTYRE

Blowguns are of several types. In the Guianas, the commonest form is made from a slender, hollow reed of *Arundinaria* grass, which is perfectly straight and smooth inside, but so thin and fragile that it must be encased in a hollow palm stem. In a second type of blowgun, the split halves of a straight length of palm wood are gouged out with a chisel to form matching, semicircular channels about 12 millimeters (half an inch) in diameter. These channels are carefully smoothed to reduce friction, and the halves are then joined together, wrapped spirally with a thin strip of vine, and covered with resin to make the barrel airtight, so that none of the breath will escape when the blowgun is shot.

A sight is usually fixed to the blowgun about 30 centimeters (12 inches) from the mouthpiece. Most commonly, it consists of two curved rodent incisor teeth placed side by side, convex side up, on a piece of beeswax.

Poisoned Darts

The missile shot from a blowgun is a thin dart no thicker than a matchstick and about 30 centimeters (12 inches) long, made from the midrib of a palm leaf or a sharp palm spine. To provide sufficient resistance to the puff of air that expels it from the tube, the butt of each dart is wrapped in a wisp of kapok. Being silky smooth, this fiber is well suited to the purpose, since it creates little friction as the dart travels along the barrel of the gun. Moreover, the cell walls of kapok are watertight, which means that, unlike ordinary cotton, kapok does not become soggy and useless if darts get wet.

Even if it hits its target, a blowgun dart alone would be ineffectual. To make it lethal, the dart is poisoned with curare, a thick paste consisting essentially of the boiled-down sap of the vine *Strychnos toxifera* (an alkaloid related to, but different from, the strychnine derived from deadly nightshade). Curare works by blocking the nervous impulses to the muscles. Unable to breathe, the wounded animal asphyxiates. Death is relaxed rather than spastic; when a monkey is hit, its limbs go flaccid and it falls from the tree, sometimes landing at the hunter's feet.

The making of curare is often surrounded with a great deal of secrecy, and it is not uncommon for as many as 15 or 20 ingredients to go into it. While a few of these may add some toxicity to the mixture, only the sap of the *Strychnos* vine is essential.

A Hunter's Equipment

A hunter going into the forest with his blowgun takes a quiver containing 30 or more darts, as well as a small calabash or gourd, stuffed with kapok. Most darts will be wrapped ready to shoot, but should the hunter need to prepare more, he pulls out a small tuft of kapok and, with a deft twist of his fingers, wraps it around the dart. The mandible bone of the piranha fish also forms part of a hunter's equipment. With this tool, before setting out, the hunter cuts a groove around the tip of each dart, just below where it has been smeared with curare. A monkey struck by a dart will try to pull it out, but the dart will break off at the groove, leaving the poisoned tip embedded.

Silent and Stealthy

When a hunter spies a troop of monkeys in the trees, he stealthily makes his way to a spot directly beneath them. Shooting straight up at his target, he does not need to allow for any curvature in the dart's trajectory.

The range of a blowgun varies with the hunter's skill and the density of the surrounding foliage. Generally, a lethal shot is possible up to about 35 meters (120 feet). One of the blowgun's major advantages is that, unlike a bow, it is virtually noiseless. A hunter is thus able to pick off one monkey after another before the troop finally becomes alarmed and scampers off.

The blowgun is never used in warfare, some tribes asserting that if it were, the weapon would lose its effectiveness against game animals. No one knows when the blowgun was invented, but its use has spread mostly within post-Columbian times.

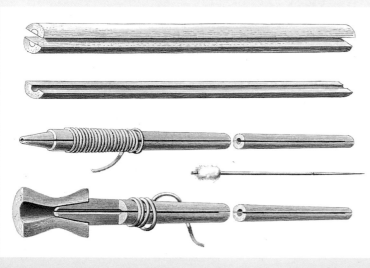

ILLUSTRATION: RAY SIM

Stages in the manufacture of a Yagua blowgun. After being split, the two halves of a section of hard wood are scored, and the groove is polished. The halves are then cemented together, a mouthpiece is applied, and the barrel of the blowgun is wrapped with a thin, flat vine.

VICTOR ENGLEBERT

A Yagua man, from Peru, shows how a blowgun is held when shooting at monkeys or birds in the trees above.

⚫ Wearing feather headdresses and holding war clubs, Kayapó men chant and dance in their village plaza, in Brazil. Such dances are held on a number of occasions, including naming ceremonies, corn ceremonies, and when warriors return from battle.

➤ Made by the Tapirapé Indians, of Brazil, this mask of wood and feathers resembles a giant face covered with many-colored feathers. It represents the spirits of enemies killed in battle.

R.P. SHERIDAN/AMERICAN MUSEUM OF NATURAL HISTORY, NO. 3220 (2)

Ceremonies and Social Life

Ceremonies are an important part of life in Amazonia. The Kuikuru, for instance, have no fewer than 17 ceremonies, each with its own set of performers. Singing, dancing, and feasting are essential parts of most ceremonies. People from other villages are often invited to a feast, and conviviality may be heightened by the free flow of alcoholic beverages. These are made from manioc or maize mash, which women first chew to induce fermentation (by the action of the ptyalin present in saliva).

Puberty initiations for both sexes are common, and the rites associated with them are often grueling and even dangerous. Among several Guiana tribes, the puberty ritual for both boys and girls involves the "ant ordeal". A straw plaque, with a hundred or more stinging ants inserted into its mesh, is placed against the chest of the candidate, who is expected to bear the excruciating stings with fortitude. At puberty, a Kuikuru boy faces a different ordeal: he goes with his father to a swamp to catch an anaconda, and then has to wrestle bare-handed with the giant snake. After killing it, the boy smears its fat over his body to acquire the constrictor snake's power as a great wrestler.

Social organization among Amazonian tribes is relatively simple. Only among a few tribes—along the upper Rio Negro, for example—are villages

◀ Most Amazonian Indians, like these Kayapó women, of Brazil, wear body paint every day, sometimes in intricate designs. The favorite colors are red from *urucú* seeds and black from the *genipa* fruit.

➤ *Opposite page*: The Kayapó chief, Raoni, wears the characteristic lip-plug and a large feather headdress on a frame at the back of his head. He has been an active and effective defender of Brazilian Indian rights.

A Kayapó man wearing a feather headdress. Brazil's Kayapó Indians are known for their spectacular headdresses and other ornaments, made mostly from red and blue macaw tail feathers.

organized into a system of interrelated clans. Where they occur, clans are kin groups in which descent is reckoned in either the male or the female line. Clans are generally exogamous, which means that members are required to marry outside the clan. The Kayapó have an elaborate system of moieties—social groupings that form two complementary halves. The moieties have reciprocal functions, such as burying each other's dead, thus helping to integrate the unusually large villages of 500 to 600 people in which, until recently, the Kayapó lived.

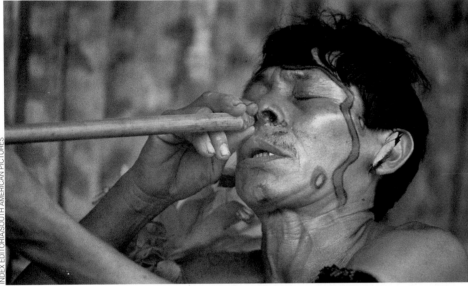

Throughout Amazonia, shamans use some kind of drug to help them establish contact with the spirit world. In common with many other tribes, the Yanomami, who inhabit the border area of Venezuela and Brazil, favor *ebene*, a powder scraped from the inner bark of a tree of the genus *Virola*. Here, a Yanomami man receives a "hit" of snuff, blown into his nostril through a cane tube by a companion.

After taking *ebene*, an hallucinogenic snuff, a Yanomami shaman calls to the spirits. Known to the Yanomami as *hékura*, the spirits may be invoked benevolently, to cure illness within the village, or malevolently, to kill the children of enemy villages.

While in every Amazonian village some people are regarded as more able, intelligent, or industrious than others, and accordingly enjoy greater respect and prestige, the societies of this region are essentially egalitarian. There are no significant differences in rank; nor are there distinct social classes. Even the village chief is usually no more than "the first among equals", and so his power is sharply limited.

Myths and Shamans

The supernatural beliefs of Amazonian Indians are expressed through a rich mythology. Sun and Moon, universal mythological characters in Amazonia, are often represented as twins. Born on Earth, they went through a series of adventures, distinguishing themselves as culture heroes by imparting knowledge or inventing things before finally ascending into the sky to assume their permanent places.

Shamanism continues to be a prominent feature of virtually all Amazonian tribes. Above all else, the shaman (almost invariably a man) is a healer, but he may also be asked to locate lost or stolen objects, to divine the future, or to identify sorcerers. In time of war, he may be expected to help his village by sending evil spirits to attack the souls of its enemies.

Shamans throughout Amazonia use some kind of drug to help them establish contact with the spirit world. Among the denizens of the supernatural world, the shaman has his own tutelary spirit, who provides answers to his questions and helps him effect his cures. The most widely used narcotic in shamanistic practice is tobacco. A Kuikuru shaman smokes tobacco in the form of a long cigarette, inhaling deeply and swallowing the smoke with audible gulps to help him achieve a state of trance. Among other narcotic plants used for this purpose, the most notable is the vine *ayahuasca* (*Banisteriopsis caapi*). In western Amazonia, infusions made by boiling lengths of this vine are drunk not only by shamans, but also by other men, in order to experience vivid, colorful, and sometimes frightening hallucinations, which are often regarded as portents of impending events. It has even been known for a man to kill someone in an adjacent village in the belief, imparted by a spirit during a séance, that the man was planning to kill him.

CHIEFDOMS OF AMAZONIA

When Europeans first arrived in Amazonia, not all the Indians they encountered lived in small, autonomous villages. In certain bountifully endowed areas, such as along the Amazon and the middle Orinoco rivers and on the Mojos Plain of Bolivia, large, complex chiefdoms had emerged. Typically, such societies consisted of a number of villages brought under the permanent control of a paramount chief, usually a successful war leader. The chief had great power, including, as a rule, the power of life and death. He was, therefore, able to surround himself with supporters and retainers. Paramount chiefs were shown a proportionate respect, being carried in litters and spoken to deferentially. They were able to accumulate considerable wealth, and enjoyed the company of many wives.

Some Amazonian chiefdoms, such as those of the Omagua and the Tapajó, had extensive domains. While these were established by force of arms, they also found a strong economic base in the bountiful environment offered by the banks of the Amazon. Their territories encompassed what Brazilians call *várzea*, strips of land along the larger rivers whose fertility is replenished every year by silt-laden floodwaters. As well as enriching the soil, the river waters provided fish, manatees, turtles, and turtle eggs in prodigious quantities.

The chiefdoms of the Mojos Plain were somewhat smaller than those along the Amazon. But here, too, paramount chiefs enjoyed great power and high status. Writing about the Manasí as they were 300 years ago, ethnologist Alfred Métraux noted: "Nobody dared leave the village without the chief's permission. Young people never sat in his presence, but stood respectfully at a distance. Commoners addressed the chief in a very formal manner … The main chief lived in a huge house built by the people in the middle of the plaza. Each chief had two large fields which were tilled by his subjects." These chiefdoms lasted until the coming of the Jesuits in the seventeenth century.

The areas of Amazonia where chiefdoms flourished were also those that Europeans found most attractive. It was these societies, therefore, that bore the brunt of European conquest and colonization. If not destroyed outright, chiefdoms were generally fragmented into their component villages. Seeking security, their inhabitants fled from the banks of the Amazon up its various tributaries.

Today, in some remote areas of Amazonia, difficult of access and not well endowed with such coveted resources as gold or diamonds, rubber or Brazil nut trees, Indian tribes live on with some semblance of their traditional culture. But the quickening pace of deforestation, road building, and economic development in general throughout Amazonia poses a critical threat to their survival. Unless these processes are drastically slowed, it is likely that within a few decades no tribe will remain with more than a vestige of the culture that, for thousands of years, allowed Indians to flourish in the world's largest area of tropical rainforest.

LUIZ CLAUDIO MARIGO/BRUCE COLEMAN LTD

The chainsaw, the successor to the steel axe, has played a major role in the rapid destruction of the Amazonian rainforest. A government resettling project in the Brazilian state of Rondônia, for example, involved the felling of some 40,000 square kilometers (about 15,000 square miles) of rainforest.

Men of Brazil's Suruí tribe standing amidst the devastation of their land, much of which has been cleared, exhausted, and finally abandoned by settlers and miners. Unknown to the outside world until the 1960s, the Suruí now face the threat of cultural, if not physical, extinction.

MICHAEL K. NICHOLS/MAGNUM

THE YANOMAMI: AMAZON SURVIVORS IN PERIL

GABRIELE HERZOG-SCHRÖDER

IVE HUNDRED YEARS AGO, before the arrival of Europeans, the South American continent was inhabited by nearly 50 million people. When the two worlds came into contact, the resulting clash of cultures was catastrophic. South Americans perished in staggering numbers. The devastation began with biological invasion: the illnesses and infections the foreigners brought with them met little resistance from the immune systems of the indigenous peoples. Prolonged social interaction with the conquerors contributed further to the demise of these civilizations. It has been reliably estimated that during the first 100 years of contact, the population of South America declined to as little as 10 percent of its previous size.

⚥ Women join with one another to make gathering trips into the forest. Blackened cheeks express mourning for a loved one.

⚕ Apart from shamans, no one specializes in particular arts or skills. Everyone knows how to make what he or she needs to survive. Interestingly, the fruits of the Yanomami's labors are rarely used for themselves but exchanged to create social ties.

Wherever they prevailed, the Europeans beat the local Indian populations into submission. Depending on their own traditions, different Indian communities reacted differently to the foreigners' attempts to enslave them. The highland civilizations had a complex social and political structure not unlike that of medieval Europe. As a result, they were able to adapt their lives to their new rulers without entirely abandoning their cultural identity. The cultures of the Amazon lowlands, in contrast, were divided into hundreds of small, largely egalitarian, societies, which lived by foraging and gardening. Unable to submit to foreign rule, they chose instead to withdraw into remote areas—or they perished.

One of the few peoples of the Amazon lowlands who have managed to remain in relative isolation until recent times is the Yanomami, who live on

➤ In egalitarian societies, positions of status are continually in flux. This gives rise to sudden conflicts, as well as to ways of making peace.

⬆ Men hunt individually or, before a feast is to be held, in a group. Nearly all the game killed for a feast will be given to the visitors who come to the village for the occasion.

the rugged frontier between Venezuela and Brazil. Traditionally, the Yanomami settled around the rivulets feeding into the headwaters of the Orinoco, Rio Negro, and Rio Branco rivers. In the twentieth century, some communities moved closer to the larger rivers, and since the 1950s, these groups have lived in regular and well-documented contact with other societies—notably, Western civilization in the form of missionaries and anthropologists.

A Close Community

The Yanomami live in small, self-contained communities of between 40 and 200 people. Family homes are built in a circle, close to each other, and feature a high, palm-thatched roof sloping steeply to the ground. Family members work, sleep, and socialize around a central hearth.

Each kin group is represented in a council of elders by the man considered to be most competent. Political issues are decided within the council by consensus. The attributes by which a man gains prestige and respect within his group are his charismatic ability to influence the opinion of others and his ability to settle quarrels, uphold group morals, and weigh up the consequences of conflicts with other communities. Such men are promoted to a position of shared leadership in negotiations with outside groups. In critical situations, it is their task to motivate the warriors of their village to take action against other Yanomami communities. Despite their responsible position, these leaders do not assume

permanent command, nor do they enjoy any material privileges in return.

The Yanomami subsist by simple agriculture and by hunting and gathering. Traditionally, plantains were cultivated, but in recent years, manioc has become a more common crop, usually supplemented by maize, sweet potatoes, and sugar cane. Women collect small catfish, crabs, crayfish, caterpillars, and large insects, which are the major sources of protein, as well as nuts, mushrooms, and wild fruits. Men clear and plant garden sites, and specialize in hunting, for which they use a long bow and arrow fitted with a variety of points made from bamboo, wood, or bone.

Yanomami material culture is meager and functional. Baskets, calabash gourds, forked sticks, and fresh leaves serve as their cooking utensils.

A Warrior Tradition

Courage and confidence are considered admirable virtues in both men and women, and children are taught from an early age not to show fear. One should never, if provoked, withdraw silently from conflict, but must immediately make a verbal stand. If this does not resolve the issue, the Yanomami readily resort to fists and weapons. Expressions of ferocity are governed by strict rules, however, and threats and menacing display are a central strategy.

When a family or village member dies, a spectacular feast is held to mourn the dead, and relatives and friends from other villages are invited. On these occasions, Yanomami men perform long and

highly ritualized duets—a kind of competitive singing, in the course of which they communicate news, ask for goods, negotiate marriages, and assure each other of mutual loyalty.

Funeral ceremonies take place in two stages. Immediately after death, the corpse is burned, and later, at the feast, the remaining bones are ground to powder and mixed into a soup made from plantains, which is then eaten by close relatives. The Yanomami believe that this communal act frees the soul of their beloved.

⬆ Children are free to explore their community and the surrounding jungle, but generally stay close to their mother, who represents the core of the family.

⬅ A hunter dries the poison curare (*Strychnos toxifera*) on his arrow tips.

A Grim Future

About 10,000 Yanomami currently live in Venezuela. In the early 1980s, there were a further 8,000 to 9,000 living in Brazil, but about 15 percent of these, mainly young people, have since died as victims of an unrestrained gold rush. The national interests of these countries are so varied and conflicting that, despite genuine and sustained efforts on some authorities' part to uphold Indian rights, injustices are rife and disaster is imminent. In our own time, the last remaining traditional peoples, like the Yanomami, are falling victim to the same kinds of destructive forces we deplore when looking into the historic past.

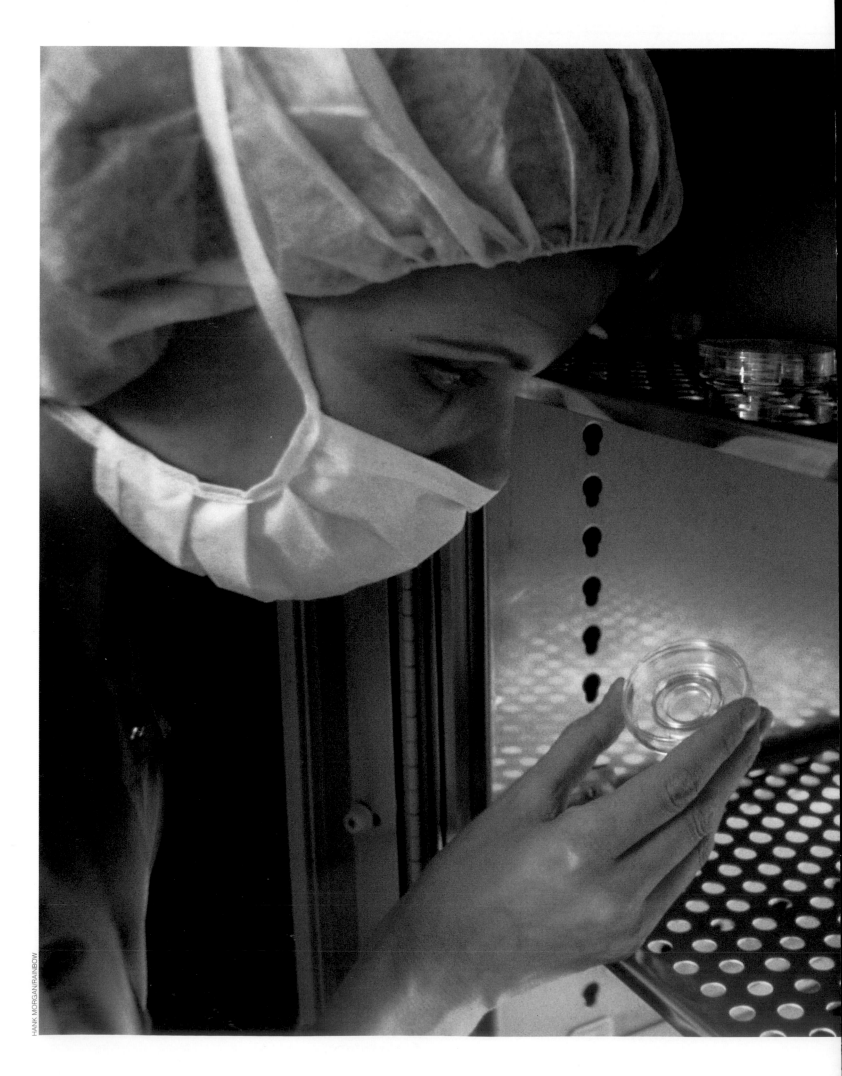

THE FUTURE OF HUMANKIND

Prologue or Epitaph?

FRANK KEMP SALTER, WULF SCHIEFENHÖVEL, AND GÖRAN BURENHULT

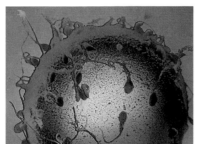

What a piece of work is a man! How noble in reason! how infinite in faculty! in form, in moving, how express and admirable! in action how like an angel! in apprehension how like a god! the beauty of the world! the paragon of animals! (Shakespeare, Hamlet, *Act 2, Scene 2)*

Evolutionary biologists tell us that no species is perfect, that all the millions of forms of life are, to varying degrees, only approximately adapted to their niches—niches that are changeable and therefore capable of upsetting the "perfection" of any species' adaptation. Yet, when one surveys the history of our species, and tries to comprehend the diversity of living cultures, Shakespeare's words echo with authority. Evolved during millions of years, *Homo sapiens* has survived, thanks to something close to biological perfection. Vigilant, strong, and enduring, with reactions swift as lightning, a highly developed sense of curiosity, and surpassing ingenuity, our ancestors conquered every continent and every habitable region of the Earth. Our muscles can function in perfect coordination, controlled by commands from our brain, the complexity of which far surpasses even the most sophisticated computers. We can put our minds to patiently solving the most intricate problems; are able to precisely gauge the feelings of fellow humans and to deal competently with the complexity of our social environment. After nearly four million years, a unique being has evolved with no parallel in the animal world.

◄● In vitro fertilization: with advances in genetic engineering, will it become normal practice for humans to begin their lives in incubators? And what kinds of people will we choose to breed?

◖ A (color-enhanced) microscopic view of human sperm competing to fertilize an egg. Modern technology allows us to rig the race, if we choose.
DAVID PHILLIPS/SCIENCE SOURCE/
PHOTO RESEARCHERS INC.

W. JESCO VON PUTTKAMER/HUTCHISON LIBRARY

☝ Humans evolved as hunter-gatherers, with an extraordinary ability to survive in a wide range of environments.

☟ Today, the environment many of us are adapted to is urban and densely populated: as here in Hong Kong.

JOHN YATES/THE PHOTO LIBRARY, SYDNEY

During this long period, we have hunted game, caught fish, and gathered plants, and in the course of time also learned to domesticate both plants and animals. Dangers in nature and, particularly, danger coming from other humans have shaped our senses and the reactions of flight and attack. In overcoming these challenges, humans, as a species, have become extraordinarily well adapted for survival in a wide range of environments, both mentally and physically. As Konrad Lorenz has said, humans are the only creatures that can swiftly walk 30 kilometers (about 20 miles), then swim underwater for 15 meters (about 15 yards), while picking up a few things from the riverbed, and, finally, climb a rope up a cliff face.

Yet, over the course of a few generations, in most parts of the world, humans have completely abandoned the way of life to which they have adapted during their long past. We can only guess what consequences—psychological as well as physical—this artificial way of life will have for humankind's future biological evolution. Muscles and senses that developed for walking, running, and climbing in forests and fields tend to atrophy in people who spend most of their time in chairs, cars, and offices.

The methods humans have evolved for dealing with conflict—flight, aggression, and reconciliation—are often out of kilter with the large-scale, anonymous world of the city. We developed in small, intimate communities, where a stranger was something rare. The deficiencies of the anonymous society may lower our threshold for aggressive acts. Our biological and psychological heritage is not always well matched to the environment we have created. Our species changes extremely slowly: it takes hundreds of generations to bring about a new trait, while culture can produce major changes in just one or two.

What can be done to improve the match? Clearly, humans are highly adaptable, but we need to learn more about our limits and long-term needs. With such knowledge, short-term perspectives will appear less viable. Our values have to be put into a far wider, and longer, perspective. A species-wide view, one that envisions humans in the context of the animal kingdom, will also enable us to interact without prejudice with cultures differing from our own in a constantly shrinking world.

A knowledge of history, and prehistory, is most important for understanding why contemporary peoples live and behave the way they do in different parts of the world. Because 99 percent of our past is prehistory, most of our knowledge of human behavior and social structures in the past comes from the findings of archaeology, human ethology, and biology. This knowledge will better prepare us to cope with future problems of the survival of humankind in a world worth living in. Those who lack the perspective gained by looking back in time are handicapped in looking forward. An impoverished awareness of the past is one of the great threats to our technocratic society. This chapter looks at some scenarios of future social developments on the basis of what we know today about the nature and cultures of humankind.

Our crystal ball will become less cloudy if we allow ourselves to make some relatively safe assumptions about certain important future social developments. What significant aspects of the future can be assumed with relative certainty? Most people will be surrounded by large numbers of other human beings, because that is the present situation, and one that is unlikely to change. Population growth is still substantial, and experts are in agreement that by the year 2100, even with a decline in the rate of increase, the world's population will have doubled, from the present 5,000 million to more than 10,000 million.

The natural environment will bear the brunt of this population explosion. Technology has allowed human populations to defy the constraints of living space and naturally occurring resources that operated in the past. Our species has occupied most land niches, leaving the Antarctic as the sole continent still (almost) empty. The world's shipping lanes

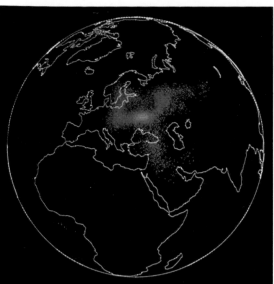

unlimited energy without contributing to chemical air pollution or the so-called greenhouse effect. However, the major problems of how to guarantee the safety of reactors and dispose of large amounts of radioactive waste are yet to be solved. Exposure to levels of radiation considered harmless some years ago has been shown to increase the incidence of cancer and chromosome damage, which may be carried over to future generations. Nuclear weapons, presently stored or developed by an increasing number of countries, pose another grave danger.

The nuclear problem is hard to fully comprehend. We have difficulty thinking beyond the span of a few generations, but we must if we are to act as optimizers, balancing a multiplicity of factors rather than seeking to maximize a few to the detriment of the delicate web of life. Nuclear technology has

◀● This computer-generated map of the northern hemisphere shows the spread of radioactive material from the power station at Chernobyl, in Ukraine, on the fourth day after the devastating nuclear accident in 1986.

carry the oil slicks and debris of burgeoning international trade, and already schemes are being devised to colonize the oceans with floating airports and cities. Pollution poses a direct threat to existing and future generations, but there are also significant indirect dangers. It is not known how many species are driven to extinction each year, but 20 percent of all bird species have been lost forever, and the endangered list is growing. This is not surprising, considering that major ecosystems such as the Amazonian basin are shrinking under the impact of human settlement and the continued global warming attributed to the burning of coal and oil.

Of the alternatives to fossil fuels, nuclear technology has received the lion's share of research and development funds. It is correctly argued that uranium power plants can provide

♠ Water pollution is one of the major problems in industrialized countries, with their rapidly growing, largely urban populations. Yet clean drinking water is one of the basic necessities of life.

◀● The world's rainforests are rapidly diminishing. Here, in Ecuador, a section of Amazonian rainforest in a wildlife reserve has been burned off in preparation for the construction of a settlement. The site was chosen because of its proximity to the transport links used by the oil industry. An oil pipe runs across the foreground. Short-term convenience of this kind often translates into cumulative ecological disaster.

innate traits with deep evolutionary roots. Unless human nature is interfered with artificially, it is a safe prediction that, in terms of central tendencies, it will remain fairly constant for the next 10,000 years.

The relative permanence of human nature provides at least one set of fixed points that can be projected into the future. The phenomenal enlargement of the hominid brain from the size of a chimpanzee's 500 cubic centimeters (30 cubic inches) to about 1,400 cubic centimeters (85 cubic inches) over a mere three million years continues to amaze scientists. In that same period, humans developed a unique, adaptive quality of flexibility, based on culture. They domesticated plants and animals, in the period often referred to as the Neolithic transition; built civilizations; invented writing; landed on the moon; and have developed the capacity to reinvent themselves through genetic engineering.

Barrels containing radioactive waste from the Savannah River nuclear plant in South Carolina, in the United States. The containers will be buried in the ground, out of sight. Are we planting time bombs?

The development of writing is a striking example of human ingenuity. One of the earliest scripts known is cuneiform, shown here, which developed in Mesopotamia from the pictographs invented by the ancient Sumerians some 5,000 years ago. More angular than pictographs, the symbols were impressed into wet clay with a split reed, giving them their characteristic wedge shape.

extremely long-lasting and complex effects, some of which we are just beginning to understand.

Considering such environmental dangers, it is not unreasonable to ask how pleasant or dignified the future will be. On present trends, it is possible that we shall make the planet inhospitable or even uninhabitable. In the last 150 years or so, we have, at an ever increasing speed, initiated a vast number of artificial environmental changes that threaten our very future.

The firmest foundations for extrapolating the social future, and those of most general interest, are the demographic variables of sex and age and the universal ties of kinship. Social patterns formed by these three basic variables differ between cultures, but have a common basis in universal,

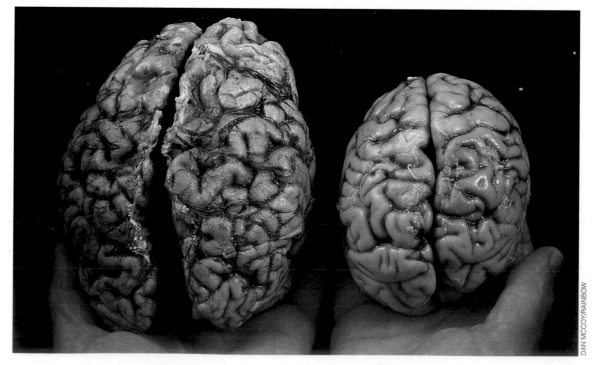

20 July 1969: "... one small step for a man, one giant leap for mankind."

A human brain (left) compared to a gorilla's. Some experts believe artificial intelligence systems to be the next step in the evolution of intelligence, perhaps even programmed with drives and emotions.

THE FIRST TIME I SAW YOUR PLACE WITH MY OWN EYES

Tomalala Moluboda

TOMALALA MOLUBODA, usually called Tom, is a Trobriand Islander from Tauwema village. He was born about 1944 and went to a village school for two years. He can read and write his mother language, Kilivila, well and speaks basic English. As a young man, he worked for an Australian company in Samarai, near the coast of mainland New Guinea, where he acquired skills in mechanics and other fields. His furthest journey was to Port Moresby, the capital of Papua New Guinea. He returned to Tauwema, where he married and now has four children. Since 1979, he has been local assistant to a team of scientists. In 1992, he came to Germany to work on the translation of the original sound tracks of films made by Irenäus Eibl-Eibesfeldt.

The following account of some of Tom's experiences in Australia and Europe was translated by Wulf Schiefenhövel, maintaining Tom's phrasing.

⚓ Tomalala Moluboda beside a Stone Age skeleton at the Ajvide burial ground, on the island of Gotland, Sweden.

We arrived in Sydney. I saw it and I run really out of words. Because there is no earth, we are walking on sheer cement. Neither sand nor rocks are anywhere, we are walking on cement and this other cover. We are rolling over it almost like a plane. Earth and sand are not spoiling our trousers and our shoes.

I was not afraid because Frank and you and Sibylle we were going around together. Today we went up on this very tall house [*the Centre-point Tower*] and it was a little bit like a tall coconut palm, but the coconut palms on the Trobriand Islands are short compared to this. This is a house, but it almost touches the clouds.

I am watching everything in Sydney. Today when we were riding in the bus I saw a man. He was picking up a metal [*a soft drink can*] and he was crushing it with his foot and he stuck it in his bag. And I was thinking, well, he is probably going to the factory to sell them the metal, so that they give him some money. And I thought this man was similar like some people in Port Moresby who are collecting bottles on the road and sell them. I saw this man, he was very tall and very strong, but he must be a little bit poor. And I thought, really, these people are not staying very well, they are just moving around. Because I have seen it with my own eyes, and it is true. Before I was thinking, all the white people are working for money and they don't just roam around.

Now we have traveled through Germany and Holland and we were going around a lot and I saw that the things are all right here. Because there are forests and fields. The people are growing food and it is growing very well. Sydney does not have space. And then we went on the road to Amsterdam and I thought we would not reach this place because there were so many roads. I saw that this city is similar to Sydney, because also here is no open space where we could make gardens and grow food. There is no space, there are narrow roads and no space.

About these ships [*in a museum*], they have told us that long time ago they were fighting wars with them. Grete bought a book and I kept looking at it. It is really something because they are writing about the time long ago and they have repaired all the old things so that they are still there until today. And we can see the change.

These channels [*in and around Amsterdam*]—how were they dug? My words run out. Because they dug such enormous channels. And I think they were using prisoners to do this work. Because in the old time it was like this in our islands. Did your forefathers do it because they wanted the ships to have channels? Because I see how many there are. Like roads on the ground. I am amazed, I have never seen something like that.

From my country probably no one came to see this. It is only the big bosses who visit your countries. And they stay two or three days and return.

Today we came and I saw this dam [*the Afsluitdijk, separating the low-lying areas of the Netherlands from the North Sea*] and somehow I run out of words. When I'll return I will give my people a report on this. The bay is really very, very wide and still they have made a dam and a road. When we arrived I saw that the sea was much higher than the land. We were standing below the sea.

I went to the house with the showers [*on a camping ground in Sweden*]. I thought they would be like the ones which we have used before. But these ones were different. They worked only with money. I put a coin in and then it opened the hot water and it kept coming out and I was washing with the two waters mixing. And the water went and went and when it had reached the limit of the money the hot water was shut off. In our place we have to use our hands to cut firewood and make fire and boil the water and then we take the hot water and pour it and wash ourselves and when the hot water is finished, it is really finished. But here we have just to put in another coin and new hot water will come.

I have seen the people in your places. There are very many of them. We don't know, are they friends, relatives, or what. They are walking around just by themselves, and also we are walking around among them. If one of them knows us a little bit we can start to talk, if not, not. We came to this place [*Gotland*] and we met friends. It was very good because we went to their house. We ate together and we talked and we told all kinds of good stories and later we returned and slept.

[*At the newly excavated archaeological site of Ajvide on Gotland, where Tom easily identified Neolithic tools and other grave goods*] Your forefathers and we Trobrianders are alike. When somebody dies all the belongings are put in the grave. We do this out of sorrow. You white people have changed this custom and keep the belongings of the dead persons. That is why you have businesses and become rich.

When I see those TV pictures in your house I feel sorry and I get afraid. Because they are fighting [*in former Yugoslavia*] for such a long time. In our place fighting is different. After one day it is over. One day only. But the white people are fighting war without rest.

Some people in Africa are dying. They are dying for nothing. I have seen it [*in TV reports*]. It is very bad. You see, with us there is always some food. When the sun has destroyed the taro in the gardens, then only the taro will die, but other foods like yams, coconuts, and banana are OK. There is always a little bit of that. Our children don't have to cry.

THE URBAN WORLD

ROLAND FLETCHER

W E LIVE in a rapidly urbanizing world. In the last decade of the twentieth century, more people will be living in towns and cities than in the country-side. How did this come about, and where will it lead?

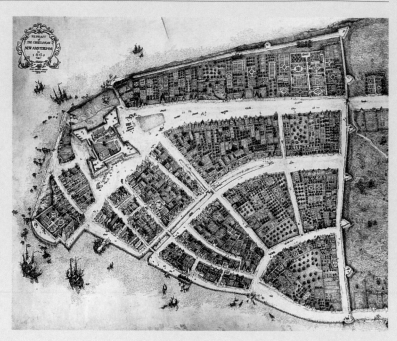

One view is that, for such settlement growth to be possible, changes have to take place in the ways communities interact and communicate. Economic changes are then required to enable and sustain this growth.

Over the past 15,000 years, there have been three great jumps in the growth of compact (as opposed to dispersed) settlements. The first, occurring at different times in different regions, was sustained by the development of agriculture. This allowed the compact settlements established by permanently sedentary communities to expand from a previous maximum size of between about 1 and 2 hectares (2 and 5 acres) to areas of about 100 hectares (250 acres). The second jump, often referred to as the rise of urbanism, also began independently in different places at different times. Sustained by the development of more intensive agricultural practices, such as large-scale irrigation works, it allowed compact cities to reach sizes of up to 100 square kilometers (about 40 square miles). The third jump occurred in the 1800s, when industrialization in Europe began to sustain a massive rate of urban growth that has since extended around the planet. Cities today can be as large as several thousand square kilometers and contain as many as 15 million people. However, while their centers often have high

☞ Industrial urbanism is producing vast, dispersed urban regions. The East Coast megalopolis will soon link up with the Chicago–Gary urban complex around the Great Lakes. In Europe, a single urban region may eventually extend from the Midlands of England, through the Netherlands, to the Ruhr, in Germany.

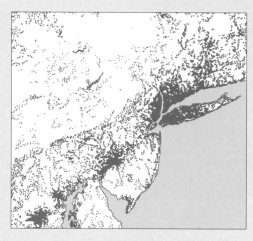

☝ New York was founded by Dutch immigrants in the seventeenth century. Originally named New Amsterdam, it was a typical compact European town of the period.
THE GRANGER COLLECTION

♀ New York has grown from a compact town into an extensive, dispersed city.

☝ The Central Business District of New York: a world architecture.

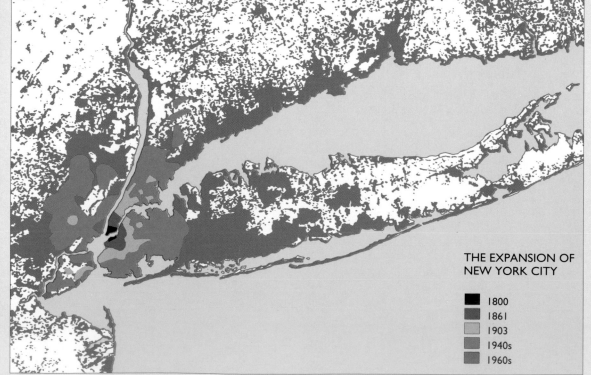

THE EXPANSION OF NEW YORK CITY

■ 1800
■ 1861
□ 1903
■ 1940s
■ 1960s

JOHN W. REPS, HISTORIC URBAN PLANS OF ITHACA, NEW YORK/NATIONAL LIBRARY OF AUSTRALIA

very large settlement areas with low-density, dispersed populations. Such areas can vastly exceed the maximum extent possible for any single compact settlement using the same communication structure. In the case of industrial urbanism, this growth trajectory is dramatically exemplified by the developing so-called East Coast megalopolis in the United States and the great conurbations of Europe.

The city of Edo, shown here about 1854, was established as the capital of Japan by Shogun Ieyasu Tokugawa in AD 1590. In the eighteenth and early nineteenth centuries, it was one of the largest cities on Earth, with more than a million inhabitants. It has been repeatedly devastated by fires and earthquakes. Following the Meiji restoration in the 1860s, the emperor came to reside in the city, which was renamed Tokyo.

The Central Business District of Tokyo: a world architecture.

population densities, their average densities are usually quite low.

Each of the three great size increases has been associated with changes in communication methods. Early urbanism, for instance, was linked to the development of material forms of information storage, including writing. Similarly, the current wave of urban expansion was linked to the advent of mechanized means of communication, such as newspapers and railways.

Each of these growth jumps has allowed a hundredfold increase in the size of the largest compact settlements. If industrial towns and cities can be assumed to grow at the same rate, compact cities of up to 10,000 square kilometers (about 4,000 square miles) are feasible with our existing social and communication infrastructure. The alternative growth trajectory, which also occurred during all the previous growth phases, is towards

In the 1980s, Tokyo was concentrated around Sangama Bay and had already linked up with Kawasaki and Yokohama (left). If it expands to cover an area of 10,000 square kilometers (4,000 square miles), it will cover the entire Kwanto plain (right), and could contain more than 100 million people. We do not know whether a compact city of this size could be sustained by the current global economic system.

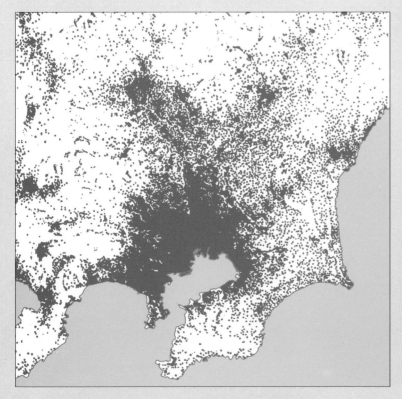

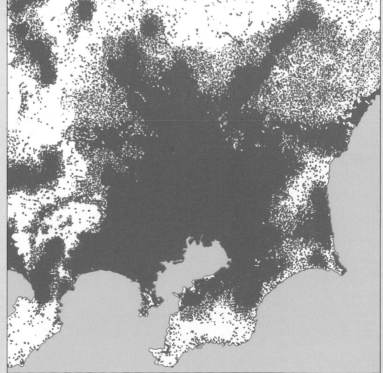

Marriage and Family

The nuclear family made up of wife, husband, and children has been characteristic of Western societies in the twentieth century, especially in the more industrialized countries. Will the future see a return of the extended family, with three and even four generations living together and grandparents contributing to a domestic division of labor? It depends on individual and community priorities.

The argument for more decentralized societies rests partly on their social advantages in terms of lower crime rates, less delinquency, and greater family stability. Similarly, a return to extended families is seen by some analysts as a natural counter to the modern-day problems of isolated mothers,

Extended families, as in this scene in Mexico, were once the rule in all societies. Many people today argue for the return of the extended family, on the grounds of its social and economic benefits. As well as offering greater family stability, it would relieve governments of much of the cost of providing social services for the children of working parents and the aged alike. But in industrialized societies, many people value the mobility afforded by the nuclear family. It is not easy to predict what the predominant family pattern will be in the future.

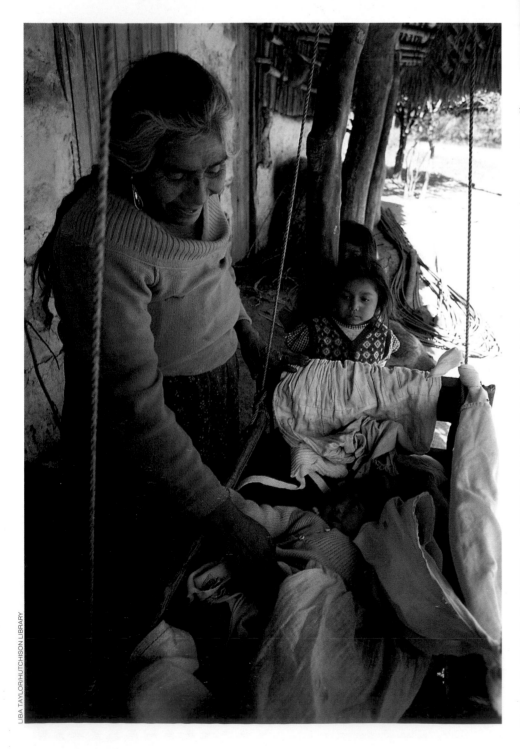

The first countries to grant women the franchise were New Zealand (1893), Australia (1902), and Finland (1906). Many other countries have since followed suit. This photograph was taken in London in 1918.

unsupervised children, and abandoned grandparents. This would have economic benefits as well, since these social problems contribute to the everescalating costs of social infrastructure, in terms of facilities for the aged, shelters for homeless young people, various psychiatric and counseling services, extra police, and so on.

The fortunes of families have had a heavy impact on women, for whom children and kin have traditionally been the center of social and work life. The women's movement has enjoyed spectacular success in the twentieth century, since women in New Zealand gained the vote for the first time, in 1893. But even in the handful of Western societies that pioneered this development, a large measure of sexual inequality remained. Women next won equal pay for equal work, at least in government jobs and large corporations, whereas they had previously been passed over for jobs with career potential in favor of men, who were seen as the primary breadwinners. Now, some are arguing for equal outcomes as well as equal opportunities.

As women's status improves, will the political phenomenon of feminism become a permanent feature of the political landscape? Some women, like some men, will always feel frustrated with their status and will attribute their grievance, rightly or wrongly, to discrimination. Will this dissatisfaction remain sufficiently high to fuel militant feminism as it did the 1960s, 1970s, and 1980s? Demands for reform will probably persist while the accepted symbols of success remain those of career and high income, and the traditional female role is insufficiently rewarded financially and in public esteem.

GÖRAN BURENHULT

NANCY DURRELL MCKENNA/HUTCHISON LIBRARY

♦ A father and child in a Trobriand Islands village, in Papua New Guinea. Infants in traditional societies enjoy much more body contact than those in Western countries. While children usually bond most closely with their mother, fathers and other family members, including grandparents, play an important role in children's socialization.

An Ageing Society?

Industrial societies are now ageing as the "baby boom" of the late 1940s and 1950s works its way down the generations like a dissipating shock wave. Under the impact of contraceptives and lifestyle competition favoring small families, modern industrial societies are now returning to something like the steady-state mix found in traditional societies, although with the following two differences. First, fewer children will be born per woman. In several industrialized countries, the average figure is now less than 2.2 children. This is, in the absence of immigration, the rate at which births balance deaths over a period, usually referred to as zero population growth. Also, as a result of antibiotics and other achievements of modern medicine, many more people will live to old age than at any time in the past. The effect of these two factors will be to distort the traditional population pyramid by narrowing the base and widening the top, producing, instead, a mushroom-like shape. What are the implications of this shift in age distribution?

One effect of an older electorate might be to swing the balance of social and political forces

GÖRAN BURENHULT

♦ Large families are valued in many parts of India, especially in rural areas. Here, a mother feeds her children in the courtyard of their house in West Bengal.

◄● An old man in southern Vanuatu. Many more people survive to old age in industrialized societies, with modern methods of health care, than in traditional societies. This trend is likely to result in a major demographic shift in the future, with greater social and political power vested in senior citizens.

CHRISTINE PEMBERTON/HUTCHISON LIBRARY

♦ Under Indira Gandhi, an official program to reduce India's birth rate was a threat to civil liberties, and failed. Contraception involves more than technology.

behind the extended family. As noted, a return to greater family self-reliance would help governments to unburden themselves of the costs of health and other social services devoted to the aged. Politics might undergo a drift to conservatism, dampening the volatility that often characterizes more youthful societies. A secondary political effect could emerge from a greater emphasis on families and parental authority. The politics of patriotism, including extreme nationalism, are asociated with cultures in which family bonds are strong.

MALE AND FEMALE: WHY ARE WE DIFFERENT?

NANCY WILMSEN THORNHILL

CHARLES DARWIN published his theory of sexual selection in 1871, in *The Descent of Man and Selection in Relation to Sex*, proposing that the extent of sex differences within species depends on the mating system, monogamous species exhibiting none, whereas in polygamous species, the sexes are markedly different. Yet it was not until the twentieth century that researchers suggested that behavioral differences between the sexes arise as a consequence of the fundamental physiological differences between them. In essence, females produce eggs and males produce sperm, and this basic biological fact underlies the whole range of characteristics by which we distinguish female and male. These behavioral differences are, quite simply, the result of females making the bigger investment in offspring from the outset: eggs are larger, more nutritious, and, in the long term, more costly in terms of energy than are sperm.

THE HUTCHISON LIBRARY

♂ Men in most societies compete with each other, often in the form of physical contact. One-to-one shows of strength, as here among the Dinka, of Sudan, in Africa, can be important in establishing a man's status.

♀ In the Peruvian rainforest, in South America, as in many other hunting-gathering societies, a man's hunting skill is critical to his eligibility as a mate. Good hunters often have the most wives.

For many mammals, especially the higher primates, including humans, females' involvement in reproduction minimally includes pregnancy, gestation, parturition, and lactation—and, in some cases, prolonged years of caring for the young. For males, on the other hand, the minimum involvement is a short period of time and the relatively small amount of energy involved in the act of mating and the process of sperm production. As a result, men and women evolved with different motivations. Men sought to mate as often as possible, and were, therefore, more promiscuous and less discriminating, while women, for whom the consequences of mating were greater and longer-term, were less promiscuous and more discriminating.

Because women were more discriminating in their choice of sexual partners, men competed for the opportunity to become one of these partners. Inevitably, some men were chosen for sexual relationships and some were not, and this had

JOE CAVANAUGH/D. DONNE BRYANT STOCK

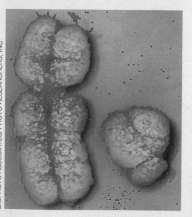

BIOPHOTO ASSOCIATES/ PHOTO RESEARCHERS, INC.

♂ Human X (left) and Y chromosomes. Females carry two X chromosomes, and males carry one of each.

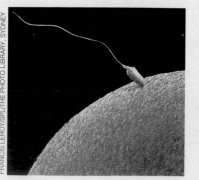

FRANCIS LEROY/SPL/THE PHOTO LIBRARY, SYDNEY

☞ The difference in size between egg and sperm is clearly evident. This is, in part, what defines the sexes.

In the Amazonian rainforest, in South America, Yanomami women take care of children, and also forage for food, while men do the hunting. These women are collecting termites.

men have had to compete with each other for access to mates and have thereby developed a more aggressive psychology, making them more inclined to take risks. This is supported by statistical studies showing that, in every society in the world, men (particularly young men) are more likely than women to die as a result of accident or violence. Psychologists Martin Daly and Margo Wilson have documented sex differences in the occurrence of homicide, revealing that homicides are overwhelmingly committed by men against men in the United States, Australia, Europe, and India, and also among three groups of North and South American Indians and eight African tribes.

In contrast, women generally provide the vast majority of care, protection, and daily food for children. To do this effectively, they must have reliable access to food and shelter, both for themselves while pregnant and lactating and for their children after weaning. Over the long course of evolutionary time, men have provided women with these critical resources in exchange for sexual access and paternity.

two consequences: more men than women never reproduced, and some individual men had far more offspring than did any woman.

Sexual Division of Labor

Beginning in the 1970s, evolutionary theorists began to study behavioral differences between men and women in earnest. The sexual division of labor was already a widely known phenomenon, largely through a study published by anthropologist G.P. Murdock in 1949. Murdock evaluated ethnographic data from 250 societies, and found that, in most of these cultures, women look after the children and acquire most of the food—by gathering and gardening—and men do the fighting and hunting.

Evolutionary explanations for this division of labor focus on the different behavioral "strategies" that men and women are thought to have pursued, each triggered by a complex of psychological mechanisms that also seem to have been different for each sex.

Evolutionary Psychology

Men and women differ in their inclination to fight and hunt because, from the earliest times,

Because of this, one of the things for which men compete with each other is control of the resources women desire. Women, in turn, have evolved a psychological propensity to evaluate and select men according to their ability to accrue such resources. In a recent crosscultural study of 37 societies, psychologist David Buss found that women, significantly more than men, value wealth and high status in a potential mate.

The legacy of psychological and behavioral differences men and women have inherited need not be viewed as immutable. As we gain insight into the environmental circumstances that molded these differences over thousands of generations, we become better equipped to judge their appropriateness in our rapidly changing world.

A !Kung mother, her baby on her back, fishes in the Okavango swamp, in Botswana, southern Africa. Women often provide most of the family's daily food.

Like many other animals, humans have a strong instinct to band together in groups. National and ethnic identities, often symbolized by flags, are a powerful expression of this human need. This "support our troops" rally was held in Pittsfield, Massachusetts.

Nuclear tests are still conducted, albeit underground. The proliferation of nuclear weapons raises the specter of an unthinkable future. We must rein in this threat.

PHOTRI INC.

Near Belet Huen, Italian and Nigerian United Nations troops prepare to destroy surrendered arms used in the Somalian civil war that raged between 1991 and 1993. While aggressive nationalism is re-emerging as a potent force in the post-Cold War era, it is to be hoped that rising standards of living and global organizations such as the United Nations will bring to bear the moderating influence of interdependence and the rule of law.

DAN MCCOY/RAINBOW

Kinship and the Nation-state

Patriotism, the emotional underpinning of the nation-state and the tragic conflicts of the twentieth century, is still with us. Its continuity is remarkable, considering the influence of antinationalist movements, the crushing of many small nations by post-Second World War communism, and the progressive globalization of the economy. How long will national feeling remain a significant political factor when one of the effects of huge trading blocs such as the European Union is to allow the unimpeded movement of people between member countries?

Politicians of the Left and Right have extolled and decried patriotism. Yet loyalty towards and special affection for one's own people and land have proved to be as durable as, and often stronger than, that wellspring of socialism, pity for the downtrodden. Group loyalty has been a feature of our species' social life probably from its inception.

While small-scale human societies, such as those of the Kalahari Bushmen (San) or traditional Australian Aborigines, are relatively open to migrants, they also identify strongly as a group and observe territorial boundaries. In all traditional societies, sharing and exchange are crucial strategies for insuring against famine. But defence of territory has also been a necessity, since for hunters and gatherers land is the only economic resource, and defense is a group activity in which the defenders are bound together by a sense of loyalty to one another and by love of the land.

The intimacy of contact with the land might be diminished in farming communities, but the need and propensity for group coherence and mutual aid remains. Religion, a universal feature of traditional societies, has helped to integrate people into cooperative communities and provided emotional support. Simultaneously, it has been a force for ethnocentrism, since tightly knit groups tend to view the world through the lens of their own society, with its assumptions and practices. For thousands of years, group differences in language and custom that the citizens of modern, cosmopolitan societies would consider minor have compounded this sense of difference, fostering group solidarity and hence group survival. Throughout all the changes that have taken place in the subsistence base of different societies, it has remained advantageous to belong—and is, therefore, natural to want and seek to belong—to a mutually supportive group.

One reason why patriotism continues to flourish in the modern urban environment may be that it provides a layer of meaning, in the form of group identity, for people living in an ever more secularized world, often stripped of the bonds of family and community. Belligerent nationalism and other aggressive ideologies are unacceptable in the emerging global village. But before we can humanely curb ideological excesses, we need to better understand, and to learn to live with, the social needs and structures that underpin them.

The massive destructive potential of nuclear and mechanized warfare makes peace the first imperative in international affairs. Despite continuing armed conflicts in various parts of the world, the trend appears to be towards international integration and the diffusion of the extreme superpower polarization of the Cold War era.

The reduced likelihood of warfare between the great powers still leaves room for relatively minor squabbles, which nonetheless inflict terrible suffering. The rapid fragmentation of the former communist bloc is the most recent example. This trend is being balanced, however, by large, overarching, and unifying bodies, such as the United Nations Organization and the European Union, which facilitate diplomatic alternatives to war and exert the cohesive force of shared economic interests.

CRISPIN HUGHES/HUTCHISON LIBRARY

Biotechnology: Extending Life and Selective Breeding

The threat and promise of biological manipulation of society is at least as old as Aldous Huxley's *Brave New World* (published in 1932), which foresaw the possibility of cloning and of doping citizens to fit docilely into a totally planned society. Science has added to Huxley's vision. The era of recombinant DNA manipulation, embryo transplants, in vitro fertilization, and effective contraception has arrived. It is now possible to manipulate offspring genetically, adding, subtracting, or shuffling lengths of DNA to produce a child (or 10 or 1,000 identical children) whose every cell contains the new arrangement. Fortunately, this is illegal, but it *is* done routinely with other mammals. Laboratory mice used in cancer research are often produced by means of gene manipulation and cloning, allowing scientists to experiment on any number of identical individuals. At present, this is done rather clumsily, although the recently invented "gene shears" point to a future of precise gene surgery.

Genetic engineering and organ transplant techniques have given new life to those two perennial topics of speculation and wishful thinking: increasing longevity and selective breeding of humans. If knowledge continues to accumulate at its present rate, human life might become extendible in much the same way an automobile can be repaired. With sufficient expenditure, a car need never be abandoned. Instead, worn-out pieces can be replaced ad infinitum. But car maintenance presents no moral dilemma, while the prospect of extending human life spans to hundreds of years does.

Central to this dilemma is the future possibility that we may be able to double or triple the present 100-year limit on life by such means as transplant-ation and genetic engineering. The former could lead to some individuals becoming "walking transplants", with replacement human, animal, and artifical organs and limbs outnumbering their original "parts". The final step will be to replace the brain, perhaps piecemeal. In the future, new neurons might be obtained through cloning. It will then be fair to ask: who is this new person, the recipient or the donor? The question might be fair, but it will be immaterial to patients faced with progressive loss of memory, social facility, and intelligence. In such matters, the morality of the armchair is often very different from that of the sickbed.

If an antidote is possible to the cellular breakdown believed to cause ageing, it will be based on genetic engineering. As more than one critic has cautioned, however, tinkering with the human genetic code is not something to be done lightly. It would be a dangerous step to introduce into the human gene pool sequences of DNA taken from animals. Yet this is what scientists are beginning to do with animals and plants. How might these developments affect humans?

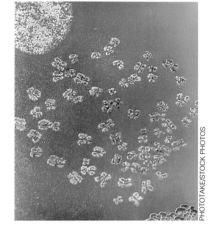

A geneticist holds up genetically altered cancerous cells. In 1991, the first attempt was made to immunize a patient with terminal cancer by injecting him with his own modified diseased cells. While still highly experimental, this application of genetic engineering is set to continue humankind's march towards the eradication of disease.

Human chromosomes seen through a powerful electron microscope. From Gregor Mendel's first breeding experiments in the late 1800s, the science of genetics has progressed to the point where it can screen out hereditary disease and even design the next generation. This new technology presents profound ethical challenges.

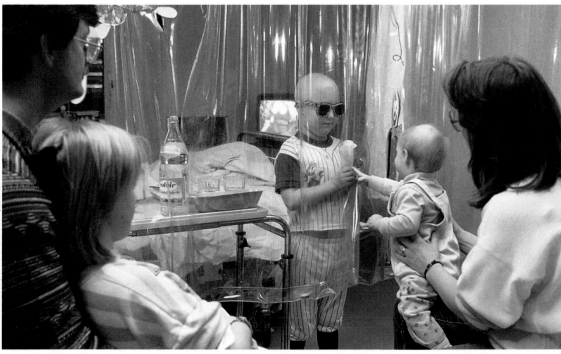

Matthew lives in a sterile environment, separated from his family by a plastic wall. He received a transplant of bone marrow and blood cells in an effort to cure him of Fanconi disease, an inherited form of anemia. Situations such as Matthew's, and the material and human costs of treating symptoms, provide the impetus for negative eugenics, aimed at screening out dangerous genes before they can do harm. Who should make such choices, and should they be allowed at all?

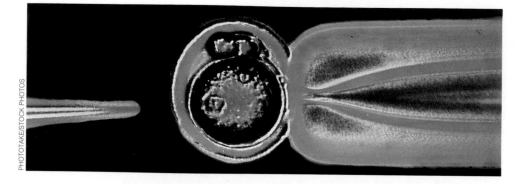

PHOTOTAKE/STOCK PHOTOS

♨ Transferring foreign DNA into a mouse embryo. One of the big issues in genetic engineering is whether it is safe—and also morally defensible—to transfer genetic material from one species to another. The long-term consequences of such profound interference in evolution are almost beyond comprehension.

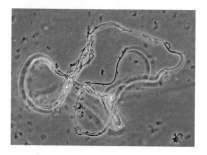

♨ A light micrograph of human DNA (desoxyribonucleic acid), the "code of life" that carries genetic information from one generation to the next.
PHILIPPE PLAILLY/SPL/THE PHOTO LIBRARY, SYDNEY

♀ Modern medicine is using genetic engineering to fight disease. Here, lymphocytes are genetically altered to boost their immune power. Methods such as this instill hope in some hearts, and strike fear in others.

Sir Francis Galton, the pioneer of experimental psychology and behavioral genetics, coined the term "eugenics" to describe the science and practice of good breeding. Until recently, eugenics was confined to limiting the reproduction of individuals with undesired traits (typically, some forms of genetic pathology) and promoting the reproduction of individuals with desired traits—so-called negative and positive eugenics.

As noted, recent developments in genetic engineering make it possible, in principle, to design human genomes (an individual's genetic code) to order. Cautious experiments are already being conducted and have produced novel animals and plants, to the consternation and outrage of some critics. At the same time, the human genome is being mapped in ever greater detail, and the function of individual genes and gene combinations analyzed. The Human Genome Project at Stanford University, in California, led by L.L. Cavalli-Sforza, will go much further, describing the precise DNA structure of all 46 chromosomes (the structures in the cell nucleus, consisting of a long, coiled and folded strand of DNA, that carry the genes). Some day fairly soon, scientists will know which genes code for the various development processes, and how the genetic recipe produces the final outcome—the range of human "phenotypes", or different physical charac-

teristics. It will be possible to say with varying degrees of accuracy how a certain embryo will appear and behave at different stages in life. Humanity will then be the first species able to deliberately shape its genetic future.

If genetic engineering technology becomes cheap and accessible to general practitioners, market forces will place decisions about the future of the species in parents' hands. Government control will be practicable only if such technology remains the province of institutions. History shows, however, that determination and money are almost always sufficient to connect demand with supply. If choice comes to reside in individuals, the only precaution possible will be education. Who knows, the safest course might be a democratic one, keeping momentous decisions about our genetic future out of the hands of a powerful few while providing the many with the knowledge necessary to exercise responsibility for future generations.

The Next Step?

It would be overly negative to end on a cautionary note. Admittedly, much travail would seem to lie ahead for our species, but it will be mixed with great achievements, adventures, and plain good living. In addition to the cognitive capacities in which we take pride, humans are endowed with strong emotions and motivations, which have so far helped us find our way from hominid times to the space age. We are an optimistic species, for whom optimism is appropriate. Our forebears did not lose hope when glaciers covered the land and other major global changes occurred. They always rebuilt their shelters when they had been destroyed by floods, earthquake, or war. We modern humans can take hope in this heritage, and in our growing knowledge of ourselves—of our strengths as well as our weaknesses, especially our unsurpassed ability to think and to cope with the enormous problems and opportunities that lie before us.

In these speculations, our intent has been not so much to issue dire warnings as to reflect on the apparently inexorable tide of evolution. Every one of the millions of species now living is merely, and magnificently, the latest chapter in a family history reaching back through thousands of extinctions. And that includes humans. In a process that took about 15 million years, *Homo sapiens sapiens* replaced *Homo neanderthalensis*, which, in turn, had replaced *Homo erectus*, *Homo habilis*, *Australopithecus africanus*, and the original ancestor we shared with the apes. In this account, humans are but a page in their lineage's history. But they are unlikely to be the final chapter.

☞ *Opposite page:* A young mother in a Sudanese village, in Africa, communicates joy and good cheer in a language people everywhere can understand. The remarkable similarity of all the populations making up our planet-wide species is one of humankind's main hopes for unity of purpose in meeting the challenges that lie ahead.

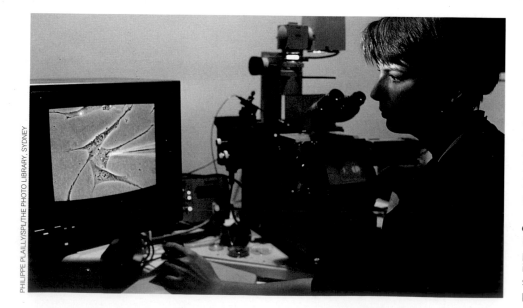

PHILIPPE PLAILLY/SPL/THE PHOTO LIBRARY, SYDNEY

GLOSSARY

animism
A belief in the existence of classes of supernatural spirit beings, usually including both ghosts (wandering, disembodied souls of deceased humans) and nonhuman spirits. Both types may inhabit the surrounding environment. Most are bipedal and may appear in human form. They are not worshiped, but rather are feared and avoided by the local people, except for the religious specialists, who know how to placate them or pray to them. They may be malignant or benevolent, and are believed to have some influence over many aspects of the natural world and human life.

Arawak language family
A widely distributed language family of South America and the Caribbean, including the Taíno of the West Indies.

Austroasiatic language family
A major language family of northeastern India and the Southeast Asian mainland, comprising about 150 languages spoken by some 60 million people. It has two major groupings: the Munda languages of northeastern peninsular India and the Mon–Khmer languages of the Southeast Asian mainland. The Mon–Khmer languages include modern Vietnamese and Khmer (Cambodian), as well as many fairly isolated languages from southern China to as far south as Malaysia and the Nicobar Islands. The Austroasiatic language family appears to be the most ancient in its area, having been superseded in places by Indo-European, Tai, and Austronesian languages.

Austronesian language family
A major language family to which the languages of Taiwan, the islands of Southeast Asia, the Pacific (excluding much of New Guinea), Madagascar, and parts of the Southeast Asian mainland belong. Although all Austronesian languages are related, they are not necessarily mutually understandable.

Bêche-de-mer

bêche-de-mer
A marine invertebrate (*Holothuria*, also known as sea cucumber or trepang), found in shallow water. It was gathered and smoked for sale as a food item exported to China. Significant in the nineteenth century, the bêche-de-mer trade has since declined in importance.

blackbirding
A term used to describe the recruitment of plantation labor in the nineteenth century. Islanders were often kidnapped or tricked into boarding blackbirders' ships, and many died on plantations or were stranded on foreign islands after their work was completed. Reactions to blackbirding abuses provided an impetus for the establishment of colonial protectorates in the western Pacific.

breadfruit
Breadfruit (*Artocarpus altilis*) is a significant crop in Micronesia and Polynesia especially, since its starchy fruit may be stored for long periods of time. On small Micronesian atolls, breadfruit is often the predominant variety of tree, providing an indispensable source of building materials for houses and canoes.

candelabra model
One of the theories of human development, also known as the regional continuity or multiregional model. Modern humans are seen as descending from *Homo erectus* in Africa, Europe, and Asia. The opposing theory, known as the Noah's Ark model, and the more recent "Eve" theory, hold that modern humans originated in one single area of Africa.

Carib language family
One of the three major language families of South America, represented by the languages of tribes located as far north as the Lesser Antilles and as far south as northern Mato Grosso.

circumcision
In the Australian Western Desert, the ritual involving the removal of the foreskin is the most important one an Aboriginal male experiences. It truly sets him on the road to manhood. It also gives him access to country other than his own, and the place where he is circumcised becomes, in a sense, his place. Moreover, the men who perform the operation are obliged later to provide him with a wife (one of their daughters or sisters).

coconut
Found in coastal areas throughout the Pacific, the coconut (*Cocos nucifera*) is a source of moisture, carbohydrates, fats, and oils, as well as providing building materials. Extensive coconut plantations were established throughout the Pacific in the nineteenth century in order to produce copra (the dried meat), which is used as a source of edible oils and in the manufacture of soap.

depilation
The removal of body hair. In Aboriginal Australia, indications are that depilation was traditionally engaged in by males in areas where circumcision and subincision were not practiced.

DNA
The abbreviation for desoxyribonucleic acid, a complex molecule found in the nuclei of the cells of all living organisms that contains, in chemically coded form, the genetic information necessary to build, control, and maintain life. The characteristic form of the DNA molecule is a double helix.

Dravidian language family
A language family spoken in southern India to which the Tamil, Telegu, Malayalam, and Karmada languages belong. It is thought to have been spoken in northern India before the spread of Indo-European languages in the second millennium BC, and was probably the main language of the Harappans.

ethnoarchaeology
Sometimes called "living archaeology", ethnoarchaeology unites the disciplines of enthnography and archaeology. Ethnoarchaeologists study the technologies and ways of life of contemporary peoples (particularly hunter-gatherers), with the aim of arriving at a more comprehensive picture of earlier cultures.

ethnobotany
The study of the botanical folk knowledge of a native people: how they name, classify, and use the various plants in their environment.

ethnography See *ethnology*.

ethnology
The division of anthropology devoted to the analysis and systematic interpretation of present-day cultural data. Often contrased with ethnography, which is restricted to the descriptive recording of present-day cultures.

"Eve" theory
The hypothesis that all modern humans are descended from a common first mother who lived in southern Africa about 200,000 years ago. The theory is based on genetic research showing that as modern humans spread throughout the world, they rarely, if at all, interbred with existing, but more archaic, humans, such as the Neanderthals. The "Eve" theory does not imply a creationist view, only that there has been a chance survival of a single line of mitochondrial DNA.

evolutionary clock
The theory that genetic mutations (if they have no survival value) occur at random and therefore at the same rate in all pop-
ulations. If this is true, the genetic distance between two populations is a measure of how much time has elapsed since the populations diverged, and, therefore, of how closely related they are to one another. If the rate of genetic change can be estimated, the length of time since the populations diverged can be calculated.

Finno-Ugric language family
A language family spoken by some 22 million people in northern Eurasia. The Finnic branch comprises Finnish, Estonian, and Saami (Lapp), while the Ugric branch consists of Hungarian. Finno-Ugric is also related to the Samoyed language of northern Eurasia, and, more distantly, to Yukaghir, which is spoken in Northeast Asia. All these languages are grouped into the higher-level Uralic–Yukaghir language family.

founder effect
Rare genes can be common in some populations that have grown from small, closely related groups. Sometimes, a rare gene, and its phenotypic effect, can be traced back to an individual "founder" of a lineage, who had many offspring.

freshwater "lens"
Rain falling on coral atolls percolates below ground level and forms a layer of fresh water "floating" on the surface of the underlying salt water. The fresh water does not dissipate through the coral, because it is contained by pressure from the denser salt water. Also known as the Ghyben-Hertzberg lens.

funerary mask
Mortuary rituals are highly elaborated in many parts of island Melanesia, and masks are often used to represent the presence of spirits on such occasions. The distinctive Malanggan masks of New Ireland were traditionally destroyed at the end of the ceremonies in which they were used.

Malanggan **funerary mask**

gaucho
An Argentinian cowboy. The gaucho method of riding horseback was borrowed from the style developed by the Puelche and Tehuelche Indians of the Pampas and Patagonia.

gene pool
All the genes in an interbreeding population. The genetic make-up of each individual and each new generation is drawn from this pool.

genetic drift
A term used to refer to random changes in a population's genetic make-up. These changes are not due to natural selection. Genetic drift is strongest in small populations, and can occur as a result of either mutation or the loss of individuals and families who fail to reproduce for some reason or who emigrate.

genome
The complete genetic material for any cell carried by a single set of chromosomes. The chromosome are the structures in the cell nucleus, each consisting of a long, coiled and folded strand of DNA, that carry the genes.

genotype
The genetic make-up of an organism.

hominid
A member of the Hominidae, the family that includes both extinct and modern forms of humans and, in most modern classifications, the Great Apes.

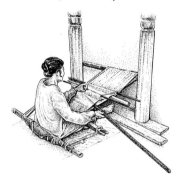

Horizontal backstrap loom

horizontal backstrap loom
A loom is a device for weaving cloth. Its basic components are a rod or beam at either end to hold the warp threads and keep them under tension, and a mechanism for opening a so-called shed between selected warp threads to facilitate the passage of weft threads from side to side. In a backstrap loom, the warp is stretched horizontally, or at a slight angle to the ground, with one warp rod fixed to the ground or to a post and the other attached to the weaver's body by means of a belt or strap that passes around his or her back. Warp tension is thus maintained during weaving by the weaver's body weight. Horizontal backstrap looms are found in South and Central America, Japan, and Nepal, as well as in Indonesia.

hula
Although now familiar as a tourist entertainment, Hawaiian hula dances traditionally had political and religious significance. Performed on ceremonial occasions, the dances were accompanied by chants, which included supplications to deities, the recitation of chiefly genealogies, and spontaneous compositions expressing grief, admiration, or ridicule. Contemporary Hawaiian nationalists are attempting to restore some of this former significance to the performance of hula.

hunter-gatherers
Groups of humans who subsist by gathering wild plants and hunting wild animals. Although many hunter-gatherers regularly move their camps to be near seasonally available wild foods, others remain virtually sedentary throughout the year.

Indo-European language family
A group of Old World languages with related grammars and vocabularies, which diverged from a common ancestor several thousand years ago. It encompasses the Germanic languages (including English) and most other languages spoken in Europe, the Caucasus, and Persia and on the Indian subcontinent. Among the major extinct branches is the Hittite language of Anatolia. Languages of the Indo-European family are today spoken by more people than those of any other family. Indo-European was the first major language family to be recognized by scholars, in the late eighteenth century.

ikat
The term *ikat* comes from *mengikat*, a Malay–Indonesian word meaning to tie or bind. In *ikat* textiles, the pattern is determined by a resist dye technique before weaving begins. Warp and/or weft threads are wound around a frame, and the pattern is created by tightly binding small groups of threads so that they will resist penetration by the dye. After the first dyeing, bindings are added or removed for additional colors. *Ikat* is used to pattern traditional textiles in India, Japan, central Asia, and Central America, as well as in Indonesia.

kachina
A Hopi word meaning "life father" or the "sitter": one who reclines to hear petitions for rain, fertility, and other blessings. A religious figure, the kachina is a supernatural being believed to visit the pueblo-dwelling Indians of the southwestern United States at the beginning of the year. On ceremonial occasions, local Indian leaders dress in spectacular kachina costumes and impersonate the spirits in dances, when they are traditionally regarded as the physical embodiment of these powerful beings. The word is also sometimes used to refer to kachina dolls—small, painted representations of kachina dancers—but these are more properly called *tihü* (figurines) by the Hopi people. Membership of the various kachina cults is determined by kinship.

kaolin
A fine white clay formed by the weathering of volcanic rocks. Kaolin is named after a mountain in China that yielded the first clay of this type sent to Europe; it is also known as china clay.

land dive
The *gol*, or land dive ritual, of southern Pentecost Island is performed on the occasion of the local yam harvest. Men construct a large tower, from which individual men jump with their ankles secured by vines, which arrest their fall just before they reach the earth. Success in the land dive and in yam cultivation were closely linked in traditional culture, but the character of the land dive has changed since it became a popular tourist attraction in the 1970s.

lip-plug
A carved stick or stone worn as an ornament through an opening in the lower lip. Among the Kayapó of the Amazon, lip-plugs were meant to instill fear in the enemy.

manioc
Also called cassava, manioc (*Manihot esculenta*) is a starchy root crop that can be processed into an important food. It was the staple diet throughout most of Amazonia and the Caribbean at the time of European contact. Manioc is the source of tapioca.

matrilineal descent
A system of tracing affiliation through females: a person inherits through his or her mother, who, in turn, would have inherited through her mother, and so on. Sometimes termed uterine descent.

megalith
A stone of great size, particularly one used in ancient construction work or forming part of monumental remains. The name comes from the Greek words *megas* (large) and *lithos* (stone).

Melanesia
The westernmost of the three traditional groupings of Pacific island cultures, Melanesia includes New Guinea, the Admiralties, the Bismarcks, the Solomons, Vanuatu (formerly the New Hebrides),

Kachina

and New Caledonia. Fiji is on the border between Melanesia and Polynesia, and different scholars sometimes include it in one or the other area.

Micronesia
Occupying a broad band of islands just north of the equator, Micronesia consists of the Belau (formerly Palau) group, the Marianas, the Carolines, the Marshalls, Kiribati (formerly the Gilbert Islands), and Nauru. Ethnologists traditionally divide the region between western Micronesia, including Belau, the Marianas, and Yap, and eastern Micronesia, comprising the rest of the region. Western Micronesia is believed to have been settled from the Philippines or Indonesia, while eastern Micronesia was probably settled from somewhere in the eastern Solomons–Fiji–Vanuatu region.

mithan
A small bovine animal (*Bos frontalis*) kept by the Naga and their neighbors in India and Myanmar (Burma). The flesh of the *mithan* forms a part of ritual feasts, and the horns are symbols of high status when worn on headdresses or displayed on house walls.

Megalith

mitochondria
The minute granular organelles present in living cells that are responsible for respiration and energy production. Sometimes referred to as the "powerhouses" of the cell.

mobile
The settlement pattern of social groups who move from place to place within a given territory, building camps at each site.

moiety
Either of two distinct, but more or less equal, parts into which a society is divided, often on the basis of clans. Each moiety has reciprocal rights over, and responsibilities towards, the other.

Mon–Khmer language group
A language family that includes Vietnamese and Cambodian, as well as numerous other languages spoken from northern India, through Thailand, to Laos and Vietnam.

monogamy
Being married to, or having a long-term sexual relationship with, only one person.

music-bow

The simplest of string instruments, played in many cultures around the globe. An ordinary hunting bow can be used. The player's lips encircle the string at one end, and the string is either tapped with a small stick or plucked with a fingertip. Different tones are produced by the player varying the position and shape of the lips. As well as the string vibrating between the player's lips, the stave may be held against the player's mouth. A special bow is often used, however, varying in length from 0.5 to 3 meters (about 20 inches to 10 feet), with the addition of a resonator consisting of a gourd, a pot, or a wooden box to reinforce the naturally faint tone. A further variation is to divide the string into two segments of unequal length by encircling the stave and the string with a simple noose.

Music-bow

mutation

A random change in the genome, resulting from environmental damage (from chemicals or radiation, for example) or from replication errors in a length of DNA. Most mutations are not adaptive and are either weeded out by cellular self-repair mechanisms or cause spontaneous abortion of the affected fetus. Some mutations, however, do help their carriers to adapt and thus to have more offspring: a process that underlies natural selection.

natural selection

A major mechanism of evolutionary change. Natural selection occurs when one genotype in a population is more successful than another in transmitting its genes to the next generation. Success is due to the organism (the phenotype) being better adapted to its physical or social environment. This insight was contributed by Charles Darwin in the mid-nineteenth century.

Neolithic

Literally, the "New Stone Age". The term refers to the final phase of the Stone Age, when farming became an essential part of the economy.

nomadic

A term used by ethnographers to describe the movements of whole social groups of pastoralists who utilize different parts of a given territory in different seasons, usually summer and winter pastures, and build camps for those periods.

obsidian

A black, glassy volcanic rock, often used to make sharp-edged tools.

paddle-and-anvil method

A technique of pottery production in which the sides of the pot are formed and smoothed by beating a wooden paddle against a stone held inside the pot. Sometimes, the paddle is carved, to produce decorative designs on the pot's surface.

Paleoindians

The big-game hunters of the Americas from the earliest known, about 12,000 years ago, to about 8,000 years ago. Some investigators regard the term as referring to all hunting groups involved with now-extinct mammals, in which case the peoples who hunted the species of bison that became extinct about 6,500 years ago would also be classified as Paleoindians.

Paleolithic

Literally, the "Old Stone Age". It began some two million to three million years ago with the emergence of humans and the earliest forms of chipped stone tools, and continued through the Pleistocene Ice Age until the retreat of the glaciers some 12,000 years ago. The Paleolithic is equivalent to the Stone Age in sub-Saharan Africa.

Papuan language family

A series of possibly related languages spoken in the western Pacific, particularly in New Guinea. There are at least 700 languages in the family, but they are spoken by only three million people in total. Papuan languages may derive from those spoken by the earliest settlers in this region.

patrilineal descent

A system of tracing affiliation through males: a person inherits through his or her father, who, in turn, would have inherited through his father, and so on. Sometimes termed agnatic descent.

peyote button

The top portion (flower) of the peyote plant (*Lophophora williamsii*), a small, tap-rooted cactus native to Central America and Texas, in the United States. Containing several narcotic elements, the "button" causes hallucinations and long periods of wakefulness when ingested. The practice of eating the buttons probably originated among the Lipan Apache, and is a central feature of tribal religious life throughout much of Native North America. A typical peyote meeting lasts all night, punctuated by praying and the eating of peyote, and

ending with a ceremonial breakfast of parched (sun-dried) corn. The Native American Church was formed in 1918 to give the peyote cult protection against drug laws, and combines elements of the ceremony with the teachings of traditional Christianity.

phenotype

The product of the genome (or genotype) interacting with its environment. Plants and animals show only their phenotypes to the world, and genetic causes can only be inferred from these. Some phenotypic characteristics, such as height, are greatly affected by environment. Others, such as body plan and eye and hair color, are insensitive to environmental changes, and are often referred to as being innate or genetically determined.

plantain

A tropical plant (*Musa paradisiaca*) yielding a coarse, banana-like fruit, which is usually cooked before being eaten. Also refers to the fruit itself.

plaza

An unroofed, but architecturally enclosed space, around or within which are placed platform mounds and their associated buildings, such as palaces and temples.

Pleistocene

The first epoch of the geological period known as the Quaternary, preceding the Holocene (or present) epoch. It began some two million years ago and ended about 10,000 years ago, and was marked by the advance of ice sheets across northern Europe and North America. During this epoch, giant mammals existed, and in the Late Pleistocene, modern humans appeared.

polygamy

The practice or condition of having two or more spouses at the same time.

Polynesia

The most recently settled of the Pacific's three major cultural areas, Polynesia occupies a vast area within the triangle formed by New Zealand, Hawaii, and Easter Island (Rapa Nui). The ancestors of the Polynesians are believed to have dispersed from the Fiji–Vanuatu region about 3,000 years ago. A second dispersal from western Polynesia (the Fiji–Tonga–Samoa area) about 2,000 years ago ultimately resulted in the settlement of eastern Polynesia, which includes the Marquesas, Tahiti and the Society Islands, Hawaii, Easter Island, and New Zealand.

powwow

A gathering of the tribes to celebrate their culture and heritage, taking the form of competitive traditional singing and dancing. At least once each year, every viable Indian community sponsors a powwow by providing the facilities and prize money for dancers of all ages—clad in

traditional dress, highlighted with eagle feathers and deerskin—to come and celebrate life.

Quillwork

quillwork

A uniquely American Indian decorative technique utilizing porcupine quills. The quills are dyed and flattened, and then embroidered or skillfully bound onto items of clothing or other artifacts in intricate, colorful patterns and designs.

sacred flutes

In much of New Guinea, men's cults are associated with sacred flutes played on ritual occasions. The flutes are almost always played in matched pairs (often correspondng to dual social divisions, or moieties), and their music is said the be the voice of the spirits who assist in the growth and fertility of men, pigs, and crops.

sago

Both wild and cultivated varieties of the sago palm (*Metroxylon sagu*) grow in swampy areas of Southeast Asia and the Pacific. The starchy pith of the palm may be extracted by a process of pounding, washing, and settling, yielding between 110 and 400 kilograms (250 and 900 pounds) of storable flour per palm. Sago is likely to have been important in the diet of some of the earliest settlers of the western Pacific.

sandalwood

Found throughout much of the Pacific, sandalwood became a prized commodity in the nineteenth century, being valued in China as an incense wood for religious occasions. This gave it a crucial role in the British tea trade, since it was one of the few items of interest to the Chinese, who supplied much of England's tea. The sandalwood trade was a major stimulus to European colonialism in the South Pacific.

Sanskrit

A language of the Indo-European family formerly spoken in India. Vedic hymns were composed in Sanskrit as early as about 1800 BC, but were not written down until after about 500 BC. Sanskrit writings were one of the earliest indications that languages of the Indo-European family were to be found outside Europe. Sanskrit has not been spoken for many centuries, but (like Latin in medieval and Renaissance Europe) it survives as the classical literary and religious language of the Hindus.

sedentism
A way of life in which people remain settled in one place throughout the year.

shaman
A person believed to have supernatural powers. In times of sickness, shortage of game, or any other threat to a community's survival, the shaman is called upon to mediate with the spirit world on the community's behalf. The shaman presides over rituals, and may also be responsible for the keeping of laws and the continuity of traditions. Shamanism is the dominant element in the religion of most known arctic and subarctic hunter-gatherers. Most shamans are male.

Sino-Tibetan language family
The main language family of continental East Asia, spoken by nearly a billion people. It is found in China, India, Nepal, Myanmar (Burma), and the northern parts of Thailand, Laos, and Vietnam. Languages include Tibetan and Burmese, but Chinese is by far the most widely spoken. Chinese forms a linguistic continuum usually divided into about eight languages, of which Mandarin has the most speakers.

slash-and-burn agriculture
See *swidden agriculture*.

Stone Age
The earliest period of technology in human culture, when tools and weapons were made of stone, bone, and wood. The Stone Age comprises the Paleolithic, the Mesolithic, and the Neolithic (literally, the Old, Middle, and New Stone Age). In sub-Saharan Africa, the Stone Age is equivalent to the Paleolithic.

subincision
The practice of opening the underside of the penis to the urethra. In the Australian Western Desert, Aboriginal men who have undergone this rite are said to be "full men"—that is, fully initiated. They are then admitted to men's secret rituals.

sun dance
A widely practiced religious festival of the Plains tribes of North America. Held annually in the late spring or early summer, the dance lasts for several days and follows a closely prescribed format, from the choosing of the central lodge pole to the solemn placing of sacrificial gifts at an altar. Both men and women paint themselves and perform ritualized dances. Some tribal societies practiced self-mortification as a rite of purification and rejuvenation, including piercing and tearing the flesh, fasting, and dancing to the point of collapse.

swamp taro
A starchy root of the aroid family, swamp taro (*Cyrtosperma chamissonis*) is grown in artificial pits or natural freshwater bogs on many Micronesian atolls.

sweet potato
Originally domesticated in the New World, sweet potato (*Ipomoea batatas*) tubers tolerate cooler and drier weather conditions than most tropical root crops. Sweet potato is the main staple of the highland peoples of New Guinea and was very important in the traditional diet of the New Zealand Maori. It is not to be confused with yams.

swidden agriculture
A farming method in which an area of forest is cut down and burned to clear the land, after which crops are planted among the ashes, which serve as a fertilizer. After one to three years, the field (the swidden) is abandoned, to allow it to grow back into forest and rejuvenate. Technically, it is defined as a cultivation system in which fields are cropped for fewer years than they are allowed to fallow. Also called slash-and-burn cultivation or shifting cultivation.

taiga
The subarctic coniferous forest of Eurasia and North America, bordered on the north by tundra and on the south by deciduous forest or steppe.

taro
Once thought to have been introduced into the Pacific from the Southeast Asian mainland, taro (*Colocasia esculenta*) now appears to have been initially domesticated in New Guinea in ancient times. A member of the aroid family, it produces a nutritious and starchy corm, which grows best in wet, tropical conditions. Taro is favored as a food crop throughout the Pacific, but the spread of taro blight in the twentieth century has led to its replacement by sweet potato in many areas.

throw net
A small fishing net weighted with stones and designed for use in shallow water. The user casts the net to a likely spot and then wades out to retrieve the net and any fish caught in it.

Tumpline

thumb-piano
A small, portable musical instrument, with some affinities to a xylophone. Indigenous to Africa, and spread by slaves to the New World, it should be known by an African term rather than an English misnomer. *Marimba, mbiru,* and *sansa* are names that seem to have traveled particularly widely. It consists of a varying number of cane or metal lamellae, or tongues (flattened nails of different sizes are commonly used), arranged in one or two rows and sometimes grouped by pitch, fitted over two supporting bars and under a third (straining) bar to a wooden board. Often, a gourd or wooden box is added as a resonator. One end of the lamellae vibrates freely, and their varying lengths determine the pitch. Small metal sleeves are sometimes added to the base of the lamellae, or to the board, adding a rattling sound to the tone. In the Kalahari, a thin membrane may be fitted over the sound hole, producing a more buzzing sound. The player holds the *mbira* and fingers the lamellae with the thumbs and sometimes a forefinger, usually with a percussion-like attack.

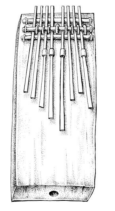

Thumb-piano

tipi
A Siouan word meaning "used to dwell", a tipi is a structure framed by a cone of peeled poles about 4 to 9 meters (15 to 30 feet) high and traditionally covered with a semicircle of tanned and sewn buffalo hides. With the introduction of the horse in the sixteenth century, bison became the center of the Plains Indian economy, and the tipi, easily constructed and transported, suited a more mobile way of life. Most tipis were family dwellings, although some Plains tribes construct much larger tipis for ceremonial or religious use.

totem
An animal or a natural object assumed by a particular kin or descent group as its symbol or emblem. In some cultures, the totemic entity is considered to be ancestrally related to the group.

tumpline
A cord, strap, or vine going around the head or shoulders from which a basket is suspended at the back to carry burdens.

Tupí–Guaraní language family
An important language family of Amazonia, especially of Brazil, where it gave rise to a trade language known as *lingua geral*.

Wigwam

wigwam
An Algonquian word meaning "bent poles", a wigwam is the traditional style of house built by the Woodland Indians of eastern North America. Saplings of hickory or elm are arranged upright in a circle 2 to 6 meters (7 to 20 feet) across and either buried in the ground or secured by horizontal crosspieces. The saplings are lashed together at the top to form a frame, which is covered with grass or reed mats in summer, or sheets of birch, elm, or chestnut bark in winter. An opening near the top of the wigwam allows smoke to escape. Men generally cut the poles and construct the frame, while women provide the covering and interior furnishings.

wild rice
An aquatic single-stem plant of the genus *Zizania*, which produces a long, cylindrical kernel of dark slate color. Native to the shallow mud flats of the upper and western Great Lakes region of the United States, it has long been gathered as a staple by the Ojibwa, Menominee, Ottawa, Dakota, Winnebago, and other Algonquian-speaking and Siouan-speaking tribes. Among the Ojibwa in particular, the gathering of wild rice has taken on sacred as well as practical significance.

X-ray painting
A form of Aboriginal art originating in western Arnhem Land in which both the internal and external body parts of humans and animals are depicted.

yam
Many varieties of yams (*Dioscorea esculenta* and *D. alata*) are found in the Pacific, some of which were probably introduced from the Asian mainland. Unlike most other tubers, yams may be stored for long periods of time, and they are often accumulated for the purposes of display or feasting. Yams demand fertile and well-drained soils, but reward skilled cultivation with tubers weighing as much as 20 kilograms (about 45 pounds) in the Sepik region of Papua New Guinea, where they are decorated and transferred to partners in ceremonial exchanges.

Louise Bäckman

Louise Bäckman is a Saami, whose family herded reindeer in the traditional way. She speaks one Saami language and reads all three. She retired in 1993 from the position of Professor and Director of the Department of Comparative Religion at the University of Stockholm, Sweden. Her main areas of interest are the religions of northern Eurasia, including the religion of the Saami of Lapland, and shamanism.

Serge Bahuchet

Serge Bahuchet is Directeur de Recherches at the Centre National de la Recherche Scientifique, Paris, and Co-head of the Département de Linguistique Culturelle at the Laboratoire de Langues et Civilisations à Tradition Orale (LACITO). His areas of specialization are the cultural anthropology of the forest peoples of Africa and the ethnoecology of Pygmies and farmers. He is co-editor of the 18-volume work *Encyclopédie des Pygmées Aka*. During 1994, he was a visiting research scholar at the Center for African Area Studies at Kyoto University, Japan.

E. Pendleton Banks

E. Pendleton Banks is Professor of Anthropology and Director of the Remote Sensing Laboratory at Wake Forest University, USA. He is currently doing research on the cultural ecology of Xinjiang and western Mongolia, using satellite images, historical documentation, and ethnographic data, and is also interested in the study of value orientations and the impact of war on the natural and cultural environments. He has conducted field research on the Island Carib, Burmese, and Chin cultures and on peasants in Bosnia, Croatia, and Romania. He has made five field trips to China, and in 1992, was an invited participant in the Nomads' Route International Scientific Expedition to Mongolia, sponsored by UNESCO and the Mongolian government. He is a member of a group of experts on space archaeology assembled by UNESCO to study ancient cultures along the Silk Road in central Asia.

M.E.F. Bloch

M.E.F. Bloch is Professor of Anthropology at the University of London, UK. His principal area of interest is Madagascan anthropology. He is the author of many books, and is a Fellow of the British Academy.

Boedhihartono

Boedhihartono is Senior Lecturer in the Department of Anthropology and Sport Medicine at the University of Indonesia, Jakarta, Indonesia. He has an MD from the University of Indonesia, a doctorate in human ecology from the University of Paris VII, France, and an oral PhD from the University of California at Berkeley, USA. His research interests include traditional medicine and healers, traditional and vernacular settlements in rural and urban areas, paleontology, and paleoanthropology. He also has an interest in the visual arts, especially Indonesian shadow puppets.

Boedhisantosa

Boedhisantosa is Professor of Cultural Anthropology at the University of Indonesia, Jakarta, Indonesia, where he obtained his doctorate. He currently holds the post of expert and adviser member to the Minister of Environmental Affairs of the Republic of Indonesia, in Jakarta. His particular interests include the sociocultural impact of the government's development program and agroeconomic anthropology.

Göran Burenhult

Göran Burenhult has been Associate Professor of Archaeology at the University of Stockholm, Sweden, since 1981 and is acknowledged internationally as a leading expert on prehistoric rock art and megalithic traditions. Between 1976 and 1981, he was director of the Swedish archaeological excavations at Carrowmore, County Sligo, Ireland, excavating one of the earliest known megalithic cemeteries, and he has undertaken field work on prehistoric rock art throughout the world, including the rock painting areas of the central Sahara Desert. Most recently, he has conducted ethnoarchaeological expeditions to the islands of Sulawesi and Sumba, in Indonesia, to the Trobriand Islands of Papua New Guinea, and to the island of Malekula, in Vanuatu, to study megalithic traditions, social organization, and primitive exchange. He is the author of numerous scholarly and popular books on archaeology and ethnoarchaeology, and has contributed to journals, magazines, and encyclopedic works. Between 1987 and 1991, he produced a series of international television programs about aspects of archaeology.

Robert L. Carneiro

Robert L. Carneiro is Curator of South American Ethnology at the American Museum of Natural History, New York, USA. He is a specialist in the Indian tribes of Amazonia, and has conducted field work among the Kuikuru of central Brazil, the Amahuaca of eastern Peru, and the Yanomami of southern Venezuela. He is particularly interested in the subsistence ecology of these tribes, and has made a special study of the cultivation of manioc, the staple food of most Amazonian Indians. He is also interested in political evolution, from autonomous villages, through chiefdoms, to the state.

Wally Caruana

Wally Caruana has been Curator of Aboriginal and Torres Strait Islander Art at the National Gallery of Australia, Canberra, since 1984, and has organized a number of major exhibitions of Aboriginal and Islander art at the gallery. He is the author of *Aboriginal Art* and several exhibition catalogues, and editor of *Windows on the Dreaming*.

C.B. Clark

C.B. Clark is Executive Vice-President of Oklahoma City University, USA. Of Creek American Indian heritage, he has taught American Indian Studies at university level throughout the western United States for the past 20 years, and has served on a number of American Indian urban boards and committees. He has also written widely on the topic of urban Indian experience.

Roland Fletcher

Roland Fletcher is Associate Professor in the School of Archaeology, Classics and Ancient History at the University of Sydney, Australia. His major fields of interest are a worldwide comparative study of the way humans use space, and the logic of archaeological theory. His theoretical concerns are with the development of long-term, large-scale models of human behavior.

Bruce Grant

Bruce Grant is Assistant Professor of Anthropology at Swarthmore College, USA. His special area of interest is the peoples and cultures of northern Asia, with particular reference to the indigenous peoples of Siberia. His current field of research is the results of cultural engineering in the far north of Siberia during the Soviet period.

P. Bion Griffin

P. Bion Griffin is Professor of Anthropology at the University of Hawaii, USA. He is a specialist in the archaeology and ethnology of humid tropics foragers. With his wife, Agnes Estioko-Griffin, and son, Marcus B. Griffin, both anthropologists, he has spent more than 20 years studying the Agta of northeastern Luzon, in the Philippines. His current research focuses on the prehistoric archaeology of the Moluccas, in eastern Indonesia.

Brigitta Hauser-Schäublin

Brigitta Hauser-Schäublin is Professor of Anthropology at the Institut und Sammlung für Völkerkunde at the University of Göttingen, Germany. Her special fields of interest are gender studies, the anthropology of space, and building traditions. She has undertaken field research in Papua New Guinea, where she worked among the Iatmul and the Abelam, and in Bali, Indonesia.

Mary Hawkins

Mary Hawkins is Lecturer in the Department of Sociology at the University of Western Sydney, Australia, where she teaches in the fields of anthropology, sociology, and Asian studies. She conducted her doctoral field work in Indonesia, and from 1986 to 1989, worked in Indonesia as a community development consultant on various projects for the World Bank, the Food and Agriculture Organization of the United Nations Organization, and the Australian International Development Assistance Bureau.

Thomas N. Headland

Thomas N. Headland is Adjunct Associate Professor of Linguistics at the University of Texas at Arlington, USA, and an international anthropology consultant for the Summer Institute of Linguistics in Dallas, Texas. His current research focuses on Holocene hunter-gatherer societies and human ecology in tropical forests. Over the past 30 years, he has conducted extensive field work among hunter-gatherers in the Philippine rainforests. He is the editor of *The Tasaday Controversy: Assessing the Evidence*, and is presently working on a volume documenting the population decline of Philippine Negritos.

Gabriele Herzog-Schröder

Gabriele Herzog-Schröder is a graduate student at the Free University of Berlin, Germany, and is attached to the Research Institute for Human Ethology at the Max Planck Society, Andechs, Germany. She has conducted field work in a Yanomami community in southern Venezuela, and has recently published a study of her focal village. Her doctoral thesis analyzes the role of women in Yanomami society.

George P. Horse Capture

George P. Horse Capture is an A'ani (Gros Ventre) Indian from the Fort Belknap Indian Reservation, in Montana, USA. He taught American Indian Studies from 1974 to 1979, and was Curator of the Plains Indian Museum at the Buffalo Bill Historical Center, Wyoming, from 1979 to 1991. He is now the Deputy Assistant Director for Cultural Resources at the National Museum of the American Indian at the Smithsonian Institution, New York.

Frederick E. Hoxie

Frederick E. Hoxie is Director of the D'Arcy McNickle Center for the History of the American Indian at the Newberry Library, in Illinois, and Adjunct Professor of History at Northwestern University, USA.

He is a specialist in the history of federal Indian policy, Plains Indian history, and contemporary American Indian life, and has served as a consultant and expert witness to the Standing Rock and Cheyenne River Sioux tribes and to the US Senate Select Committee on Indian Affairs. He is the author of *A Final Promise: The Campaign to Assimilate the Indians, 1880–1920* and *The Crow*, and is currently completing *Parading through History: The Making of the Crow Nation*.

Åke Hultkrantz

Åke Hultkrantz is Professor Emeritus at the University of Stockholm, Sweden, where he was Professor of Comparative Religion and Chief of the Institute of Comparative Religion from 1958 to 1986. He has undertaken field work in Lapland and North America, and is the author of 17 books, his most recent dealing with Native American shamanism and medicine, the peyote cult of Native Americans, and Scandinavian mythology.

M.C. Jedrej

M.C. Jedrej is Lecturer in Social Anthropology at the University of Edinburgh, UK, and was previously on the staff of the University of Khartoum, in the Sudan. He has carried out field research in the Sudan, Sierra Leone, Mali, Burkina Faso, and Ethiopia. His current research focuses on the culture of the Dar Funj people of the Sudan.

Aldona Jonaitis

Aldona Jonaitis is Director of the University of Alaska Museum, Alaska, USA. An art historian, she specializes in the art of the Indians of coastal British Columbia and southeastern Alaska.

Dan Jorgensen

Dan Jorgensen is Associate Professor of Anthropology at the University of Western Ontario, Canada, where he has taught anthropology since 1977. His special areas of interest include the study of myth, the anthropology of religion, and historical analysis of social change and economic development. Between 1974 and 1992, he conducted field research among the Telefolmin people of Papua New Guinea. His initial research concentrated on traditional Telefol religion, with particular reference to the role of secrecy in the transmission of men's cult lore. The focus of his more recent work has shifted to an analysis of social changes in the Ok region of Papua New Guinea in the wake of national independence, Christian revivalism, and the launching of the Ok Tedi mining project.

Hermann Kreutzmann

Hermann Kreutzmann is Senior Lecturer at the Institute of Geography at the University of Bonn, Germany. He has made a special study of the remote mountain societies of Asia and their adaptation to external influences. His field work includes long-term village studies in the mountain areas of the Hindukush, Karakoram, Pamir, and Himalayas. From 1989 to 1991, he served as Field Director of the "Culture Area Karakoram" interdisciplinary research project. He is the author of a book and several articles on the high mountain agriculture and irrigation systems of the Hunza Valley and the interethnic relations of linguistic and religious minorities of High Asia.

Greg Lehman

Greg Lehman is Head of the Riawunna Centre for Aboriginal Education at the University of Tasmania, Australia, an executive member of the Tasmanian Aboriginal Centre, and an Australian government nominee to the Tasmanian Wilderness World Heritage Area Consultative Committee. His current projects include developing Aboriginal heritage policy and site management strategies. He has also written on Aboriginal history, heritage, and culture. He is a Tasmanian Aborigine and has been active in Aboriginal community development all his working life.

Wilhelm Östberg

Wilhelm Östberg is Curator of African Anthropology at the Folkens Museum, the National Museum of Ethnography, in Stockholm, Sweden. He is also the scientific coordinator of a research project on the importance of local production systems in modern soil conservation work at the Environment and Development Studies Unit within the School of Geography at the University of Stockholm. He has been involved in field work in East Africa and Botswana since the early 1970s, and is the author of a number of publications and articles on African rural societies.

Lutz Roewer

Lutz Roewer is a Research Fellow in the Department of Molecular Biology at the Institute of Forensic Medicine, Humboldt University, in Berlin, Germany. His area of specialization is DNA analysis in a forensic and anthropological context. He has developed methods to analyze individual-specific DNA markers in hair and minimal blood residues and in the tissues preserved in ancient Egyptian and medieval European mummies. He is currently investigating family structures and migration patterns in populations of Yanomami Indians in southern Venezuela and northern Brazil. He is also a participant in a research project set up to analyze the DNA of Papuan and Austronesian speakers in Melanesia, in order to reconstruct the Austronesian colonization of the Pacific.

Susan Rowley

Susan Rowley is a consultant archaeologist based in Pittsburgh, Pennsylvania, USA. For the past 20 years, she has been carrying out research in the Arctic, working extensively with the Inuit on archaeology, oral history, and ethnohistory projects. Since 1990, she has been co-organizer of an archaeological field school for Inuit high school students, which seeks to integrate Inuit knowledge of their history with archaeological techniques for investigating the past.

Peter Rowley-Conwy

Peter Rowley-Conwy is Lecturer in the Department of Archaeology at the University of Durham, UK. He obtained his PhD with research on the Late Mesolithic and Early Neolithic history of Denmark, and has subsequently researched the European Paleolithic, Mesolithic, and Neolithic periods, and the origins of agriculture in Southwest Asia. He has also worked on the economic archaeology of the Nile Valley in the late and post-Pharaonic periods.

Lee Sackett

Lee Sackett is Senior Lecturer in Anthropology at the University of Adelaide, Australia. In 1972, he began working with the Aboriginal people of the Wiluna area of Western Australia, collecting information on traditional ways of life, while simultaneously investigating contemporary life on the mission and reserve there and, specifically, the reactions of the Wiluna people to government-sponsored development initiatives in the area. He has also worked with the Nunga people of the Adelaide region, with people from various tribal groups in central Australia, and, earlier, with members of the Indian Shaker Church of Siletz, in Oregon, USA.

Frank Kemp Salter

Frank Kemp Salter is a scientist and Guest Researcher at the Research Institute for Human Ethology at the Max Planck Society, Andechs, Germany, where he is furthering his postdoctoral studies. Over the course of two postdoctoral degrees at Griffith University, in Brisbane, Australia, he pursued a biological approach to the study of politics, especially bureaucracy. Central to his research is the question of why members of a primate species that evolved in small, egalitarian groups allow themselves to be subordinated in large, impersonal bureaucracies. He is the author of *Emotions in Command: A Naturalistic Study of Institutional Dominance*, in which he reports observations of several Australian organizations, including the Federal Parliament and senior law courts, and finds a common thread of natural behaviors in these artificial environments.

Wulf Schiefenhövel

Wulf Schiefenhövel is Research Associate at the Research Institute for Human Ethology at the Max Planck Society, Andechs, Germany, and Professor of Medical Psychology and Ethnomedicine at the University of Munich. He has conducted field work in Papua New Guinea, Irian Jaya, Bali, East Java, and the Trobriand Islands. His main areas of interest are the evolutionary biology of human behavior, ethnomedicine, and anthropology, especially reproductive strategies, birth behavior, early socialization, nonverbal communication, aggression and aggression control, and cultural diversity and the evolution of culture. He serves on the boards of many publications.

Christina Sumner

Christina Sumner is Curator of Decorative Arts and Design at the Powerhouse Museum, in Sydney, Australia. Her main area of responsibility is textile collection, reflecting her long-standing interest and expertise in traditional textiles and forms of dress, especially those of Asia. She taught courses in fiber arts for a number of years, and between 1979 and 1984, participated in six seasons of archaeological field work in Israel and Cyprus.

David Hurst Thomas

David Hurst Thomas is Curator of Anthropology at the American Museum of Natural History, New York, USA. He is a specialist in the archaeology of the American Indian. He discovered and excavated the Gatecliff Shelter, in Nevada, the deepest rock shelter known in the Americas, with tightly stratified deposits spanning the past 8,000 years. He is the author or editor of many distinguished publications, has written more than 60 monographs and scientific articles, is on the editorial board of several journals, and is a founding trustee of the National Museum of the American Indian. In 1989, in recognition of his services to American archaeology, he was elected to the National Academy of Science.

Nancy Wilmsen Thornhill

Nancy Wilmsen Thornhill is Assistant Professor in the Department of Communication at the University of Michigan, USA. Her main area of research is sexual conflict and sex differences in psychological design, and she has undertaken two large-scale projects in this field, studying the psychological effects of rape and women's evaluation of sexual threat. Her other major area of research is the crosscultural study of rules regarding human inbreeding and marriage from the perspective provided by evolutionary biology.

J. Peter White

J. Peter White is Reader in Prehistoric Archaeology in the School of Archaeology, Classics and Ancient History at the University of Sydney, Australia. He has a special interest in the prehistory of Australia and the Pacific, especially Melanesia. He began research work in New Guinea in 1963, excavating for prehistory and studying the technology of highlanders who grew up in the Stone Age. More recently, he has worked in New Ireland and undertaken taphonomic studies in the Flinders Ranges, Australia. He is co-author, with Professor J. O'Connell, of *A Prehistory of Australia, New Guinea and Sahul* and has edited the journal *Archaeology in Oceania* since 1981.